NOT QUITE SUPREME

Not Quite Supreme

The Courts and Coordinate Constitutional Interpretation

DENNIS BAKER

McGill-Queen's University Press
Montreal & Kingston · London · Ithaca

© McGill-Queen's University Press 2010
ISBN 978-0-7735-3650-0 (cloth)
ISBN 978-0-7735-3681-4 (pbk)

Legal deposit first quarter 2010
Bibliothèque nationale du Québec

Printed in Canada on acid-free paper that is 100% ancient forest free (100% post-consumer recycled), processed chlorine free.

This book has been published with the help of a grant from the Canadian Federation for the Humanities and Social Sciences, through the Aid to Scholarly Publications Programme, using funds provided by the Social Sciences and Humanities Research Council of Canada.

McGill-Queen's University Press acknowledges the support of the Canada Council for the Arts for our publishing program. We also acknowledge the financial support of the Government of Canada through the Book Publishing Industry Development Program (BPIDP) for our publishing activities.

Library and Archives Canada Cataloguing in Publication

Baker, Dennis Rene
    Not quite supreme: the courts and coordinate constitutional interpretation / Dennis Baker.

    Includes bibliographical references and index.
    ISBN 978-0-7735-3650-0 (bnd)
    ISBN 978-0-7735-3681-4 (pbk)

    1. Judicial supremacy – Canada. 2. Separation of powers – Canada. 3. Canada. Supreme Court. 4. Constitutional law – Canada. I. Title.

    KE4775.B35 2010   347.71'012   C2009-904567-2
    KE4483.J8B35 2009

This book was typeset by Interscript in 10.5/13 Sabon.

Contents

Acknowledgments ix

Introduction: Sharing Interpretive Power 3

1 Judicial Supremacy, Dialogue Theory, and Coordinate Interpretation 17

2 Explaining the Hostility to Coordinate Interpretation 39

3 The Separation of Powers in Canada: "Partial Agency" or Watertight Compartments"? 53

4 The Separation of Powers in Canada: "Fusion" or "Ambivalence"? 64

5 The Ambivalent Judicial Role in the Separation of Powers 83

6 Legal Pluralism after the Supreme Court Decides 102

7 Judicial Remedies and the Separation of Power 123

Conclusion: Some Final Words about the "Final Say" 145

Notes 153

Bibliography 197

Index 213

To my grandmother,
Joyce Buckley,
for a lifetime of love and support

Acknowledgments

This book would not exist without the guidance of my friend and mentor, Rainer Knopff. For his endless patience, constructive advice, and tireless work on my behalf, I am eternally grateful. I hope to repay my debt to him, in part, by meeting his high standards of scholarship and teaching.

The ideas herein have benefitted from many discussions with colleagues and friends. George Breckenridge has endured more than most and deserves special thanks. Janet Ajzenstat, Ted Morton, Grant Huscroft, Barry Cooper, David Taras, Anthony Sayers, Troy Riddell, Matt Hennigar, Jeremy Clarke, and Ray Novak have all made suggestions and comments that made this a better book. Of course, some friends have managed to avoid discussing judicial politics altogether but, through their constant friendship, contributed nonetheless. In this regard, I thank Ray Scanlan and Chris Spearin. I would also like to acknowledge the generous financial support of the University of Calgary and the Social Science and Humanities Research Council of Canada.

Finally, I would like to thank my entire family for enduring what has been a long and winding academic journey. My wife, Andra, has demonstrated far more faith in me than I have ever had in myself. Her patient and enduring love has made all the difference. My parents and brother have never wavered in their support even when they probably had reason to do so. My Mom, in particular, has been a source of inexhaustible love and encouragement. Thanks are also due to my little girls, Charlotte and Eleanor, for reluctantly accepting that Daddy has to work sometimes.

Parts of chapters 1 and 2 have been previously published by Dennis Baker and Rainer Knopff as "Minority Retort: A Parliamentary Power to Resolve Judicial Disagreement in Close Cases," in 21 *Windsor Yearbook of Access to Justice* (2002): 347–59. This material has been reworked for incorporation in the present study. A small excerpt from chapter 4 appears in Dennis Baker and Rainer Knopff, "Charter Checks and Parliamentary Balances," 16(2) *Constitutional Forum* (2007): 15–22.

NOT QUITE SUPREME

INTRODUCTION

Sharing Interpretive Power

Defenders of judicial power and constitutionally entrenched rights inevitably wrestle with what Alexander Bickel famously described as the "counter-majoritarian difficulty," namely, the awkward fact that judicial power involves unelected judges overturning the decisions of elected officials.[1] One approach to overcoming this difficulty has been to minimize the scope and reach of judicial power by exhorting courts to intervene only to protect the procedural requirements of democracy itself[2] or to exercise restraining "passive virtues" more generally.[3] A second approach – the focus of this study – is to permit courts a wide scope for intervention but to deny finality or supremacy to their pronouncements.[4] This approach emphasizes the freedom of elected actors to disagree with and even overcome the decisions of appointed judges, thus minimizing Bickel's counter-majoritarian difficulty. It has at least two major variants: "coordinate interpretation" and "dialogue theory." While dialogue theory has recently attracted considerable interest in Canada, this study attempts to make the case for the currently unpopular alternative of coordinate interpretation as a means of reconciling Canadian judicial power with the other principles and norms found in the Canadian constitution.

Both "coordinate interpretation" and "dialogue theory" are best understood as part of a continuum, one pole of which is occupied by their common enemy, judicial interpretive supremacy. Judicial interpretive supremacy posits that the constitution is only "what the judges say it is."[5] In this view, the other branches must immediately accept the judicial interpretation of the constitution as correct and adopt the judicial reading as their own. Without exception, all non-judicial actors are expected to exercise their powers in all future cases and circumstances as if the judicial interpretation were controlling. From this perspective, there is nothing discrete about the exercise of the Supreme Court's interpretive power; the judicial interpretation is constantly "active" in the sense that no alternative interpretation may be legitimately held, even provisionally.

While some jurists and legal commentators argue that the interpretive supremacy of the highest appellate court is an inevitable and necessary consequence of constitutionalism itself,[6] the suggestion that a constitutional court possesses an exclusive and authoritative power to interpret the constitutional text is a relatively recent innovation in the Western liberal-democratic tradition. Despite claims that judicial interpretive supremacy was firmly established in the United States by Chief Justice John Marshall's oft-cited *Marbury v. Madison* decision in 1803,[7] *Marbury* has been understood as standing for interpretive supremacy only since the U.S. Supreme Court's decision of *Cooper v. Aaron* in 1958.[8] Assuming that the pre-Warren court held an unanswerable power to interpret the constitution is, in the words of one scholar, "pretty clearly bad history."[9] It is necessary to make this point because Canadian proponents of judicial interpretive supremacy rely on the claim that judicial finality has a "long history, in this country and elsewhere" and reject any contrary approach as "inconsistent with our traditional institutional arrangements" and "inconsistent with over 150 years of institutional practice."[10] In fact, as this study demonstrates, the traditional Canadian (and Anglo-American) approach to judicial power runs directly against the notion of judicial interpretive supremacy and instead favours the opposite "coordinate" pole of the continuum.

Coordinate interpretation means that each branch of government – executive, legislative, and judicial – is entitled and obligated to exercise its constitutional powers in accordance with its own interpretation of what the constitution entails. Contrary to such critics as Peter Hogg and Allison Bushell Thornton, coordinacy can hardly be reduced to simple "legislative finality" on matters of constitutional controversy.[11] Instead, coordinate interpretation envisions a process whereby "constitutional interpretation takes place over time, not in a single instant at a fixed and privileged institutional locus of interpretive authority," and where "the institutional competitors for interpretive authority [are] linked together in an inextricably nested relationship, so that each would see its interdependence with the others and all would accordingly work toward mutual accommodation."[12] In other words, the interpretive power is shared between institutions in the course of an unfolding process of constitutional interpretation (in stark contrast to the unilateral "lightning strike" of interpretive authority claimed by judicial supremacists). For the coordinate theorist, it is only through repeated inter-institutional exchanges that enduring constitutional principles emerge.

Even under a coordinate system of constitutional interpretation, it is quite likely that the judicial branch will be at the forefront of most constitutional controversies. Since no other Canadian institution entertains constitutional arguments as directly or as regularly as the Supreme Court of Canada, it has acquired a comparative advantage in interpretive expertise that surely warrants such a leading role and therefore it is unsurprising that Canadians have readily accepted its decisions as authoritative. A leading role, however, does not necessarily mean an exclusive or determinative role and it does not mean that other institutional actors cannot play significant roles. It is the extent of the Court's interpretive authority that this study explores: Is the judicial branch's interpretation of the constitution binding upon all other branches as a rule without exception (judicial interpretive supremacy) or are there opportunities for exceptional inter-institutional disagreement over the correct interpretation of the constitution (coordinate interpretation)? To put it bluntly, when it comes to constitutional interpretation, does the Court enjoy unanswerable obedience from the other branches or is it "not quite supreme"?

While judicial interpretive supremacy is unquestionably the orthodox position of legal scholars in both the United States and Canada, a significant minority of American legal theorists (from all parts of the political spectrum) advocate a coordinate approach of some flavour. They include John Agresto,[13] Robert Burt,[14] Mark Tushnet,[15] Robert Nagel,[16] Larry Kramer,[17] Walter Murphy,[18] Michael Stokes Paulsen,[19] Christopher Eisgruber,[20] and Neal Devins and Louis Fisher.[21] In Canada, save for a very few scholars – Christopher Manfredi[22] and Grant Huscroft[23] being the most prominent – the idea of coordinate interpretation has failed to attract serious consideration.[24] Instead, the focus in Canada has been on formal constitutional mechanisms for non-judicial participation (emphasizing the "reasonable limits" [s.1] and "notwithstanding" [s.33] provisions of the Charter of Rights and Freedoms), especially as incorporated in the middle-ground position of "dialogue theory."

Dialogue theory, as it is most commonly expressed in Canada,[25] emphasizes the fact that legislatures can use section 33 of the Charter to override rights *as judicially construed* or impose "reasonable limits" on those rights *within judicially determined boundaries*. Dialogue theory thus exhibits the inter-institutional give and take of coordinate interpretation but rejects the latter doctrine's premise that courts and legislatures can legitimately come to different, even conflicting, understandings of the essential meaning of constitutional rights or the boundaries of "reasonable limitation." Dialogue theory maintains judicial supremacy as far as *interpretive* authority is concerned, understanding the contribution of legislatures to inter-institutional "dialogue" as being one of helping to determine the appropriate balance between rights (*as judicially understood*) or between judicially defined rights and other, non-rights considerations.[26] "If 'genuine dialogue' can occur only where legislatures share coordinate authority with the courts to interpret the constitution," the authors of the dialogue theory write, "then by definition it cannot exist in Canada."[27] "Dialogue theory" simply recognizes that the representative branches are free to exercise their constitutional (but non-interpretive) powers so long as they are consistent with the always-operational and always-trumping judicial interpretation. On the other hand, as we shall see, coordinate interpretation allows for a degree of power sharing by treating judicial interventions as discrete and finite acts to which the non-judicial branches can respond using alternative interpretations in future cases. Unlike dialogue theory, then, coordinate interpretation contemplates inter-institutional "dialogues" *about*, not merely *within*, judicially defined limits.

On the whole, Canada's jurisprudential culture rejects the coordinate-interpretation end of the continuum.[28] This is shown by the strongly negative reaction to two Supreme Court judgments that flirted with limited forms of coordinate interpretation in circumstances that seemed particularly favourable to it. The first concerns a legislative sequel enacting the dissenting opinion in a very close (5–4) Supreme Court decision. While it is clearly one thing for the legislature to persist in pursuing a policy rejected by a strong majority of the Supreme Court, it might be considered another thing altogether if it enacted the policy preference of the minority in such a closely divided decision (what I will call the "minority retort"). The Court seemed to think so when, in *R. v. Mills*,[29] it upheld such a "minority retort" to an earlier precedent (R. v. O'Connor[30]), arguing that this represented a legitimate form of inter-institutional "dialogue." Most dialogue theorists strongly disagreed or found *Mills* "difficult to rationalize,"[31] maintaining that the Court had wrongly bowed to political pressure and abandoned its role as constitutional guardian. It was not legitimate dialogue, they insisted, for the legislature, through ordinary legislation, to side with four of the judges against five, and for the Court to change its mind as a result.[32] The only legitimate form of dialogue, in this view, would have been for the legislature to use the section 33 override to implement the judicial minority's view. For these critics, the legislation at stake in *Mills* had gone beyond legitimate dialogue and fallen into the error of coordinate interpretation. The Court has not repeated this "error."

The second flirtation with coordinate interpretation came in *R. v. Hall*,[33] which concerned the legislative enactment of the plain language of the constitution itself in response to a judicial interpretation (in *R. v. Morales*)[34] that transcended that language. Here, again, we confront a situation in which the claims of coordinate interpretation seem particularly attractive. Surely, it might be thought, the legislature can legitimately seek to preserve the very language of the constitution itself against judicial revisions to that language. When the Court confronted such restorative legislation in *Hall*, the majority opinion did not as clearly capitulate to the legislative response as the Court had done in *Mills* – indeed, it struck down the new legislation – but it suggested an alternative policy that came close to the one struck down in *Morales*, claiming that this kind of fine-tuning represented appropriate "dialogue." Nevertheless, this decision, too, was strongly criticized as transforming "dialogue into abdication."[35] Using *Mills* and *Hall*, among other cases, chapter 1 will set out in more detail the continuum from judicial supremacy through dialogue theory to coordinate interpretation.

Clearly, coordinate interpretation has met strong resistance even in situations where its claims might appear strongest and most tempting. *Mills* stands out as the lone instance in which the Supreme Court clearly gave in to that temptation. The fact that the majority in *Hall* tries so hard not to appear to be "abdicating" its original opinion in *Morales*, but is nonetheless charged with doing exactly that, says much about overall level of hostility to coordinate-interpretation pole of the continuum. The hostile reaction to these cases is important because future exceptions to judicial interpretive authority are less tenable if previous non-judicial interpretive exercises are perceived as illegitimate aberrations from a judicial supremacy norm. Chapter 2 attempts to explain the hostility to such coordinate responses exhibited by Canada's leading constitutional theorists. This study's attempt to recover the case for coordinate interpretation, at least in the kinds of limited circumstances represented by the *Mills* and *Hall* situations, runs strongly against the grain.

The project may seem especially problematic inasmuch as I propose to defend coordinate interpretation as being more compatible than its alternatives with the Canadian doctrine of separated powers and checks and balances among the legislative, executive, and judicial branches. Such a claim surely risks incredulity, if not outright ridicule, given the conventional wisdom that Canada has no functioning separation of powers between the legislative and executive branches, and thus no effective checks and balances within and between those branches. "There is no general 'separation of powers' in the Constitution Act, 1867," writes Peter Hogg, Canada's leading constitutional scholar.[36] Political scientist James Kelly even attributes Canada's "distinct political culture" to, at least in part, "the absence of a separation of powers theory."[37] Patrick Monahan agrees, and his well-regarded text, *Constitutional Law*, features a section boldly entitled "No Separation of Powers between the Executive and the Legislature."[38] According to these constitutional scholars, the "separation of powers" and Canada's convention of "responsible government" are mutually exclusive: "Any separation of powers between these two branches would make little sense in a system of responsible government," explains Hogg.[39] Federal Court judge Barry Strayer, a key legal adviser during the drafting of the Charter, similarly argues that the separation of powers is the "antithesis" of responsible government and thus not a prominent part of the Canadian constitution.[40] So does law professor Marilyn Pilkington, who considers any "assertion of a doctrine of separation of powers [to be] inconsistent with Canada's historical, legal, and political organization."[41] That Canada's system of responsible government precludes a separation of powers between the executive and the legislature has clearly become the orthodoxy among scholars.[42] The main reason is that, under responsible government, the executive dominates the legislature far too much to consider the two as separate institutions. Nothing has done more damage to the reputation of Canada's constitutional doctrine of separated powers than the fact of executive control of the legislature. The overstatement (or formalization) of this fact has skewed Canadian constitutional theory to the point that it can be seriously suggested that no institutional separation of powers exists in Canada but that between the judiciary and the elected institutions.

A corollary of the orthodoxy is evident in Eugene Forsey's assertion that, while checks and balances were "a basic feature of the United States Constitution, *with its separation of powers*, it is no part of ours"[43] – that is, where there is no separation of powers, there can be no checks and balances.[44] Since unchecked governmental power is almost universally considered to be a bad thing, it is therefore fortunate that there *is* after all *some* separation of powers in the Canadian system, and thus some opportunity for checks and balances. The separation lies, not between the executive and the legislature, but between these two political bodies and the independent judiciary. Thus, while Hogg believes that "the close link between the executive and legislative branches which is entailed by the British system is utterly inconsistent with any separation of the executive and legislative functions,"[45] he concedes a "little separation of powers doctrine" to protect the judicial functions in sections 96 to 100 of the 1867 British North America Act.[46]

It is the separate and independent judiciary that is thought by many scholars to provide some of the desirable but otherwise missing checks and balances. In this view, the augmentation of judicial power by the 1982 Charter of Rights and Freedoms was a good thing in part because it improved the ability of this checking institution to counterbalance the obviously substantial power of the executive-legislative complex. Thus, Ian Greene et al. upbraid Charter sceptics for failing "to recognize the essentially corrective role of the courts in a system of parliamentary majority rule where the executive dominates the policy process."[47] Lorne Sossin argues that "a robust and independent judiciary" is one of the few "external checks" on the "very small group of very powerful individuals [who] shape the policy and politics of the country."[48] In parliamentary systems, T.R.S. Allan similarly argues, "it seems necessary ... to match executive discretion with judicial discretion" so that judges can offer "genuine protection from abuses of executive power."[49] With executive-dominated legislatures failing to hold the government accountable, this argument runs, the judiciary plays a vital role in restraining what would otherwise be an unlimited and unchecked executive.[50]

In sum, the prevailing orthodoxy holds that, there being no separation of powers, and thus no effective checks and balances, between the executive and legislative branches of government, we should welcome the strong judicial check that comes from a separate judiciary armed with the trumping powers established in the Charter of Rights; an unchecked executive warrants an unchecked judiciary, they argue. Among other things, this perception of the all-powerful executive undergirds the widespread resistance to coordinate interpretation. To treat the already too powerful executive-dominated legislatures as equal interpretive partners with the judiciary would undermine a desirable institutional balance, tipping too much power back into the very institutional complex that most needs to be checked. Contrary to the claim I wish to make, in other words, the orthodoxy holds that a proper understanding of the Canadian separation of powers actually weighs against the claims of coordinate interpretation, which would enhance the power of otherwise unchecked political institutions and rob us of the salutary counterweight of strong judicial checks. In this view, the intermediate position of dialogue theory is as far as Canadians can prudently go along the continuum from judicial supremacy to strong coordinate interpretation. Some degree of inter-institutional partnership may well be justified, but it must be limited to dialogue about how best to limit rights under section 1 of the Charter or whether to override them under section 33.[51] There can be no legitimate interpretive debate about the essential meaning of rights themselves; on those questions, the courts must reign supreme.

Obviously, my defence of coordinate interpretation cannot get off the ground unless it mounts a credible critique of this orthodox view of the Canadian institutional system. The orthodoxy is wrong, I maintain, insofar as it rests on two mistaken assumptions: first, that there can be no separation of powers without a watertight compartmentalization of functions between the separate branches; second, that any formalities of separation that might exist in our constitutional rules are "mere" formalities – or even "myths" – that have been replaced by behavioural realities which effect a practical "fusion" of the executive and legislative branches. If I can establish that these two assumptions are indeed mistaken – as I propose to do in chapters 3 and 4 – then the orthodoxy and its implications for the appropriate forms and limits of judicial power can legitimately be reconsidered; that will be the task of chapters 5 through 7.

The first of the two orthodox assumptions – that a separation of powers requires the complete compartmentalization of governmental functions into the branches that bear their names – is the easier one to lay to rest. As I will demonstrate in chapter 3, this watertight-compartments assumption subscribes to what M.J.C. Vile has called the unrealistically "pure" or "ideal type" model of separation.[52] It is a model, Vile emphasizes, that has rarely been attempted and never succeeded, and that finds little support among major theorists of the separation of powers. Some degree of mixing of functional powers across branches – some "partial agency" in each other's affairs, to use James Madison's terminology[53] – has been generally acknowledged not only as inevitable but also as highly desirable in helping to generate healthy inter-institutional checks and balances. Such mixtures characterize all successful separation-of-powers regimes, including the archetypical United States. Simply put, to the extent that Canadian constitutional theorists rely on the watertight-compartments or "pure" model to ground their claim that Canada has no separation of powers – as they demonstrably do (see chapter 3) – they have introduced an unhelpful red herring into the discussion.

And, indeed, the formalities of the Canadian constitution, both legal and conventional (in their complex interactions), contemplate just such an arrangement of "partial agency" by the conceptually separate executive and legislative branches in each other's affairs. The executive is explicitly given significant control over the activities of the legislature. For example, all "money bills" must originate in the executive. On the other hand, the executive must retain the "confidence" of the elected legislative assembly, thus giving the latter considerable formal control of the former. This regime of "responsible government" was explicitly understood by its most prominent founders to mix the powers of two separate branches in order achieve a system of effective checks and balances.

At this point, the second assumption – that the actual relationship between the executive and legislative branches in Canada has gone well beyond any "partial agency" originally contemplated to outright "fusion" – comes to the apparent rescue of the orthodoxy. This assumption, it must be said, poses a greater challenge. The rejection of the watertight-compartments theory of institutional separation notes that the separation is compatible with a *degree* of mixing of functional powers across the branches. This clearly implies that such mixing can go too far, that what Madison calls "partial agency" may no longer be sufficiently "partial." Wherever the implicit boundary between appropriate and inappropriate degrees of mixing lies, the "fusion" of branches would surely overstep it. Indeed, even something short of complete fusion – an excessive "concentration of power,"[54] say, or an overly "close link"[55] – might arguably go too far. If the formalities of "partial agency" have indeed been overcome by the reality of "fusion," then the orthodoxy remains fundamentally intact, even if its "pure separation" formulation is plainly wrong. This appears to be the view of political scientist Graham White, who, despite the obvious mixing of powers, is prepared to concede a formal "constitutional separation of legislature (Parliament) and executive (Cabinet)" but then insists that "the political reality is very different."[56] Political scientist James Kelly relies upon a similar distinction to argue that "the perception of a Supreme Court as a political actor is quite different in a parliamentary democracy based on fusion than it is in a system based on the separation of power."[57] Fellow political scientist Tom Flanagan declares that "our system of responsible government depends on the fusion, not the separation, of power between the executive and legislative branches."[58] Similarly, dialogue enthusiast Kent Roach finds that Canada's "responsible government" means that "the executive and the legislature are fused."[59]

I will show in chapter 4, however, that the formalities of partial agency have not been overcome by the "very different" reality of fusion. The claim that they have been rests on the radical depreciation of institutional forms and formalities characteristic of "realist" or "behavioural" approaches to political science. In this view, whatever formalities of separation of powers are found in the constitution are dismissed as having no reality in the age of executive-dominated legislatures. However, while realist and behavioural approaches have much to recommend them in comparison to the deterministic legal formalism they replaced, they have themselves been effectively challenged by the neo-institutionalist revival of interest in forms and formalities. Without relapsing into legal determinism, neo-institutionalists have taught us to appreciate afresh the subtle and nuanced interaction between formal rules and informal behaviour. Indeed, as Harvey Mansfield has so brilliantly shown, the "ambivalent" interplay between powers formally assigned and those actually exercised is essential to the "partial agency" contemplated by mainstream separation-of-powers theory.[60]

I maintain that the "fusion" dimension of the prevailing orthodoxy about the separation of powers in Canada reflects residual blindness to the lessons of neo-institutionalism, and that Mansfield's analysis in particular will bring to light the reality of "partial agency" – and hence real checks and balances – in the interaction between the executive and the legislature in Canada.

When the interplay of formal and informal power is accorded its real significance, a fully realized Canadian doctrine of the separation of powers can be discerned. That doctrine may be stated very simply: no institution may *wholly* assume the formal powers of another. Thus, the executive might wield broad and substantial powers over legislative outputs but, so long as there is at least a theoretical opportunity for the legislative rejection of executive plans, the executive cannot be said to possess the *entire* legislative power. The ambivalent model, therefore, allows for considerable inter-institutional participation in the exercise of any power but only within the limits of the formal assignment of power. This doctrine accounts for a great many Canadian political phenomena beyond the paradigmatic case of responsible government, including the constitutional limits on direct democracy,[61] the persuasive but non-binding nature of reference decisions,[62] the strong but emphatically informal power of political parties,[63] and the strong-on-paper but weak-in-fact powers of the Senate,[64] among others. Indeed, once the doctrine is properly understood, it appears to be one of central motifs of Canadian constitutional thought.

If the orthodoxy is wrong about the lack of checks and balances between the executive and the legislature, then one of the chief supports for the widespread rejection of "coordinate interpretation" in favour of "dialogue theory" is undermined, and the possibility of rethinking that issue becomes more plausible and legitimate. This, of course, returns us to our opening set of questions, which will occupy the rest of the book. Once Canada's separation doctrine is properly understood, two clear implications for the judicial power to interpret the constitution emerge: (1) the legislature may exert partial agency over the judicial power to interpret and (2) the judicial interpretive power may not exceed partial agency over the assigned powers of the other branches.

Chapter 5 begins this analysis by considering how the judicial power might be incorporated in the ambivalent separation-of-powers model set out, with respect to the legislature and executive, in Chapters 3 and 4. Chapter 5 shows that the ambivalent interplay between the law-creating institution (the legislature) and the law-implementing institutions (the executive and judicial branches) is such that each institution is required to exercise some interpretive power. As the separation of powers suggests, however, no institution in this scheme is granted the exclusive authority to say what the law means; instead, the inter-institutional relationships provide an opportunity for each to answer the interpretive exercises of the others.

While these inter-institutional relationships emphasize the equality of each institution in terms of its status as a constitutional actor (meaning that no institution can exclude any other from participating in the exercise of power), the institutions are not treated as interchangeable. Rather, the relationships between them are structured upon the notion that each institution contributes to the operation of the rule of law in a functionally distinct manner. While legislatures are formally consigned to the enactment of general laws and the executive is hedged by both the formal legislation it is required to enforce and the judicial supervision over its discretion, the courts are both empowered and limited by their jurisdiction over discrete cases and controversies. Chapter 4 clarifies the essentially "ambivalent" quality of the judicial role by construing any exercise of judicial power as intimately connected to the particular case before the bench. Without this restriction to discrete cases, judicial interpretive supremacy, as A.V. Dicey warned, "substitutes litigation for legislation, and none but a law-fearing people will be inclined to regard the decision of a suit as equivalent to the enactment of a law."[65] This crucial distinction between the "decision of a suit" and the "enactment of a law"– "to anyone imbued with the traditions of English procedure," Dicey notes, it is "impossible to let a Court decide upon anything but the case before it" – has been far too obscured in modern constitutionalism.[66]

Confining the formal effect of the judicial interpretive power to discrete cases makes it possible for competing interpretations of the law to be held by other branches of government. This interpretive pluralism is an accepted and manageable component of the institutional arrangements found in "ordinary law" and I propose that it might be productively applied to constitutional law. Such legal pluralism is a considerable virtue if the accommodation of law and politics is a worthwhile objective. As Chapter 6 argues, the notion of constitutional interpretive pluralism was central to the classical constitutional theories of James Madison and Abraham Lincoln. Both Madison and Lincoln understood that a degree of interpretive pluralism is necessary, for at least a period of time, to allow for robust and enduring constitutional principles to emerge from the political accommodations arrived at through interpretive conflicts. These productive interpretive conflicts, however, can be short-circuited by judicial rulings if those rulings are treated as beyond the range of any inter-institutional response, as they would be if a rule of formal judicial interpretive supremacy existed. As the negative reaction to the minority and textual retorts illustrates, in contemporary Canada, judicial decisions are afforded this privileged position for what I argue is a misguided effort to impose judicial finality upon ongoing political debates.

Chapter 7 argues the Court's interpretation of its remedial powers under the Charter have resulted in a judicial control of the executive and legislative powers that goes beyond permissible "partial agency." Specifically, these decisions have allowed for (a) the judicial exercise of legislative power without an opportunity for formal legislative consent (via "reading-in" remedies as contemplated in *Schachter v. Canada*[67] and employed in *Vriend v. Alberta*[68]) and (b) the judiciary's direct control over the enforcement of their own decisions without executive consent (as in the extraordinary "supervisory" remedies in *Doucet-Boudreau v. Nova Scotia [Minister of Education]*[69]), as well as for (c) the unilateral judicial assumption of the joint executive-legislative power of spending public funds (as the Court has done on a number of occasions but paradigmatically in the *Eldridge*[70] case). All of these cases rely upon the Court's questionable interpretation of the combined effect of the supremacy clause (s.52) and the remedies clause (s.24) whereas, as Chapter 7 makes clear, a more plausible coordinate reading of the two sections could easily conform to the separation doctrine. As judicially construed, however, the remedial sections of the Charter run afoul of the notion that powers must be formally separated even if they are informally mixed. In each of the above cases, a comparison to the ambivalent executive control of the legislature might be drawn, and one might ask whether any of those remedial decisions could have been legitimately rejected by the formally assigned institution in a manner analogous to the way in which a revolt of legislators could thwart the executive. The separation doctrine insists that a formal opportunity for rejection must be presented, but one would be hard pressed to find a legal academic (or even a political scientist!) who would accept that the Court's remedial decisions could be similarly resisted. When legislators refuse to approve the bills advanced by the executive, there is no question of their legitimacy to do so. Legislative recalcitrance to judicial decisions, however, is portrayed as illegitimate and a threat to the rule of law. Therefore, even a seemingly deferential remedy – like the delayed declaration of invalidity in *Eldridge* – fails to respect the separation doctrine because any legislative decision that wavers from the judicial preference (in that case, to supply sign-language interpreters to deaf patients) is open to the charge that it is acting not only foolishly (or niggardly) but also *illegally*. If no expression of disagreement is possible in the face of the judiciary's interpretive usurpation of its competitors' formal powers, then how can judicial power be considered checked? From the standpoint of the separation doctrine, therefore, an exclusively judicial power of constitutional interpretation appears to be an aberration from Canada's general institutional design of separated and checked power.

1

Judicial Supremacy, Dialogue Theory, and Coordinate Interpretation

The appropriate relationship between the judiciary and the other branches of government with respect to the interpretation of the constitution has long been a matter of controversy. The three main alternatives fall along a continuum from "judicial interpretive supremacy" (where the constitution is what the courts say it is) to "coordinate interpretation" (where courts, legislatures, and executives are partners or competitors in constitutional interpretation). In Canada, an attempt to bridge these poles has produced a middle-ground position, referred to as "dialogue theory," which grants legislatures a degree of freedom in tailoring the policy outcomes required by judicial interpretations of Charter rights – through the imposition of "reasonable limits" or outright overrides under section 33 – while denying them any share in the interpretive task of defining the meaning of the rights themselves. This chapter uses two pairs of cases – one Canadian and one American case in each pair – to clarify what is at stake in the conflicting claims of judicial supremacy, dialogue theory, and coordinate interpretation.

Both pairs of cases arise from circumstances in which coordinate interpretation seems a particularly attractive and tempting option. In the first pair – *R. v. Mills* (the Canadian case) and *City of Boerne v. Flores*[1] (the American case) – both national legislatures had enacted legislation that explicitly conflicted with a Supreme Court precedent (*R. v. O'Connor* in Canada; *Employment Division v. Smith*[2] in the United States). The rejected judgment, however, was not that of a unanimous Court, or even a substantial majority, in which case the claims of judicial supremacy might seem prima facie stronger, but of a narrow five-judge majority. Moreover, in rejecting the view of these five judges, the legislatures chose very carefully from the menu of contrary policies presented to them, adopting in each case the policy preference of the dissenting four-judge minority. I refer to this kind of legislative sequel as a "minority retort." In effect, a minority retort chooses the side with slightly less judicial support from a policy menu set by the Supreme Court itself, and in which the relative strength of judicial support for the two alternatives could easily have been reversed had a single judge gone the other way. For the legislative majority to enact the option preferred by the judicial minority in such circumstances is the most limited (and most intuitively plausible) form of coordinate interpretation imaginable, and thus serves as a good test of how receptive the jurisprudential culture is towards this end of the continuum.

In the second pair of cases – *R. v. Hall* (the Canadian case) and *Dickerson v. United States*[3] (the American case) – both high courts confronted legislation that mimicked the language of their respective constitutional texts. Normally, such legislation would be uncontroversial (if the legislature is free to act within constitutional boundaries, then it is difficult to see how a legislative restatement of the constitution could be unconstitutional), but each was enacted to overcome a judicial decision (*R. v. Morales* in the Canadian context; *Miranda v. Arizona*[4] in the American one) that arguably added to the minimal requirements of the constitution. I refer to these statutes as "textual retorts" since they attempt to restore the constitutional text itself against judicial glosses that go beyond that text. In this respect, a textual retort challenges the notion that judicial supremacy is a necessary and unavoidable aspect of constitutional supremacy. With the textual retort, the legislature is not granted the same scope of interpretive freedom that the judicial branch holds; rather, insofar as this legislative power is restricted to simple restatements of the constitutional text, it merely establishes, as U.S. Supreme Court Justice Felix Frankfurter put it, that "the ultimate touchstone of constitutionality is the Constitution itself and not what [judges] have said about it."[5] The strong connection of the textual retort to constitutional supremacy and the narrow range of potential responses available to non-judicial actors makes it an attractive and moderate form of coordinate interpretation.

Even these most two most intuitively plausible forms of coordinate interpretation, however, have failed to garner the support of constitutional scholars. Indeed, the *Mills* and *Hall* cases have provoked harsh accusations that the Court was abdicating its constitutional duty and that such legislative manoeuvres were "dangerous" and "likely to compromise entitlements and destabilize *Charter* jurisprudence."[6] Others have tried to minimize the precedential value of *Mills* and *Hall* by suggesting that they are rare and quirky "hard cases" that, if taken as establishing inter-institutional rules, could "wear down the gears of the Constitution."[7] If the Supreme Court of Canada was indeed flirting with coordinacy, it is safe to say that its flirtation has ended in rejection. Providing an explanation for this hostility to coordinate interpretation is the task of the next chapter. First, it is necessary to place the cases in their proper institutional context and, by using the American cases as comparators, understand their significance for the debate between judicial interpretive supremacy and the shared interpretive power that characterizes coordinate approaches.

THE MINORITY RETORT CASES

Of the two minority retort cases, *City of Boerne v. Flores*, the American case, is universally considered a stark representation of judicial supremacy. *R. v. Mills*, the Canadian decision, was justified by the Supreme Court itself in terms of "dialogue theory" but is thought by prominent dialogue theorists to fall into the errors of coordinate interpretation. Although they emerge from very different facts, *Flores* and *Mills* share the following pattern of institutional interaction: an issue has three potential preferences, x, y, and z. Let x represent the status quo, whether it is created by statute or judicial decision (or merely the absence of any policy whatsoever). Assessing the status quo (through judicial review of a statute or an earlier/lower court decision), the Supreme Court rejects preference x but splits five-four, favouring preference z over preference y. In response to the decision, the legislature passes a second statute (a "legislative sequel" in the parlance of dialogue theorists), which enacts the judicial minority's preference y. Naturally, this second statute, the minority retort, comes before the Court. Should the Court invalidate the new legislation because it fails to conform to the preference expressed by the earlier five-justice majority? Or should the Court, in light of its own internal disagreement, defer to the legislature?

Presented with this problem of institutional authority, the *Flores* court insisted on judicial supremacy while the *Mills* court tended towards coordinate interpretation. *Mills*, in other words, stands for the rule that legislatures are free to reject the constitutional interpretation of the Court's majority and adopt that of the minority in cases where the Court is quite evenly divided. The critics of *Mills* are quite right in seeing elements of coordinate interpretation in the decision, but the fact that the Canadian Court found this a tempting option underlines its intuitive plausibility in a minority-retort context. That the critics almost universally rejected the Court's flirtation with even this limited form of coordinate interpretation says much about Canada's jurisprudential culture. In order to understand the coordinate subtleties of *Mills*, however, it is useful first to consider the judicial-supremacist treatment of a minority retort. For this purpose, the U.S. Supreme Court's decision in *Flores* is instructive.

The Smith-Flores Sequence

The *Smith-Flores* case sequence arises from the continuing controversy over the constitutionality of legislation that limits religious practices. Laws of general application that unintentionally burden religious practices have long been the subjects of litigation in the United States.[8] Since the 1963 case of *Sherbert v. Verner*,[9] the First Amendment has been interpreted as meaning that such laws are permissible only if they promote some "compelling state interest." Thus, a law forcing everyone to work on Saturday is an undue burden for Saturday Sabbath observers and unconstitutional since any such law could not be said to advance a compelling state interest.[10] In the 1990 case of *Smith*, the U.S. Court reconsidered the "compelling state interest" test in the context of an employee fired for the ritual consumption of peyote as prescribed by his Native American church. Justice Antonin Scalia, writing for a five-justice majority,[11] abandoned the existing test, ruling that the First Amendment protected only against regulations that directly targeted religious practices and offered no shield against "incidental effect[s] of a generally applicable and otherwise valid provision."[12] The doctrinal change announced in *Smith* resulted in considerable popular pressure for Congress to respond by reinstating the pre-*Smith* status quo.[13] In the *Religious Freedom Restoration Act* (RFRA) (1993), the U.S. Congress used its powers under section 5 of the Fourteenth Amendment[14] to reverse *Smith* and reinstate the "compelling state interest" test.[15] Significantly, the House passed the act unanimously and the Senate passed it by a vote of 97 to 3.[16]

The constitutionality of the act quickly became the subject of litigation, and in *Flores* the U.S. Court found itself evaluating the legislative rebuttal of its earlier decision in *Smith*. Writing for the majority, Justice Anthony Kennedy denies any legislative role in constitutional interpretation. "If Congress could define its own powers," he argues, "no longer would the Constitution be 'superior paramount law, unchangeable by ordinary means.'"[17] Judicial supremacy is necessary, Justice Kennedy reasons, because "shifting legislative majorities could change the Constitution."[18] Justice Kennedy concludes as follows: "When the Court has interpreted the Constitution, it has acted within the province of the Judicial Branch, which embraces the duty to say what the law is ... When the political branches of the Government act against the background of a judicial interpretation of the Constitution already issued, it must be understood that in later cases and controversies the Court will treat its precedents with the respect due them under settled principles, including *stare decisis*, and contrary expectations must be disappointed ... it is this Court's precedent, not the *RFRA* which must control."[19] Kennedy's assertion of judicial supremacy is striking in its reluctance to give any weight to non-judicial interpretations of the free-exercise clause. Michael McConnell notes that Kennedy's argument can be boiled down to a simple proposition: "Because the meaning of the Free Exercise clause has already been the determined by the Court in *Smith*, there was no room for congressional interpretation."[20] For McConnell, this is a "startlingly strong view of judicial supremacy ... [adopting] the most judge-centered view of constitutional law" in over four decades.[21] The issue of institutional priority transcended the usual ideological voting blocks on the Court. As Ronald Kahn puts it, "that Justices Kennedy, Stevens, Thomas, Ginsburg, and Chief Justice Rehnquist, all of whom hold quite different views on issues of religious freedom and church-state separation, joined the majority opinion ... suggests the importance of the institutional norm that Congress adhere to legislative tasks while the Supreme Court remains the final arbiter of Constitutional questions."[22] Even Justice Sandra Day O'Connor's dissenting opinion does not disturb the assumption of judicial supremacy. She dissents not because she thinks a legislature can legitimately disagree with a majority opinion but because she believes that *Smith* was wrongly decided (she was part of the *Smith* minority) and that the Court, not the legislature, now had an opportunity to correct its earlier mistake.[23] No one on the Court, in other words, suggested that the interpretation of the constitution was anything other than an exclusively judicial prerogative.

The O'Connor-Mills Sequence

The *O'Connor-Mills* interaction is slightly different from the *Smith-Flores* pattern, where the long-standing status quo was altered by the judiciary and then restored by the legislature; in *O'Connor-Mills*, the judiciary and the legislature offer equally novel policy alternatives to fill what was, at the time of *O'Connor*, a lacuna in the law. In the 1995 case of *R. v. O'Connor*, the Supreme Court of Canada confronted the sensitive issue of medical and counselling records in sexual-assault cases. Bishop Hubert O'Connor had been accused of sexually assaulting several students at the native residential school he had presided over in the 1960s. In mounting his defence, O'Connor applied for the complete medical, counselling, and school records of the complainants. The question of whether such records should be admitted at trial presents a difficult conflict between the accused's right to full answer and defence (guaranteed by s.7 of the Charter) and the privacy rights of the victim. Without any relevant statutory regime for guidance, the Court interpreted the constitution as requiring trial judges to administer a balancing test for admitting records when in the possession of the crown or third parties (e.g., rape-counsellors or other caregivers). The Court split five to four[24] over the factors to be taken into consideration with respect to third-party records. While the entire Court recognized the need for judges to balance the rights of the accused against the interests of the victim, the dissenters suggested that the decision maker must also consider equality rights and the need to encourage the reporting of sexual assaults. In general, Justice Claire L'Heureux-Dubé's minority opinion argued for a narrower or tougher test for the production of third-party records than the majority believed necessary.[25]

Two years after *O'Connor* was decided, Parliament amended the Criminal Code by passing Bill C-46, which provided a statutory framework for the production of records in sexual-offence proceedings for the first time. Instead of following the majority decision in *O'Connor*, however, Parliament essentially enacted L'Heureux-Dubé's opinion, sometimes word for word,[26] making it more difficult for the victim's records to be admitted at trial. One commentator described the legislation as "vindicating the approach taken by the minority."[27] When the inevitable constitutional challenge to the Criminal Code amendments arose in *Mills* (a case where the accused, and later acquitted, Brian Mills was seeking access to the medical and counselling records of a twelve-year-old complainant whose credibility was in question), the Court, taking an approach very different from Justice Kennedy's in *Flores*, upheld the legislation, despite its "significant differences" from the policy prescription offered by *O'Connor* majority.[28] Tellingly, two justices from the *O'Connor* majority – Frank Iacobucci and John Major – joined the *Mills* majority, thus allowing parliamentarians to enact a policy they had voted against when it was originally put forward by the *O'Connor* dissenters.[29]

In justifying its *Mills* ruling, the Court, speaking through an opinion jointly authored by justices Beverley McLachlin and Frank Iaccobucci, relied heavily on the influential theory of institutional dialogue advanced by Peter Hogg and Allison Bushell,[30] suggesting that the *O'Connor* regime was merely one of a "range of permissible regimes"[31] and that Parliament was free to devise its own constitutional procedures. Perhaps worried about the institutional implications of their judgment, the Court awkwardly suggested that *O'Connor* was simply "judicially created common law" that "embodies *Charter* standards,"[32] though there is no indication in the earlier judgment that it was anything less than a full constitutional ruling (and it was treated as such by lower courts applying it[33]). Regardless of the "common law" rhetoric, the Court clearly thought that its *O'Connor* scheme could be improved upon by listening to Parliament, especially since the issues "involve policy decisions regarding criminal procedure and its relationship to the community at large."[34]

Strikingly, prominent advocates of the dialogue metaphor reject its use in justifying *Mills*. Thus, Kent Roach, while condemning *Flores*-like judicial supremacy,[35] believes that *Mills* goes too far in the other direction, collapsing into unwarranted coordinate interpretation.[36] According to Roach, rulings like *Mills* undermine the necessary minoritarian protection that the courts provide; Roach argues that "political opposition to a controversial decision does not make legislation reversing that decision constitutional."[37] Like other dialogue theorists, Roach emphasizes sections 1 and 33 of the Charter as the appropriate mechanisms for inter-institutional exchanges. When a court rejects a policy, the legislature is usually free under section 1 to achieve the same purpose through legal means more carefully tailored to minimize the infringement of rights. Such section 1 "dialogue" does not apply to *Mills*, however, because the law at issue was *more* restrictive of rights than the previous Court majority would have countenanced. In Roach's evocative phrasing, the law represented an "in your face" disagreement with the *O'Connor* majority.[38] Although Roach does not rule out such "in your face" disagreements, he insists that the section 33 override is the appropriate way of expressing them.[39] "To the extent that one of the Court's concerns in *Mills* was to make room for dialogue between it and the Parliament," he argues, "the s. 33 override also would have accomplished this task by preserving the Court's decision in *O'Connor* and ensuring further public discussion of this difficult and evolving subject in five years time when the override would expire."[40] Obviously, "preserving the Court's decision in *O'Connor*" is key. If judicial supremacy means that the Court gets the final word on policy, Roach rejects it. But he clearly thinks that judges must be supreme in matters of constitutional *interpretation*. Section 33 allows "in your face" derogations from rights; it does not allow legislatures to disagree with judges about the correct meaning of rights. *Mills* is deficient, for Roach, precisely to the extent that it departs from *interpretive* judicial supremacy.

THE TEXTUAL RETORT CASES

The question of judicial interpretive supremacy is directly at issue in the "textual retort" cases. These cases address a simple problem: Can a law that essentially enacts a provision of the constitution be unconstitutional if it runs afoul of a Supreme Court ruling that goes beyond the constitution? There are two defining elements to a textual retort: (1) it is enacted in response to a judicial addition to the constitution; and (2) it uses little more than a restatement of the constitutional provision to defeat the judicial addition. From the perspective of judicial interpretive supremacy, the textual retort is at best ineffective (and, at worst, constitutionally invalid) because a judicial addition to the constitution is no less authoritative than the text itself. The second element – the legislature's employment of language directly taken from the constitutional text – does nothing to alter, in the judicial supremacist's mind, the fact that ordinary law must yield to the constitutional dictates of the Court. Still, only the most committed judicial supremacists can be comfortable with the idea that a legislative restatement of the constitutional text is itself unconstitutional.

In such circumstances, the textual retort is an attractive means of ensuring that judicial "interpretations" remain close to the meanings plainly codified in the constitutional text. As Justice Gérard La Forest notes, the legitimacy of judicial review is "imperiled ... when courts attempt to limit the power of legislatures without recourse to express textual authority."[41] This is not to suggest that the "plain meaning" of a text is always the single correct interpretation of the text. Indeed, there may even be multiple plain meanings of the same constitutional text. Consider the Charter guarantee that "every citizen of Canada has the right to vote" (s.3). That seemingly uncontroversial section has been the subject of considerable disagreement even though it appears, on the surface, to be straightforward: every citizen votes. The application of section 3, however, is not quite so simple, as demonstrated by the long-running controversy over the right of prisoners to vote.[42] One approach might follow the simple logic that prisoners, as citizens of Canada, are entitled to vote. Such an approach would quickly run into a substantial problem: children are citizens but they are (rather uncontroversially) denied voting privileges.[43] The age exclusion reflects the notion that the right to vote is subject to reasonable limits upon which one might reasonably disagree. Simply because an interpretation is obvious or "plain" does not mean it is a better interpretation. Why, then, should the legislature's "more plain" interpretation prevail over the more elaborate judicial one?

From the coordinate perspective, the textual retort would be upheld by virtue of its closeness to the constitutional text and in recognition of the legislature as the primary source of positive law within constitutional boundaries. With respect to section 3, for example, consider hypothetical legislation that extended the franchise to children over ten years of age. Any attempt to invalidate such an act using section 3 would be absurd, even if the Court found that the "purpose" or "values embodied" by section 3 required that the vote be restricted to more mature citizens. This result follows from a simple premise: when legislatures act *with* the constitution, they cannot be acting unconstitutionally. Legislatures, in other words, are entitled to deference when they clearly act within constitutional boundaries. This suggests an asymmetry with respect to the competing interpretations: a plain-meaning interpretation advanced by the legislature supersedes any judicial interpretation, plain or otherwise. If one is committed to the idea of constitutional – as opposed to judicial – supremacy, then the textual retort offers a particularly plausible means of securing it.

This abstract argument, with its hypothetical examples, benefits from a discussion of actual cases where the legislature has sought to preserve the very language of the constitution itself against judicial additions. As with the minority retort, two case sequences, one American and one Canadian, demonstrate the potential of the textual retort and the judicial responses the manoeuvre might provoke. Like its decision in *Flores*, the American Court in *Dickerson* asserts a strong judicial supremacist line, this time to protect the celebrated *Miranda* decision against a legislative revision. When the Canadian Supreme Court confronted the textual retort in *Hall*, the majority opinion did not as clearly capitulate to the legislative response as the Court had done in *Mills* – indeed, it struck down part of the new legislation – but it suggested an alternative policy that came close to the one struck down in *Morales*, claiming that this kind of fine-tuning represented appropriate "dialogue." Nevertheless, this decision, too, was strongly criticized as transforming "dialogue into abdication."

The Miranda-Dickerson Sequence

Having been saturated with American legal (and pop) culture, Canadians are no doubt familiar with the U.S. constitution's Fifth Amendment guarantee that no person "shall be compelled in any criminal case to be a witness against himself." This formal guarantee does not mean that one cannot be a witness against one's self since the accused maintains the ability to waive this right (in order to confess, for example). What the amendment plainly prohibits is *compulsion*; a confession is admissible so long as it is made voluntarily. In 1966, in one of its most famous rulings, *Miranda v. Arizona*, the Warren Court decided that a warning must be given before all police interrogation to inform suspects in custody of their constitutional rights. The Court suggested that this rigid warning, now popularly known as reading a suspect's "*Miranda* rights," was sufficient to ensure that any statement made by the suspect was voluntary. By making the warning mandatory, the *Miranda* Court went further than the constitution required since a confession that was entirely voluntary but without the prescribed warning (or with a defective warning) was to be excluded from trial.[44] Writing for the Court, Chief Justice Earl Warren expressly recognizes this extra-constitutional dimension of *Miranda* when he admits that the Court "cannot say that the Constitution necessarily requires adherence to any particular solution."[45] After noting that "it is impossible for us to foresee the potential alternatives for protecting the privilege which might be devised by Congress," Warren claims that the mandatory warning policy "in no way creates a constitutional straitjacket."[46] On the contrary, the Court "encourage[s] Congress and the States to continue their laudable search for increasingly effective" alternatives as long as they "are at least as effective in apprising accused persons of their right of silence."[47]

Presented with this invitation to continue the legal-political dialogue, Congress responded with ordinary legislation intended to overrule *Miranda* in 1968.[48] Instead of the warnings, the statute simply made voluntariness the sole criterion for the admissibility of a confession. In determining the issue of voluntariness, according to the statute, the trial judge "shall take into consideration all the circumstances surrounding the giving of the confession," and, after a list of concerns specifically identified in *Miranda*, the statute continues by declaring that "the presence or absence of any of the above-mentioned factors ... need not be conclusive on the issue of voluntariness."[49] Therefore, the legislative sequel to *Miranda* poses the difficult theoretical question of interpretive supremacy in the context of a judicial addition to the constitution as discussed above. This intriguing aspect of the *Miranda* response remained an abstract one for over thirty years, as successive justice departments declined to invoke the legislation directly.[50]

Spurred on by victims' rights groups[51] and University of Utah College of Law Professor Paul Cassell,[52] the legislation was finally subsequently to judicial review in the case of *Dickerson v. United States*.[53] In June 2000 the Supreme Court ruled, in a 7–2 decision, that *Miranda*, "being a constitutional decision of this Court, may not be in effect overruled by an Act of Congress."[54] Chief Justice William Rehnquist, not typically a "rights of the accused" enthusiast, claims that the case "turns on whether the *Miranda* Court announced a constitutional rule or merely exercised its supervisory authority to regulate evidence in the absence of congressional direction."[55] In order to buttress *Miranda*'s constitutionality, Rehnquist, writing for the majority of the Court, contends that the "prophylactic" *Miranda* warnings minimize the risk of admitting an involuntary confession and, in what appears to be the crux of his argument, identifies these warnings as a long-standing "part of our national culture" and thus properly protected from congressional abolition.[56]

Justice Scalia dissents from Rehnquist's decision with his typical combination of bombast and clarity.[57] Scalia opens by noting that the majority refuses to state explicitly that the legislation is unconstitutional. Such a statement is absent, according to Scalia, because "it would be absurd, inasmuch as [the legislation] excludes from trial precisely what the Constitution excludes from trial, viz., compelled confessions."[58] To reach their result, the majority must "adopt a significant *new*, if not entirely comprehensible, principle of constitutional law."[59] This principle, Scalia explains, means "statutes of Congress can be disregarded, not when what they prescribe violates the constitution, but when what they prescribe contradicts a decision of this Court that 'announced a constitutional rule'" and thus the Court has "the power, not merely to apply the Constitution, but to expand it."[60] For Scalia, the only way legislation can be disregarded by the Court is when "the Constitution *requires* the result that the decision announces and the statute ignores."[61] Any other understanding of the judicial function amounts to a "power of the Supreme Court to write a prophylactic, extraconstitutional Constitution, binding on Congress and the States."[62]

The power of Scalia's textual argument is grudgingly acknowledged even by defenders of the majority position. Legal commentator Craig Bradley, for example, argues that "[Scalia] is right that the statute sticks closer to the literal constitutional mandate than does *Miranda*."[63] Scalia's argument fails, according to Bradley, because the Fifth Amendment was intended to be a right for witnesses (as the text says) and is silent on the matter of custodial interrogations. One need not be an "originalist" to see the error of Bradley's next move: "Once it is recognized that neither side's view is commanded by the constitutional language, it becomes easier to justify the majority's impression that effective enforcement of the Constitution requires that the defendant be informed of the *Miranda* rights."[64] Can one consistently argue that the constitution is silent on a matter and then suggest that the "effective enforcement" of the supposedly silent provision necessitates a constitutional invalidation? This seems especially dubious when the statute enacts the very terms of the constitution.

For Scalia, the Court's conflation of its interpretation with the text amounts to a rewriting of the text such that the legislature cannot depend on the explicit textual guarantees of *its own* powers.[65] The very essence of textual constitutionalism requires institutions to have the right to exercise the powers assigned to it by the document. For example, the Sixteenth Amendment grants Congress the "power to lay and collect taxes on incomes," plainly establishing the congressional authority to establish an income-tax system. While this does not decide every peripheral tax issue – can an excessive tax be considered a cruel and unusual punitive measure? – it does provide considerable scope for unobstructed legislative action. Regardless of its own policy preferences, the Court cannot invalidate an income-tax scheme even if it finds it to be inefficient or irrational.[66]

Similarly, with respect to the Fifth Amendment, the government is granted the power to regulate the rules of evidence so long as it does not permit involuntary confessions to be admitted. In this view, by constitutionalizing the *Miranda* decision, the Court has abrogated a legislative power, clearly assigned by the text, by prohibiting the admission of not only involuntary confessions but foolish ones as well. Scalia puts it this way in the conclusion to his decision: "I believe we cannot allow to remain on the books even a celebrated decision – *especially* a celebrated decision – that has come to stand for the proposition that the Supreme Court has the power to impose extraconstitutional constraints upon Congress and the States. This is not the system that was established by the Framers, or that would be established by any sane supporter of government by the people."[67]

The *Miranda-Dickerson* sequence illustrates the central theoretical problem with an exclusive judicial power to interpret the constitution. Faced with a judicial decision that required more protection than the Fifth Amendment required, Congress sought to curtail the additional requirements in a manner consistent with its understanding of the constitution. Certainly, as the *Miranda* Court itself understood, nothing in the text of the Fifth Amendment requires that voluntary confessions made in the absence of a *Miranda* ruling must be excluded. Reasonable people can disagree about the correct policy – perhaps a *Miranda* warning best insures voluntariness, perhaps not – but the Court forecloses all such debate when it acts to uphold its interpretative supremacy over other institutions.

The Morales-Hall Sequence

Facing its own *Dickerson*-like dilemma, the Supreme Court of Canada struggled in *R. v. Hall* to reconcile a legislative restatement of the constitution with its assumed interpretive supremacy. This tension fractured the Court into a 5–4 split over the appropriate limits of "dialogue" for interpreting of section 11(e) of the Charter and arguably resulted in the Court's abandonment of the "dialogue" metaphor altogether.[68] Section 11(e) of the Charter declares that "any person charged with an offence has the right ... not to be denied reasonable bail without just cause." This wording was used to challenge the constitutionality of section 515(10)(a) and (b) of the Criminal Code of Canada, which allowed for two conditions in which bail may be denied: (1) to ensure the accused's attendance in Court; or (2) where the denial of bail would be "necessary in the interest or for the protection or safety of the public."[69]

While the courts have consistently upheld the denial of bail to ensure the accused's attendance,[70] the public-interest ground was struck down in *R. v. Morales*. Maximo Morales, alleged to be part of a major cocaine importation network, was granted bail "without enthusiasm" by his trial judge.[71] In his majority judgment clarifying the Court's position on bail, Chief Justice Antonio Lamer ruled that the denial of bail when it is in the "public interest" constitutes a "standardless sweep" that would permit "a court [to] order imprisonment whenever it sees fit."[72] In *Morales*, and its companion case, *R. v. Pearson*, Lamer limits "just cause" to those narrow circumstance where the denial is "necessary to promote the proper functioning of the bail system and must not be undertaken for any purpose extraneous to the bail system."[73]

Justice Charles Gonthier objected to Lamer's interpretation of section 11(e). Joined by L'Heureux-Dubé, Gonthier dissented from the majority holding on the public- interest criterion in *Morales*. "Public interest," he explains, is no vaguer than the terms used in 11(e) itself: "Just cause" is itself a concept that, "though very broad, is by its very use in the *Charter* and therefore by definition not so vague as to be unconstitutional."[74] Public interest, in Gonthier's view, is simply a "particularization" that is entirely within the broad constitutional scope of "just cause."[75] Gonthier notes that "public interest" is "a concept long recognized in our legal system" that must be evaluated and elaborated only "with reference to the particular context in which it is to operate."[76] Though reluctant to engage in hypotheticals, Gonthier suggests that it might be in the public interest, for example, to deny bail to an accused who is clearly suicidal. From Gonthier's perspective, the vagueness

Lamer condemns provides the necessary flexibility for a rational and well-functioning bail system.

Despite the fact that *Morales* "[spoke] clearly in setting out the fundamental constitutional elements of s.11(e),"[77] Parliament attempted to restore the judicial discretion prohibited by Lamer's interpretation. In 1997 Parliament enacted a new version of section 515(10) that allowed for the denial of bail in three situations:

(a) where the detention is necessary to ensure [the accused's] attendance in court in order to be dealt with according to law;
(b) where the detention is necessary for the protection or safety of the public ... including any substantial likelihood that the accused will, if released from custody, commit a criminal offence or interference with the administration of justice; and
(c) on any other *just cause* being shown and, without limiting the generality of the foregoing, where the detention is necessary in order to maintain the confidence in the administration of justice, having regard to all the circumstances, including the apparent strength of the prosecution's case, the gravity of the nature of the offence, the circumstances surrounding its commission and the potential for a lengthy term of imprisonment. [Emphasis added.]

Since *Morales* had struck out the "public interest" criterion, Parliament responded by reproducing the exact wording of section 11(e), allowing for the denial of bail whenever "just cause" could be shown. To help avoid the charge of vagueness, the legislation provided a non-exhaustive list of considerations that help determine what properly constitutes just cause. By using the text of the constitution itself, Parliament provides an alternative interpretation to the expansive one given to 11(e) by Lamer in *Morales*. Professor Garry Trotter, in his well-respected text on bail procedure, argues that 515(10)(c) is "more detailed and refined" than the invalidated public-interest criterion but it "achieves the same objective."[78] Law professor Stephen Coughlan notes that the new legislation is "an extremely similar provision" to the public-interest criterion struck down in *Morales*.[79] While the new section contradicts the Court's holding in *Morales* – which permitted only two legitimate grounds for denying bail – it is difficult to characterize such legislation as unconstitutional since it employs the exact language of the constitution itself. In this respect, Gonthier's dissenting remarks about the "just cause" language in *Morales* anticipated the dilemma the Court would face in *R. v. Hall*.

In the summer of 1999, David Hall was accused of a particularly gruesome murder of the wife of his second cousin. Since there was no reasonable fear that the accused would flee or that he would reoffend, he could be denied bail only under the new 515(10)(c). Hall was denied bail because his "detention was necessary to maintain confidence in the administration of justice in view of the highly charged aftermath of the murder, the strong evidence implicating the accused, and the other factors referred to in 515(10)(c)."[80] The clear reliance on 515(10)(c) provided the Supreme Court an opportunity to review the compatibility of the new provision with the *Morales* decision.

In her majority opinion,[81] Chief Justice McLachlin notes that Hall's argument was fairly simple – the provision "amounts to substituting a new phrase for the ground of 'public interest' which the Court held unconstitutional in *Morales*."[82] Given the criticism generated by the Court's earlier flirtation with coordinacy in *Mills*, the bench in *Hall* might have been sensitive to the charge that accepting the new provision would be tantamount to allowing Parliament to overturn *Morales*. Certainly, McLachlin appears to be aware of this problem and her decision attempts to finesse the matter (unsuccessfully, as the dissent in *Hall* proves) by explicitly upholding the earlier decision but altering its central holding to match parliamentary preference. Her first move in this delicate compromise is to declare the language "or any other just cause being shown" in 515(10)(c) to be an unconstitutional deviation from *Morales* because it is too vague to provide judicial guidance.

Considering the text of the Charter provision, this is an extraordinary conclusion that cannot stand much scrutiny. As Justice Gonthier argued in *Morales*, the concept of "just cause" is hardly vague and "by its very use in the Charter" it is "by definition not so vague as to be unconstitutional."[83] The clear objective of this textual retort is to assign full discretionary authority *to the courts* so that bail can be legitimately denied in just but unforeseen cases. McLachlin's argument means that this delegation is not specific enough. If she is correct that the legislative use of just cause, with its attendant list of non-exhaustive considerations, is too vague to provide judicial guidance, then it logically follows that the constitutional language, which has no further

Dialogue Theory and Coordinate Interpretation   33

elaboration, is also too vague. This poses a considerable quandary: If the "just cause" language of 11(e) is itself vague, how can the Court interpret it in the first place? And, if the Court can interpret 11(e), why are lower courts unable to interpret it when the full scope of discretion is delegated to them by Parliament? Either "just cause" provides justiciable guidance or it does not.

The Court itself has noted that one needs to be careful with the notion of vagueness since "absolute precision in the law exists rarely, if at all."[84] Given this limitation, "the question is whether the legislature has provided an intelligible standard according to which the judiciary must do its work. The task of interpreting how that standard applies in particular instances might always be characterised as having a discretionary element, because the standard can never specify all the instances in which it applies."[85] According to McLachlin's argument, the new Criminal Code provision – and perhaps the constitution itself! – fails to provide a workable "intelligible standard." This reasoning is particularly suspect since McLachlin notes that "Parliament took to heart the Court's criticism in *Morales*"[86] and refers to the testimony of a Justice Department bureaucrat that, "as a result of representations made by a number of jurisdictions, we have attempted to substitute the public interest heading with a more precise set of criteria which would permit a judge to consider detention on more specific criteria. We think that we have accomplished that task and that judges will be able to make informed decisions. What we are proposing is neither too vague nor too imprecise."[87] McLachlin considers the specifications Parliament has offered as guides to what might constitute "just cause" but she concludes that they are not enough to immunize the open-ended provision from the charge of vagueness. Indeed, she suggests that the non-exhaustive nature of the list serves "only to confirm the generality of the phrase permitting a judge to deny bail 'on any other just cause.'"[88] Even defenders of McLachlin's decision find this argument difficult to accept: given that "Parliament stipulated a litany of four factors to be weighed," Graeme Mitchell concedes, "there can be little dispute that these indicia conform with the minimal constitutional standard laid down ... in *Nova Scotia Pharmaceutical*."[89] Moreover, one might wonder whether, if Parliament had offered an exhaustive list, it would have unconstitutionally infringed upon the bail judge's discretion by omitting conditions that the court thought relevant to the issue of bail. In any event, McLachlin's standards for vagueness appear to set a very high threshold for an interpretation of "just cause" to pass constitutional muster.

McLachlin's "vagueness" argument, however, collapses when she proposes an equally vague policy to remedy the constitutional defect in the legislation. Having declared the "any other just cause" language unconstitutional, McLachlin proceeds to revive it substantially by affirming and expanding the portion of the legislation that permits the denial of bail when it is "necessary in order to maintain the confidence in the administration of justice."[90] On this ground, the trial judge was right to deny bail to Hall even though he posed no risk of flight or recidivism. According to McLachlin, "maintaining confidence in the administration of justice," unlike public interest, "relies on concepts held to be justiciable and offers considerable precision."[91] Her analysis is remarkably similar to Gonthier's *Morales* dissent where he attempted to show that a clear, justiciable meaning of "public interest" is found in a variety of other jurisprudential contexts. With respect to "the administration of justice," McLachlin notes that the phrase is frequently employed in legislation and judicial decisions. She then argues that "if the phrase 'administration of justice' is sufficiently precise, it must follow that the phrase 'necessary to maintain confidence in the administration of justice,' amplified by the supplementary legislative direction to consider four specified factors, is not unconstitutionally vague."[92] McLachlin provides no reasoning for this conclusion. Surely there must be some vagueness in what constitutes a necessary measure even if "administration of justice" is sufficiently concrete. There is no compelling legal or semantic argument to explain why "any other just cause" is vague but "necessary to maintain confidence in the administration of justice" is not, but there is a compelling institutional reason, namely the desire to uphold the *Morales* precedent, that might account for the suspect reasoning.

Having been chastised for its capitulation to Parliament's minority retort of *Mills*, the Court is clearly unwilling to concede that its earlier *Morales* decision is anything less than a binding interpretation of the constitution. Another admission that its constitutional interpretations may be rebutted by ordinary legislation might establish an emerging acceptance of coordinate interpretation by the Court and thus make it more difficult to exert future claims of interpretive supremacy. McLachlin's opinion is therefore quite clever in upholding *Morales* in name, if not in spirit. By inconsistently employing a vagueness standard, she manages to skirt the conflict between *Morales* and the text of 11(e) and simultaneously uphold the substance but not the form of the legislative sequel. Having achieved their primary aim (maximizing judicial discretion for denying bail), legislators have little reason to insist that *Morales* be explicitly overturned. While McLachlin disguises it with a judicial invalidation, the legislature, armed with the constitutional text, has succeeded in modifying a constitutional ruling of the Court.

Justice Iacobucci, writing on behalf of the four-judge minority,[93] clearly recognizes what Parliament has achieved with its textual retort. Iacobucci rejects McLachlin's opinion because, from his perspective, the legislative response to *Morales* did not show "due regard for the constitutional standards set out in that case."[94] Iacobucci's strong dissent – characterized by one commentator as bordering on "judicial incivility"[95] – is particularly significant because he co-authored (with McLachlin) the Court's 1999 *Mills* decision that enthusiastically endorsed the dialogue approach. While the majority in *Hall* characterizes the sequence as "an excellent example" of the courts being "engaged in a constitutional dialogue,"[96] Iacobucci clearly believes that, in this instance, dialogue has gone too far. By allowing Parliament to alter the interpretive holding of *Morales*, Iacobucci alleges that McLachlin's opinion "has transformed dialogue into abdication."[97] McLachlin's broad construction of what is "necessary in order to maintain the administration of justice" violates *Morales*, according to Iacobucci, because Lamer had explicitly stated that a "public interest" criterion that "justifies denying bail whenever the public image of the criminal justice system would be compromised by granting bail" could never be constitutional.[98] By adopting an expansive notion of what is necessary to maintain confidence in the judicial system, the revised 515(10)(c), according to Iacobucci, "invokes similarly vague notions of the public image of the criminal justice system, the only difference being that ... the public image standard is expressed by the phrase 'maintain confidence in the administration of justice' as opposed to the term 'public interest.'"[99] As Iacobucci suggests, McLachlin's broad standard functions as a de facto public-interest criterion. Indeed, it is impossible to come up with circumstances that would warrant the denial of bail in the public interest but could not be construed as necessary to maintain confidence in the administration of justice. Unconvinced by McLachlin's weak vagueness argument, Iacobucci accuses the chief justice of straying from *Morales* in favour of the statutory restoration of section 11(e).

While Iacobucci was willing to defer to Parliament's enactment of a minority opinion in *Mills* (and contrary to his own preferred position), he is unwilling in *Hall* to accept a non-judicial interpretation of the constitution even if it is well grounded in the language of the constitutional text. McLachlin's hesitation to uphold the legislation outright and Iacobucci's vigourous dissent are illustrative of the hostility towards the textual retort. While *Hall* has not attracted as much academic criticism as *Mills* (presumably because the legislation was technically invalidated),[100] it is clear that the textual retort has little support among the Canadian legal elite. Graeme Mitchell offers tepid support of the majority decision in *Hall* but argues against the idea that the case offers any support for the coordinate approach because the case "is not so much about the level of curial deference due to Parliament as it was about how the principles set down in *Morales* should operate" (in other words, the Court did follow *Morales* despite all appearances to the contrary; this has the effect of minimizing the inter-institutional dimension to nothing more than an intra-Court legal dispute).[101] Criminal law scholar Donald Stuart calls the decision "disappointing" and argues that "judges should be leading rather than following the community."[102] Both Kent Roach and Jamie Cameron have cited the U.S. Court's decision in *Dickerson* approvingly as the appropriate judicial response to textual retort.[103] As with the minority retort, Roach classifies textual retorts as "in your face" legislation permissible only through the use of the section 33. Unless section 33 is invoked, according to Roach, the interpretive supremacy of the Court must prevail. This narrower account of the "dialogue theory" would soon become orthodoxy.

CONCLUSION

As Christopher Manfredi notes, Iacobucci's narrower conception of dialogue was clearly persuasive to Chief Justice McLachlin, who, three weeks after *Hall* was delivered, adopted it in her *Sauvé II* majority decision.[104] Despite the explicit invitation to Parliament to relegislate following the Court's invalidation of the previous prisoner-voting disqualification in *Sauvé I*, McLachlin emphatically rejected the notion that any legislation restricting prisoner voting rights could be deemed constitutional. "Parliament," she writes, "must ensure that whatever law it passes ... conforms to the Constitution," by which she means it must conform to the judicial interpretation of the constitution.[105] Parliamentary interpretive intransigence is not to be tolerated or, according to McLachlin, "the healthy and important promotion of a dialogue between the legislature and the courts" could "be debased to a rule of 'if at first you don't succeed, try, try again.'"[106] This characterization of the court-legislature relationship suggests that the repeated iterations of the coordinate model are illegitimate even though "trying and trying again" might be an appropriate expression of political disagreement. Coordinate theorist Robert Nagel argues that sincere inter-institutional exchanges, like those that can be described as minority or textual retorts, will likely involve precisely that: "The dignity and importance of political involvement does not consist in the formulation of neat intellectual solutions. It consists in trying, failing and learning."[107] As we shall see in chapter 6, coordinacy provides a compelling but subtle rationale for the legislature to "try and try again" that is fully consistent, not only with Nagel's approach, but with Canada's constitutional design properly understood. The Court's characterization of the *Sauvé II* legislation as "debasing" the inter-institutional relationship suggests that it has abandoned whatever coordinate impulses the "dialogue" model offers.[108]

The *Sauvé* experience suggests that the Court's flirtation with "dialogue" coordinacy is over and judicial interpretive supremacy will be asserted whenever legislative interpretive choices conflict with judicial preferences. The promise of "dialogue theory" for reconciling judicial power with democratic representation has been dashed if the Court's understanding of the dialogue excludes all non-judicial participation in the interpretive process (as, indeed, some proponents of "dialogue," such as Kent Roach, proposed from the outset).[109] The Court's move away from coordinacy and towards the supremacist pole is hardly surprising given the vociferous response of the legal academic community to *Mills* and the "uncivil" judicial dissent in *Hall*. The negative reaction to both retorts deserves more study and requires an explanation given the attractiveness of some degree of coordinacy in the particular minority and textual- retort situations. In the next chapter, I canvass several explanations for the continuing attachment to judicial interpretive supremacy to arrive at the most fundamental reason for rejecting coordinate responses in favour of judicial interpretive supremacy: deep-seated misconceptions about Canada's constitutional separation of power and its implications for the sharing of interpretive power across institutional boundaries.

2

Explaining the Hostility to Coordinate Interpretation

How do we explain the pronounced hostility to even the most modest and intuitively compelling examples of coordinate interpretation? The obvious answer is that such coordinacy conflicts with the generally accepted view that the judiciary is assigned the exclusive power to interpret the constitution. As Grant Huscroft notes, "judicial exclusivity in interpreting the *Charter* is not only well established as a constitutional norm, but ... it has become an important consideration in the political process."[1] This chapter subjects the reasons for this increasingly widespread norm to critical analysis with the aim of evaluating the basis for opposition to the minority and textual retorts.

TEXTUAL ARGUMENTS FOR JUDICIAL EXCLUSIVITY

One argument for judicial exclusivity must be dealt with forthwith and that is the contention that this judicial role is expressly required by the constitution itself. It is true that, if the constitution grants the judicial branch the sole power of interpretation, then no form of coordinacy – even the otherwise plausible minority and textual retorts – could be sustained. The constitutional text, however, is notably silent on the issue of which institution is charged with the interpretation of its provisions. The supremacy clause, section 52(1) of the Constitution Act, 1982, is often offered as textual support, but in fact this section makes no mention of the judicial branch whatsoever. Section 52(1) simply states that the "Constitution of Canada is the supreme law of Canada, and any law that is inconsistent with the provisions of the Constitution is, to the extent of the inconsistency, of no force or effect." The absence of an explicit recognition of judicial interpretive authority is particularly striking since the drafters of the Canadian Charter were well aware of the long-standing American controversy over the legitimacy of judicial review. While one cannot read too much into this omission, neither should one pretend that the provision means more than it says.[2]

As Chief Justice McLachlin observes, the supremacy clause means that there is a "very clear and very simple" answer to any confusion about the "proper roles" of courts and legislatures: "The truth lies in the Constitution."[3] Since "Canada is a constitutional democracy," she continues, "all powers, whether of Parliament, the Executive or the Courts, must be exercised in accordance with the Constitution."[4] As I hope the following chapters will demonstrate, one might accept this assertion of *constitutional* supremacy without accepting a concomitant rule of *judicial* supremacy. As the textual retort suggests, this distinction is crucial to understanding the appropriate limits of judicial power.

For some, however, the transition from the supremacy clause to exclusive judicial authority is ineluctable. Thus, despite the notable omission of a judicial role in section 52, legal scholars like Peter Hogg argue that this provision amounts to express recognition of judicial review: "Since it inevitably falls to the courts to determine whether a law is inconsistent with the *Charter*, s. 52(1) provides an *explicit* basis for judicial review of legislation in Canada."[5] Justice Bertha Wilson argues that "you cannot entrench rights in the constitution without some agency to monitor compliance. Because of its independence, relative impartiality, and security of tenure the judiciary was the obvious choice."[6] According to Justice Wilson, Canadians recognized the comparative advantages offered by the judicial branch and "decided to charge the courts with the onerous responsibility of reviewing legislative and executive actions for compliance with the constitution."[7] This view holds that the judiciary enjoys more than substantial influence, that it should have the last word on constitutional policy.

A coordinate alternative to this judicial supremacist understanding of section 52(1) is not only tenable but even more compatible with the wording of the text. Section 52(1) imposes a constitutional obligation on all political actors to act constitutionally. This could simply mean, as U.S. President Andrew Jackson once noted, that "each public officer who takes an oath to support the constitution swears that he will support it as he understands it, and not as it is understood by others."[8] In other words, legislators should not vote in favour of bills that they understand to be unconstitutional (even if they would otherwise favour the legislation on non-constitutional grounds), nor should the cabinet propose bills or undertake executive actions or commitments that they believe would violate the constitution. The judicial corollary to this principle is, of course, that judges should not apply a law they believe to be unconstitutional to the disputing parties before them. This aspect of coordinacy will be discussed in detail in chapters 5 and 6; for now I simply note that Canada's constitutional text does not expressly call for judicial interpretive supremacy and suggest that the coordinate alternative is equally compatible with the documents.

STABILITY AND THE RULE OF LAW

The prospect that the supremacy clause allows for independent, non-judicial interpretations of the constitution raises the spectre of constitutional indeterminacy. When Robert Nagel asks what might "account for the doomsdayish terms" that defences of judicial supremacy employ, he concludes that "these terms are suggestive of deep anxieties about the durability of our constitutional system, which is portrayed as being in disarray and under ferocious attack."[9] Larry Kramer notes that any suggestion of interpretive coordinacy is "perceived by legal commentators as a formula for chaos and anarchy."[10] Well-known American constitutional law scholar Laurence Tribe criticizes the coordinate position as "a grave threat to the rule of law because it proposes a regime in which every lawmaker and every government agency becomes a law unto itself, and the civilizing hand of a uniform interpretation of the Constitution crumbles."[11] Canadian responses to coordinacy also tap into this fear: Jamie Cameron, for example, describes the *Mills* decision as "dangerous" and having a "de-stabilizing effect on precedent and the protection of rights."[12] This line of critique attempts to suggest that anything less that judicial interpretive supremacy will cause the constitutional sky to crash down upon us.

This "stability" critique of coordinacy is articulated most clearly by Larry Alexander and Frederick Schauer in their oft-cited *Harvard Law Review* article, "On Extrajudicial Interpretation."[13] Alexander and Schauer conclude that "interpretive anarchy" could erupt from any displacement of judicial interpretive supremacy because coordinacy "produces no settled meaning of the Constitution and thus no settlement of what is to be done with respect to our most important affairs."[14] As Kramer notes, Alexander and Schauer's argument on behalf of the Court's "settlement function" has a particularly receptive audience in legal scholars and judges because they believe that constitutional interpretation's "critical attributes must ... be those we look for in ordinary law: certainty, predictability, uniformity, and the like."[15] The role of the courts in this view is "not so much to 'make' law as to 'kill it.'"[16] As Robert Cover argues, "confronting the luxuriant growth of a hundred legal traditions ... [judges] assert that *this one* is law and destroy or try to destroy the rest."[17] Given this outlook, it is hardly surprising that the legal elite would prefer the rigid clarity of judicial interpretive supremacy to the messy politics that can occur under a more coordinate system.

However, it is highly unlikely, considering the typical cases that come before the Supreme Court, that the uncertainty resulting from coordinate responses would fatally unhinge the rule of law or even be significantly greater than exists under a rule of judicial interpretive supremacy. Mark Tushnet argues that "what [Alexander and Schauer] establish is that the rule of law requires that a legal system have a set of institutional arrangements sufficient to ensure that degree of stability necessary to guarantee that the law's settlement function will be performed acceptably."[18] Even if judicial supremacy effectively performs a settlement function,[19] it does not follow that other institutional arrangements cannot similarly respect and maintain legal stability. Tushnet notes that "legislative inertia is a powerful force in general, which means that a legislative solution once arrived at is likely to persist for a reasonably long time" and that "there are examples of short-term oscillations in legislative policy, but then, so too are there examples of short-term oscillations in judicial doctrine."[20] It is entirely possible that a *legislative* settlement of a constitutional controversy might be more enduring than any judicial determination.[21]

In Tushnet's assessment, "it would be impossible to establish that the complex system of inter-branch interaction, in which members in each branch make their own decisions about what the Constitution requires, would be any more unstable than the system of judicial supremacy."[22] Kramer argues that history and experience prove that non-judicial approaches to constitutional interpretation are certainly capable of producing the requisite level of stability:

Most modern legal scholars and political commentators assume that leaving questions of constitutional law to the community as ultimate decision maker would destabilize a legal order. They might even be right, but this is an empirical rather than a theoretical claim. Those who make such an assumption presumably base it on the world with which they are familiar, our world, in which a constitutional system like that of seventeenth- and eighteenth-century Great Britain may seem almost fanciful. Yet this order existed and worked tolerably well for more than a century and a half before the American Revolution occurred.... one is hard put to point to another system, even in the modern era, that has worked longer or better, which is why the British constitution was so widely admired among enlightened eighteenth-century Europeans.[23]

The false choice between judicial supremacy and anarchy conveniently ignores all constitutions – those of the United Kingdom, New Zealand, Australia, and even pre-1982 Canada, for example – which manage to provide the stability necessary for the rule of law but which also deny the judiciary a final say on constitutional principles.

Whatever the merits of the claim to judicially secured stability might be in other situations, it is surely weakest in the close-case minority-retort context or when the legislature simply restates the constitutional text. Neither coordinate mechanism is likely to truly threaten the rule of law because, given that just a few statutes are invalidated each year by the Supreme Court, only a small set of laws is potentially subject to either retort.[24] Only a smaller subset, given the substantial burdens and significant hurdles of the legislative process, is actually going to attract one of the legislative sequels described here. While it is true that the coordinate opportunities that are opened will increase indeterminacy, it is unclear how this tiny amount of uncertainty is different from, say, the indeterminacy that results from legislative reversals of common law judgments or from the legal pluralism that exists between appeals.

One must bear in mind that no judicial settlement can ever be absolutely certain. This is particularly important with respect to the minority retort since the kind of split decisions that might attract such a response are themselves notoriously unstable for the obvious reason that a single change on the bench can result in a judicial reversal.[25] Given the low expectation of stability in these cases, any instability resulting from legislative participation should not catch lawyers or concerned citizens off-guard or, at the very least, not any more so than a judicial reversal of the original case. Indeed, legislative participation is perfectly in keeping with the traditional notion that a judicial dissent may be the seed of a future majority judgment.[26] If dissenting opinions can legitimately inspire future judicial majorities, surely they can also guide Parliament in its development of the law, thereby providing an additional avenue for substantial inter-institutional dialogue. In sum, it is difficult to believe that the stability argument truly (or at least completely) explains the hostility to coordinate interpretation.

RESERVING SECTION 33 FOR EXPRESSIONS OF LEGISLATIVE RECALCITRANCE

The same is true for an argument taken from the structure of the Charter itself, namely, that section 33 renders coordinate interpretation unnecessary. If the legislature really believes the Court's interpretation is wrong, it can override the Court by including the notwithstanding clause in an appropriate piece of legislation. But this is subject to several objections. First, the "notwithstanding" clause preserves legislation that is inconsistent with only some and not all provisions of the Charter.[27] Second and more important in this context, section 33 rhetorically implies that rights are truly being violated, which is precisely the question that the coordinate-interpretation option seeks to leave open.[28] A government that employs the notwithstanding clause is open to the charge that it has abandoned Charter values (as Justice Wilson put it, legislatures would give the "impression of being anti-Charter and anti-human rights"[29]).[30] Effectively, a legislature seeking to offer a sincere alternative interpretation of the Charter can be easily vilified as anti-Charter, anti-rights, and even un-Canadian. Given the grossly disproportionate political price for invoking it, section 33 is a poor vehicle for sincere legislative-judicial dialogue about whether rights have even been violated, especially when that question evenly splits the Court itself or when the legislature restores the wording of the constitution itself against judicial additions to it. It is unclear, in other words, why this burden should be placed on legislation that simply restates the constitution itself or that would have been judged constitutional with the swing of a single judicial vote. The section 33 argument is particularly specious with respect to the textual retort because it would require the legislation to engage in linguistic contortions, such as "notwithstanding s.11(e)" followed by the exact language of s.11(e)! In any case, the availability of section 33 is not the only, or the most important, reason why critics reject coordinate interpretation. A much deeper reason is a profound distrust of legislative "majoritarianism."

LEGISLATIVE MAJORITARIANISM

In assessing the suspicion of legislative majoritarianism as a foundation for hostility to coordinate interpretation, it is important to note that this suspicion does not extend to majoritarianism as such in all institutional settings. In the minority-retort context, the swing of a single judicial vote would have dramatically changed the outcome precisely because the Court, no less than the legislature, operates on the basis of simple majoritarianism. This shows that, while defenders of judicial finality frequently appeal to the dangers of simple majoritarianism, they do not actually reject such majoritarianism in principle; they simply prefer courtroom majoritarianism to legislative majoritarianism.[31]

Why, exactly, do five justices determine the law over the objection of four of their colleagues? One possibility is simply that, ultimately, a decision is necessary.[32] Still, the simple need for settlement does not in itself justify the Court's use of majority rule as its settlement device. Why not take two competing legal opinions and flip a coin to decide which becomes law?[33] There must be other aspects of majoritarian decision making that make it a preferred mechanism for arriving at a decision.

Majority decision making has a profoundly democratic defence, frequently overlooked by legal scholars, based on equality and mutual respect.[34] According to philosopher Jeremy Waldron, "the method of majority decision" is preferable to all other methods (and thus so intuitively attractive) because it "attempts to give each individual's view the greatest weight possible ... compatible with an equal weight for the views of each of the others."[35] Any other threshold for decision making increases the power of some at the expense of others. For example, requiring a super-majority of 60 per cent would favour opinion not-X over opinion X so long as not-X is favoured by over 40 per cent of the relevant population even though a majority prefers X. This effectively means that those who hold opinion not-X are given more power than those who hold opinion X.

Therefore, on the bench, five justices trump four because it is the only outcome that ensures that each of the nine justices has equal power to shape the decision. It is striking, however, that this is the *only* reason why the opinion of five justices should be treated as law and the opinion of the other four as virtual obiter dicta. Even if the five-judge opinion were intrinsically superior, that is not the reason for its victory. If it were, that opinion should win even if it attracted less than a majority. In fact, the "right" side in a divided Court is a function of its numbers, not of its being intrinsically right.[36]

Of course, one might claim that, although a majority in some institution must be counted on to make the decision, judicial majorities are *more likely* to be right.[37] And this, indeed, seems to be the claim used to justify judicial exclusivity. It is common in legal literature to find legislation frequently portrayed as the often-rash product of bargaining between interested parties, with legislators depicted as "single-minded seekers of reelection"[38] who will thus respond even to unjust public demands. As Jeremy Waldron notes, "jurisprudence is pervaded by imagery that presents ordinary legislative activity as deal-making, horse-trading, log-rolling, interest pandering, and pork-barreling – as anything, indeed, except principled political decision-making."[39] Reviewing *Mills*, Kent Roach resists any legislative participation in constitutional interpretation because legislatures, "as elected institutions ... have an interest in maximizing the rights of more popular groups" at the expense of less popular groups.[40] By contrast, judicial decisions are envisioned as the disinterested application of core, immanent principles to concrete disputes.[41] In short, defenders of judicial supremacy suggest that the Court can contribute something that the legislature cannot: an objectively principled outcome to a controversial political issue.

Some doubt the adequacy of this argument even when the Court renders a unanimous judgment,[42] but it is surely weakest in the kinds of close cases represented by *Flores* and *Mills*. Legislative resolution of close cases relies upon an assumption that supporters of the Court would be hard-pressed to deny: any interpretation of the constitution that attracts four justices of the Supreme Court is, on some basic level, a principled and reasonable interpretation. Since there is no reason to suspect that any member of the Court holds an unprincipled position, the division on the Court is best explained as a "reasonable disagreement." Therefore, legislation adopting the minority position in a closely contested judicial decision reflects the principled interpretation of the constitution accepted by four members of the Court. Under such circumstances, Jamie Cameron's charge that the minority retort grants "the government a license to ignore [the Court's] interpretations of the *Charter*" is baseless.[43] To the contrary, the enactment of the minority judicial position suggests that legislators are closely listening to the Court's arguments and limiting their own choice to one of the interpretive variants identified by the Court.[44] Catherine Kane of the Justice Department notes that "the Department of Justice drafters took the Supreme Court ruling in *O'Connor* very seriously, and put much of its insights into effect."[45] (Roach uses the fact that Parliament was "unprepared to generate a genuinely novel interpretation of the Constitution" to support his contention that legislatures are incapable of serious interpretative deliberation.[46]) If Parliament cannot side with the minority in a closely contested judicial disagreement, then any talk of inter-institutional "dialogue" amounts to very little.

It is similarly difficult to characterize the textual retort as an unprincipled majoritarian rejection of a principled judicial decision. The *Morales-Hall* sequence demonstrates that there is a potential role for the legislature in maintaining constitutional supremacy by limiting judicial additions to the text. By offering the constitutional language in legislative terms, the legislature is advancing an interpretation of the constitution that (a) differs from the judicial version and (b) is plainly obvious from the constitutional text itself. Part of the resistance to the textual retort on behalf of legalists may be accounted for by the form this competing interpretation takes. If an interpretation of the constitution must, for the legal community, mimic the form of a judicial opinion, then one can see that the legislation in *Hall* looks considerably different from the lengthy analysis and legal rationalizations that one associates with opinions of the Court. It is the *Morales* decision, not its legislative sequel, which fits the legal community's preconception of what constitutional interpretation should look like. To this end, modern legislators have occasionally attempted to meet this standard by expanded preambles[47] and detailed committee reports.[48] There is, however, little reason to accept the assumption that constitutional interpretation must take the form most amenable to the Court and its followers.

The legalists' hostility towards legislative constitutional interpretations is analogous to the contempt common law scholars once held for the statutory process, which might lead unruly and irrational legislatures to upset the elegant and rational principles of the well-ordered common law world.[49] In both cases, statutory instruments threatened to upset careful and precious judicial reasoning, but they are hardly illegitimate for that reason alone. Economist Neil Komesar is particularly critical of the idea that legitimate constitutional interpretation requires a judicial approach and cautions those looking for judicial techniques in the legislative process because

> the image conveyed is of legislators carefully deliberating and debating the meaning of the constitution. To me, this image seems quaint and naïve, at least for contemporary purposes. But the major problem is not what the image portrays; it is what it leaves out. Focusing constitutional review on those moments when legislators explicitly consider constitutional provisions ignores the essence of both legislative and constitutional decision-making ... Constitutional interpretation takes place every time the government acts ... The political process interprets the Constitution whenever it makes societal decisions. It does so whether or not the Constitution is mentioned or thought about.[50]

Komesar's argument recognizes that all acts of the legislature are constitutional interpretations by virtue of their existence.[51] As Neal Devins and Louis Fisher point out, "the legislative and executive branches first determine, through independent deliberations and joint efforts, the constitutionality of a measure ... They, not the courts, are responsible for first testing the edges of constitutionality and making the hard choices of public policy."[52] Even the Supreme Court of Canada has accepted this coordinate foundation of constitutional law: "Every law [governments] pass or administrative action they take must be performed with an eye to what the Constitution requires. Just as ignorance of the law is no excuse for an individual who breaks the law, ignorance of the Constitution is no excuse for governments."[53] The textual retort makes it clear that the legislature is keeping its "eye" on the constitution, as it is duty bound to do, and explicitly directs the Court's attention to the textual basis for their constitutional action.

CHECKS AND BALANCES

Concerns about legislative majoritarianism might account for some of the hostility to coordinate interpretation but it appears that majoritarianism is only one defect of the legislative process that defenders of judicial power rely upon. Dialogue enthusiast Kent Roach, for example, has supported judicial invalidations on the grounds that the legislative process is both overly majoritarian and overly minoritarian. When it comes to the rights of the accused, in this instance a constitutional challenge to the felony murder provisions in the Criminal Code (*R. v. Vaillancourt*[54]), Roach approves of the Court's invalidation because "Parliament was not likely to reform it ... What politician wanted to look soft on gun-wielding robbers or their accomplices?"[55] Conversely, in the context of the ban on tobacco advertising (*R.J.R-MacDonald Inc. v. Canada [Attorney General]*[56]), Roach portrays Parliament as the puppet of "rich multinationals that were able to secure significant postponements of the government's ban on sponsorship in part because of the millions they pump into cultural and sporting events."[57] As the product of either a "mob mentality" in Parliament or a corrupt catering to "special interests," legislation does not stand much of a chance in Roach's worldview. Not that Roach is necessarily wrong in either context – legislatures *do* suffer from minoritarian and majoritarian biases on occasion. But, as Komesar argues in his aptly titled *Imperfect Institutions*, "recognition of a problem in the political branches is an insufficient basis for institutional choice [in favour of the judicial process]."[58] Furthermore, courts, despite their relative independence, may also suffer from minoritarian and majoritarian biases (some judicial tests, like, for example, the fundamental-justice criterion in section 7, require judicial notice of popular sentiment,[59] and, as Rainer Knopff and F.L. Morton have argued, a panopoly of special-interest groups have sought to change policy by using the courts and the Charter.[60]) The minoritarian and majoritarian biases that affect both institutions can, however, be mitigated by encouraging "checks and balances" between the institutions. Surely this is what Roach has in mind when he applauds the judiciary for checking both Parliament's majoritarian anti-crime impulses as well as its minoritarian indulgence of powerful interests. As Komesar notes, "simple maxims that grant institutional superiority to one institution simply do not work in the complex world of institutional choice."[61]

This enthusiasm for a judicial check is also expressed in another objection to coordinate interpretation, in that any form of legislative constitutional interpretation appears to violate the well-known legal dictum that one cannot be a judge in one's own case (*nemo iudex in sua causa*). The legislature cannot fairly judge the constitutionality of its own legislation, this logic suggests, because it has a stake in the legislation being found constitutional. Alexander and Schauer, for example, claim that "there is little reason to believe that a legislature or an executive is best situated to determine the contours on its own power."[62] "True enough," Mark Tushnet retorts, "but equally true for the Supreme Court."[63] Waldron suggests that all such arguments are "facile" and notes that "unless we envisage a literally endless chain of appeals, there will always be some person or institution whose decision is final."[64] "That person or institution," Waldron points out, will always be subject to the criticism that "since it has the last word, its members are ipso facto ruling on the acceptance of their own view."[65] It is futile to try to invoke the *nemo iudex* principle when there are large societal issues at stake since such issues inevitably involve the decision maker in some other capacity.

In fact, the potentially broad impact of a judicial decision supports the involvement and participation of the legislature. Again, Waldron is enlightening. "It seems quite inappropriate," he argues, "to invoke the [*nemo iudex*] principle in a situation where the community as a whole is attempting to resolve some issue concerning the rights of *all* the members of the community and attempting to resolve it on a basis of equal participation."[66] Letting an unrepresentative body, supposedly unaffected by the decision, make the determination seems perverse when a mechanism for broader participation exists. Instead of *nemo iudex*, Waldron concludes, a more appropriate Latin tag would be *Quod omnes tangit ab omnibus decidentur* (that which affects all must be settled by all).[67]

Waldron's suggestion forces one to ask why the legislative process is seen as so bereft of reason and principle that only the judiciary can be relied upon to supply these obviously desirable dimensions of public deliberation. After all, there is a long tradition in liberal-democratic constitutionalism that expects "the mild voice of reason" to emerge within the legislative process itself because of the salutary influence of checks and balances within that process.[68] Indeed, over the course of Canada's constitutional history, it has been Parliament, not the courts, that has taken the leading role in securing civil rights and liberties. Janet Ajzenstat suggests that the open legislative process, with its constitutional guarantees of opposition participation, may protect rights just as effectively as judicial-centric models.[69] The state of civil liberties in Canada pre-1982 certainly supports Ajzenstat's view: Canadians were protected by progressive due-process legislation (the Canada

Evidence Act[70] and the Young Offenders Act[71] being two pre-Charter milestones), statutory human-rights codes (the first such legislation, the Ontario Human Rights Code,[72] enacted in 1962), and a variety of ancillary legislation. As Hogg points out, Canada's pre-1982 record on civil liberties "while far from perfect, seems to be much better than that of most of the countries in the world, although nearly all countries have bills of rights in their constitutions."[73] Hogg argues that "the basic reason for this has very little to do with the contents of Canada's (or any other country's) constitutional law" and is rather "the democratic character of Canada's political institutions, supported by long traditions of free elections, opposition parties and a free press."[74] (One might have thought that Canada's "political institutions" would be part of the "content of Canada's constitutional law" but such is the state of modern Canadian constitutional law). Hogg's admission that Canada's representative institutions are capable (but not "perfect") protectors of civil liberties again points towards a system of checks and balances, in which the elected braches can continue to play a significant role in constitutional rights in concert with the judiciary.

According to the dialogue theorists, what was true pre-1982 is not necessarily true post-1982. Kent Roach, for one, argues that "one of the unfortunate consequences of the *Charter* is that Parliament has abdicated its proactive law reform role and increasingly relies on the Court to articulate and enforce minimum standards of fairness for the accused."[75] "This situation," he adds, "is more a failure of parliamentary government than of the Court or the *Charter*."[76] In sum, Roach offers a dire picture of Canada's legislatures: executive-dominated, willing to appeal to special interests, susceptible to the tyranny of the majority, and, now, simply unwilling to provide minimum constitutional standards. It is easy to see the appeal of a judicial check in such a dysfunctional political system but is it credible to portray the minority and textual retorts as the product of such dysfunction? Given their strong connection to either a minority opinion of the Court or the text itself, do they not provide a legitimate coordinate balance to the judicial check?

The fact that judicial supremacy is so well entrenched even in the United States, where the presence of such checks and balances is widely acknowledged, shows how thoroughly it has emerged triumphant over coordinate interpretation in the modern age.

Even though some U.S. scholars attribute the rise of judicial supremacy to its "political foundations" (finding that enhanced judicial power benefits both judicial and non-judicial actors),[77] other American scholars continue to present evidence that legislative checks and balances actually do sustain the original expectation that the "mild voice of reason" can emerge from inter-institutional contests, and their work provides a foundation for advancing the case for coordinate interpretation in that country.[78] Canadian legal and political theory, by contrast, lacks this positive ground for coordinate interpretation because of the claim that we have no such checks and balances, a consequence understood to be a result of a concomitant lack of a separation of powers between the executive and legislative branches. To repeat the formulation by Eugene Forsey quoted in the Introduction, while the idea of checks and balances might be "a basic feature of the United States constitution, *with its separation of powers*, it is no part of ours," [79] because we lack such separation. This well-established orthodoxy is an especially powerful support for the claim that reason and principle will not emerge from Canadian legislatures and must thus be sought primarily from the judicial process. Given "a system of parliamentary majority rule where the executive dominates the policy process,"[80] in other words, "it seems necessary ... to match executive discretion with judicial discretion" so that judges can offer "genuine protection from abuses of executive power."[81] It is ultimately this perspective that provides the most powerful support for the widespread reluctance to concede even the most limited forms of coordinate interpretation. If this study wishes to revive the case for at least such limited forms of coordinate interpretation represented by the "minority retort" or "textual retort," it must show that this orthodoxy has, at the very least, been much overstated.

As this chapter demonstrates, most of the arguments used to justify a court-centric view of constitutional law are not particularly persuasive in the context of the limited kinds of coordinate responses suggested by *Mills* and *Hall*. The most profound reason for the legal community's hostility to even such limited coordinate interpretation – the reason posing the most serious challenge to any defence of coordinate interpretation – turns out to be the orthodox assumption that, lacking any effective separation of powers between the executive and legislative branches, the only effective checks and balances in the Canadian system are those provided by the courts. Judicial supremacy inevitably flows from this orthodoxy, it is suggested, because only a judicial branch empowered with interpretive supremacy is capable of fulfilling this checking role. Assessing the adequacy of the orthodoxy will be the task of the next two chapters.

3

The Separation of Powers in Canada: "Partial Agency" or "Watertight Compartments"?

The hostility to coordinate interpretation, we have seen, rests most fundamentally on the view that judicial power is needed to supply the lack of adequate checks and balances within and among the more overtly political branches of government in our system of parliamentary responsible government. The orthodoxy holds that, with no real separation of powers between our executive and legislative branches, we cannot expect meaningful checks and balances on that front. If this orthodoxy is correct, the claims of coordinate interpretation are correspondingly weakened. My defence of coordinate interpretation must thus question this orthodoxy. This chapter and the next will challenge the orthodoxy's two main assumptions: first, that all forms of the "separation of powers" principle require a watertight compartmentalization of functions between the separate branches; second, that any formal institutional separations that might exist in our constitution are nothing more than "mere" formalities – or even "myths" – that have been supplanted by obvious behavioural realities, including a practical "fusion" of the executive and legislative branches.

THE "WATERTIGHT COMPARTMENTS" IDEAL

What does Peter Hogg mean when he tells his readers that "there is no general 'separation of powers' in the Constitution Act, 1867"?[1] For Hogg, not only is "the close link between the executive and legislative branches which is entailed by the British system ... utterly inconsistent with any separation of the executive and legislative functions,"[2] but "it is clearly established that the [BNA Act, 1867] does not call for any such separation."[3] Hogg knows, of course, that the BNA Act employs the usual categories of executive, legislative, and judicial institutions, with Part III establishing the "executive power," Part IV the "legislative power," and Part VII the "judicature." Although the constitution conceptually *distinguishes* these functions, however, Hogg does not think it *separates* them. The constitution does not "call for" a separation of powers, he says, because it "does not ... insist that each branch of government *exercise only 'its own' function*."[4] In other words, if there is a mixing of legislative, executive, and judicial powers, so that members of each branch exercises some of the powers that conceptually belong to other branches, then there is no separation of powers.[5]

And such mixing is certainly mandated by the British North America Act. For example, section 9 of the act vests the entire executive power in the Queen,[6] while section 17 vests exclusive legislative power in a Parliament made up of "the Queen, the Senate and the House of Commons." In other words, the head of the executive (the Queen) is part of Parliament and wields a share of legislative power.[7] In practice, since the Queen's executive power is by convention exercised by a responsible cabinet,[8] and especially by the prime minister, this constitutional arrangement means that executive ministers sit in the legislature.[9] Indeed, they tend to control the legislature and its agenda and thus the executive is also the chief legislator. Moreover, members of the cabinet are individual members of the legislature in their own right, meaning that legislators also exercise executive power. Clearly, it cannot be said that each of the legislative and executive branches exercises "only its own function," the basis of Hogg's conclusion that there is no separation of powers between these branches.

Barry Strayer notes that such mixing or intermingling of functions in the Canadian constitution is a direct legacy of its British model, where "members of the Executive are [also] required by convention to be members of the legislative branch of government as well."[10] As another example, he notes that the lord chancellor "is head of the judiciary, a member of Cabinet, and Speaker of the upper house of Parliament."[11] From this, Strayer concludes that Britain's constitution contains no separation of powers, and that when Canadians adopted a constitution "similar in principle" to the United Kingdom's, they also rejected any separation of powers. Like Hogg, Strayer believes that the separation of powers requires a watertight compartmentalization of legislative, executive, and judicial powers within their branches.

This watertight-compartments view of the separation of powers embodies what M.J.C. Vile, author of the classic text *Constitutionalism and the Separation of Power*, calls a "pure" separation of powers, involving not only a conceptual separation of functions but also a separation of agencies and a separation of persons, so that each function has its own agency populated by persons who exercise only the function of that agency and do not interfere in the affairs of the other agencies.[12] To the extent that parliamentary government involves persons in one functional agency exercising the powers of another, it clearly violates the tenets of "pure" separation.[13]

THE REALITY OF PARTIAL AGENCY

It turns out, however, that this "pure" separation of powers is a red herring. As Vile himself emphasizes, the "pure" version is nothing more than an "ideal-type" that has "has rarely been put into practice"[14] and has never attracted the serious support of British, Canadian, or even American constitutional theorists.[15] Bluntly put, except for a brief period in the English Civil War period[16] and (arguably) in some pre-confederation U.S. state constitutions,[17] a "pure" separation has never been attempted nor desired.

Instead, the vast bulk of separation-of-powers theory and practice has not only permitted functions to be mixed across the branches to some degree but has also seen such mixing as essential to maintaining inter-institutional balance and generating the desirable checks and balances that healthy liberal-democratic government requires. The essential requirement for a viable separation of powers in this constitutional mainstream is a simple one, namely, that legislative, executive, and judicial power not be *wholly* vested in a single individual or single body. The idea, as Laurence Claus puts it, is to "[apportion] power among political actors in a way that minimizes opportunities for those actors to determine conclusively the reach of their own powers."[18] Born out of the English experience in the seventeenth century, this principle of separated powers has a long history that stretches from the Glorious Revolution of 1688 to include both the American founding and the Canadian confederation.[19] Indeed, it forms the core of what has been described as a "large transatlantic communion of political philosophy that has led the development of constitutionalism in the modern world."[20]

As Vile cautions, there is a great deal of confusion about the terminology employed to describe the separation principle.[21] Phrases like the "mixed" constitution and the "balanced" constitution are often linked to the ancient idea of a mixed regime (meaning that monarchical, aristocratic, and democratic elements are "blended" together) and sometimes carry an Aristotelian baggage that is unnecessary for the more basic point I am trying to make here.[22] The three members of the constitutional family I am concerned with (the English, American, and Canadian constitutions)[23] share a common trait that I call the "separation principle": they divide power between institutions along functional – but not absolute – lines and make those institutions check each other; the division is made stable by the constitutional requirement that no institution may *wholly* subsume the power of another. While the assignment of powers sometimes reflects the vestiges of the ancient mixed regime (particularly in the English case), a direct correlation between institution, power, and segment of society is not essential to the separation principle I am describing.

THE THEORY OF PARTIAL AGENCY

Given this qualification, one might search for an appropriate starting point for the discussion of the separation-of-powers principle as it relates to the Canadian context. While an historical examination of this constitutional mainstream could begin early, with the Restoration and Locke's *Second Treatise*,[24] or late, with the advent of "responsible government" in the nineteenth century,[25] the most useful starting point for the purposes of this study is Montesquieu's *The Spirit of Laws*. With his explicit adulation for the British model[26] and his oft-noted influence over both the American and Canadian framers,[27] Montesquieu makes the essential link between the seventeenth-century British proponents of a balanced constitution and the now-familiar theory and vocabulary of the American model. Indeed, Montesquieu's treatment of the principle makes clear the importance of the separation of powers for any liberal-democratic government. For this reason, chapter XI of *The Spirit of Laws*, entitled "Of the Laws Which Establish Political Liberty with Regard to the Constitution," remains essential reading for constitutional theorists and provides the necessary background for understanding Canada's particular application of the separation principle.[28]

Montesquieu begins this celebrated chapter by acknowledging many different conceptions of liberty and selecting the one he considers key – political liberty. Political liberty, in contrast to "unlimited liberty," is "a right of doing whatever the laws permit," or, in modern terms, freedom consistent with the rule of law.[29] (The selection of political liberty over other conceptions is an inherently political choice that admittedly skews one towards limited or "negative" government. Vile thinks that this foundational choice severely limited the relevance of the doctrine with the advent of "collectivist" welfare government.[30]) Montesquieu's stated objective, therefore, is to discern the institutional arrangements that will allow this lawful liberty to flourish. Political liberty, he contends, "is to be found only in moderate governments; and even in these it is not always found. It is there only when there is no abuse of power. But constant experience shows us that every man invested with power is apt to abuse it, and to carry his authority as far as it will go."[31] Montesquieu's awareness of the human temptation to abuse power and thus threaten "moderate government" leads him to the solution of dividing power. "To prevent this abuse," Montesquieu argues, "it is necessary from the very nature of things that power should be a check to power."[32] At the time he was writing (the mid-eighteenth century), Montesquieu saw only one nation, England, that had "for the direct end of its constitution political liberty," which is to say that it had adequate checks and balances.[33]

But in order for power to check power, there must be distinct sources of power with some degree of separation. Montesquieu describes the English approach as dividing governing authority into the now familiar legislative, executive, and judicial powers.[34] Simply put, the legislature creates and amends law, the executive governs according to law, and the judiciary settles disputes between the state and citizens[35] or between citizens themselves. This basic functional division of power persists throughout the development of English and Canadian constitutional law.[36] In a 1985 ruling on the authority of Canadian administrative tribunals, Chief Justice Brian Dickson plainly noted that "there is in Canada a separation of powers among the three branches of government – the legislature, the executive and the judiciary" and "in broad terms, the role of the judiciary is, of course, to interpret and apply the law; the role of the legislature is to decide upon and enunciate policy; the role of the executive is to administer and implement that policy."[37] As Dickson notes, Canada's institutional arrangement clearly matches the traditional English approach (at least "in broad terms") that Montesquieu praises for allowing power to check power.

Power thus delineated must then be assigned to different individuals. Montesquieu understood this assignment as crucial for the prevention of abuse of power: "When the legislative and executive are united in the same person, or in the same body of magistrates, there can be no liberty; because apprehensions may arise, lest the same monarch or senate should enact tyrannical laws, to execute them in a tyrannical manner ... There would be an end of everything, were the same man or the same body, whether of the nobles or of the people, to exercise those three powers, that of enacting laws, that of executing the public resolutions, and of trying the causes of individuals."[38] It is necessary to emphasize Montesquieu's point. He is concerned with the potential for a single decision maker to enforce his preferences *directly* and *absolutely* upon the citizen. He fears a king with the power to devise law (perhaps upon nothing more than regal whim) and who can also direct his police to enforce such a law (perhaps unfairly) without review or appeal. Uniting powers, Montesquieu argues, proves an irresistible invitation to tyranny. A separation of powers, on the other hand, provides opportunities for intervening checks on the power of a single individual or institution.

At the time of Montesquieu's writing, neither legislative nor monarchical absolutism was particularly appealing. While the pre-Civil War experience with Charles I confirmed the fears of a king with absolute prerogatives,[39] the subsequent experience with the Long Parliament raised serious doubts about legislative supremacy.[40] Following Montesquieu, Blackstone understood this history as confirming the desirability of *partial* executive and legislative independence since "either total union or total disjunction would in the long run lead to tyranny."[41] The functional separation of powers, for both Montesquieu and Blackstone, could provide this alternative middle ground. It could limit a tyrannical king by restricting his ability to create or amend law (acts possible only with the participation of the Houses of Commons and Lords) while maintaining an independent judiciary that could fairly adjudicate disputes. Conversely, a tyrannical legislature, pandering to an ill-motivated majority, can be tempered by a king who chooses to under-enforce the law or by a judiciary that mitigates the law through interpretation.[42] In the English system, absolute power is given to no one; and thus no institution can directly infringe political liberty alone.[43] By establishing three rival institutions with limited powers to intercept the legal effect of each other, the Montesquiean gamble is that at least one will favour political liberty and intervene for its protection.

This checking function does not rely upon an absolute separation of powers or persons in order to achieve the end of "moderate government" and "political liberty." In contrast to Vile's "pure" separation, Montesquieu follows Bolingbroke and other early English constitutionalists by conceiving the separated powers as a mixture of institutional independence and interdependence.[44] Bolingbroke's approach (and Montesquieu's), Vile notes, favours interaction to ensure stability rather than isolation: "Without a high degree of *independent* power in the hands of each branch, they cannot be said to be interdependent, for this requires that neither shall be subordinate to the other. At the same time a degree of interdependence does not destroy the essential independence of the branches."[45] In the American context, the necessary connections between separated powers is axiomatic: "While the Constitution diffuses power the better to secure liberty, it also contemplates that practice will integrate the dispersed powers into a workable government. It enjoins upon its branches separateness but inter-dependence, autonomy but reciprocity."[46]

Legal scholar Laurence Claus finds the idea of interdependence deeply embedded in Montesquieu's design because assigning "the primary exercise of a power in one actor did not give that actor *carte blanche* in the exercise of the power, it just denied the primary exercise of that power to others."[47] The important aspect of this coordinacy is therefore not a strict equality or strict separation of constitutional *power* but, rather, an equality of constitutional *status* amongst the branches. Branches can be unequal in power – indeed, one branch may be clearly dominant – but all branches must be able both to maintain their *status* as legitimate constitutional agents and to exercise some limited (though not determinative) influence over the others. For this reason, as James Madison noted in 1789, "there is not one government on the face of the earth ... in which provision is made for a particular authority to determine the limits of the constitutional division of power between the branches of government."[48] In the British context, Parliament is considered the dominant institution but English law puts the constitutional status of the judiciary and executive beyond doubt: "The British constitution has entrusted to the two Houses of Parliament, *subject to the assent of the King*, an absolute power untrammeled by any written instrument, obedience to which *may be compelled by some judicial body*."[49] This formulation requires three constitutionally separated branches capable of exercising a degree of independent judgment even if one branch is clearly more powerful. Such an institutional arrangement meets Montesquieu's standards for a separation of power in pursuit of moderate government.

Montesquieu's views in this regard are reproduced and explained by Madison in the *Federalist Papers*. While some Canadian scholars worry that "too much of the works of James Madison ... [have] been used in the Canadian debate,"[50] here Madison is instructive as an expositor of Montesquieu's views on the English constitution and thus directly relevant to Canadian constitutional theory. In the *Federalist Papers*, Madison defends the proposed American constitution from the Anti-Federalist charge that its particular arrangement of "check and balances" subverted the principle of separated powers by allowing branches to interfere with each other.[51] Against this charge, Madison argues that the Anti-Federalists have misunderstood the doctrine. Montesquieu simply meant, according to Madison, that the separate branches are each equal in constitutional status. His concern is that "where the *whole* power of one department is exercised by the same hands which possess the *whole* power of another department, the fundamental principles of a free constitution are subverted."[52] Montesquieu's logic, Madison argues, "did not mean that these departments ought to have no *partial agency* in, or no *control* over, the acts of each other."[53] Joint executive and legislative power over judicial selection is an obvious example of permissible inter-branch interactions despite the "control" this places the judiciary under. Again, recall Montequieu's aim: to prevent any single institutional actor from having the power to create, enforce, and adjudicate law. "Partial agency" and even some degree of "control" maintain openings (however narrow) for competing institutions to defeat or mitigate tyrannical acts. To fulfil its purpose of moderate government, the separation of powers might permit significant inter-branch interactions, even exertions of influence and control, but must prohibit arrangements that place one power entirely in the hands of another.

PARTIAL AGENCY AND CANADIAN PARLIAMENTARY GOVERNMENT

This is precisely the kind of mixed arrangement between the legislative and executive branches that is found in the Canadian constitution. Peter Hogg tells us that "any separation of powers between these two branches would make little sense in a system of responsible government,"[54] but the separation principle, in the sense that the branches must be equal in constitutional status, is a necessary element of responsible government. One of the early advocates of responsible government in Lower Canada, Pierre Bédard, argued that such a separation was already embedded in the Constitution Act, 1791 and linked "the argument that the ministry must command the support of the majority in the legislative assembly with an argument for the 'independence' of the assembly."[55] In other words, the founders of responsible government believed the "assembly is to have constitutional powers that mark it as a branch of government distinct from the political executive."[56] This does not mean, as both Bédard and Lord Durham recognized, that the "popular house is dominant" (Ajzenstat notes that Bédard "is always at pains to say that he is not attempting to reduce the powers of the political executive") but simply that "each has its powers under the constitution" and thus the executive and the legislature are "inseparable but, at the same time, distinguishable."[57] Far from being antithetical to responsible government, then, the executive-legislative separation is logically necessary for responsible government to work.[58] By 1867, responsible government had already been enshrined in the constitution by a series of royal instructions from 1839 to 1847 and, as a result, its incorporation in the BNA Act was assumed and uncontroversial.[59] Even so, the separation of the legislative and executive branches was explicitly recognized by sections 44 to 47 (limiting executive interference over the choice of the speaker)[60] and by sections 53 and 54 (regarding public finance).

Nowhere is the finely tuned interaction between the executive and legislative branches more apparent than in their respective influence over the power of the purse, as laid out in sections 53 and 54 of the BNA Act. Section 53 requires any bill "appropriating any Part of the Public Revenue, or for imposing any Tax or Impost" to "originate in the House of Commons," thus ensuring that any matter of public finance must face the judgment of the popular House (as Ajzenstat puts it, "the Commons cannot be ignored"[61]). Section 54 limits an individual legislator's power over the purse by requiring all appropriations of public revenue[62] to be introduced by the executive.[63] "It's because of s.54," Ajzenstat notes, "that the Commons is presented with a coherent program of spending and taxing legislation rather than a shopping list of competing demands from individual representatives."[64] While the power of the purse in liberal democracies is notoriously a legislative prerogative ("no taxation without representation,"), the BNA Act prescribes a combination of both executive control and legislative affirmation.[65]

Working together in classic Madisonian fashion – that is, through the "partial agency" of separate institutions in each other's affairs – these "crucial sections of the 1867 constitution"[66] enact an elegant scheme for effective but shared control over finance: the Commons may reject the cabinet's tax and spending plans but it may not initiate its own; cabinet can propose a cohesive plan but cannot enact it without the approval of the people's representatives.[67] The proponents of responsible government, and later the drafters of the BNA Act, did not envision a legislature – like the American Congress – that would make frequent and detailed interventions into taxing and spending plans of the executive.[68] Judged against the log-rolling and pork-barrel politics that characterizes the American congressional budgetary process, the Canadian system is definitely centralized and "executive-dominated," as its critics like to note, but in its formal structure it is certainly a system of checks and balances between conceptually separated legislative and executive powers.

Are sections 53 and 54 emblematic of the Canadian constitutional design or are they the exceptions that prove that, in general, Canada has no separation of power? Some, like Hogg, suggest the latter by arguing that any checking or balancing occurs only in this context (of money bills) and not in any more general sense.[69] Hogg's approach, however, diminishes the intended significance of sections 53 and 54. The Canadian proponents of responsible government considered the collection and expenditure of public funds to be among the most critical and sensitive aspects of governance.[70] The explicit identification of the separation principle in this "taxing and spending" context might plausibly have been thought sufficient to ensure that all legislation of any consequence would require legislative and executive acquiescence.[71] Furthermore, Hogg's denial of a general system of checks and balances makes the grant of legislative power in section 17 difficult to understand. Recall that section 17 bestows the entire legislative power to Parliament. This is not to say, however, that section 17 grants legislative power to the House of Commons since the text explicitly defines Parliament as being composed of the House of Commons, the Senate, and the crown together.[72] The "legislative" power, that is, the power to make positive law, requires the consent of all three institutions and therefore the legislative power is split between institutions explicitly. Understood from this perspective, there is *no* domestic power of Canadian governance in the BNA Act that is unchecked.[73]

That claim is sure to raise doubts in the minds of modern Canadians because of the equation of "Parliament" with "the House of Commons," an institution that is understood to be under executive control. From this perspective, section 17 includes no real check because the executive can wield legislative power without interference from members of the House (because those who are aligned with the prime minister's party are subject to his control over their careers and advancement in the party[74] and those who are not are, at least in the context of a majority government, denied any substantive role in lawmaking), senators (because they are typically beholden to the executive who appointed them), or the formal crown (because royal assent is a mere formality[75]). As I argue in the next chapter, however, the assumption that power is "fused" in the executive as a matter of political "reality" is flawed because of its denigration of formal checks. From the perspective of the "formal" constitution, section 17 remains a powerful constitutional statement of the separation principle.

4

The Separation of Powers in Canada: "Fusion" or "Ambivalence"?

Even if it is quite true that a *formal* separation of powers (of the mainstream "partial agency" rather than "watertight compartments" variety) exists in the BNA Act, the orthodoxy can fall back on a deeper claim: that there are underlying and more fundamental realities than the superficial forms of the constitution. The "reality" is that the conventions of responsible government have the effect of centralizing power almost completely in the hands of the executive. In an age of party discipline and bureaucratic centralization, the separation of powers might be thought of, as one British administrative law scholar put it, "that antique and rickety chariot ... so long the favourite vehicle of writers on political science and constitutional law for the conveyance of fallacious ideas."[1] The legislators of constitutional fiction may have the power to check the executive, but the "trained seals" of constitutional fact most emphatically do not. In *Wells v. Newfoundland*,[2] the Supreme Court of Canada declared that the separation of powers "is not a rigid and absolute structure" and suggested that the "reality" of executive domination is relevant to constitutional law: "The Court should not be blind to the reality of Canadian governance that, except in certain rare cases, the executive frequently and *de facto* controls the legislature."[3]

It is possible to call upon Montesquieu himself in support of the claim that executive domination of Parliament could subvert the separation of powers. Montesquieu wrote that "if there were no monarch, and the executive power should be committed to a certain number of persons selected from the legislative body, there would be an end then of liberty; by reason the two powers would be united, as the same persons would sometimes possess, and would be always able to possess, a share in both."[4] However, we have seen that Montesquieu's full argument suggests that this kind of arrangement would violate the separation of powers only to the extent that it shifted the *whole* legislative power to the executive.[5] Is this the case, as the critics maintain, or does "partial agency" remain a better description of the reality of modern Canadian responsible government? If "partial agency" does remain a more adequate description of our system than "fusion," it can only be because the forms and formalities of the constitution are less "rickety" and "fallacious" – that is, more real and meaningful – than the critics suppose. The fusion error – as I maintain it is – clearly involves the kind of radical depreciation of forms and formalities that one typically finds in stringently "realist" or "behavioural" social science. While the neo-institutionalist rediscovery of the often subtle but nevertheless significant relevance of forms and formalities has shed valuable new light on many aspects of Canadian politics, its insights have not yet been brought to bear on the fusion orthodoxy. I propose to do just that, using the particularly illuminating gloss on neo-institutionalist thought provided by the political theorist Harvey Mansfield.

FROM LEGAL FORMALISM TO BEHAVIOURISM

The behavioural or realist social science on which the fusion error is grounded emerged in Canada, as elsewhere, in understandable reaction to the obvious failings of earlier legal formalism. As Peter Russell notes, until the 1930s, the Canadian constitution was generally understood exclusively in terms of its own formalities, with the scholarly literature tending to emphasize the descriptive "examination of historical documents of a legal nature"[6] and often assuming that the formal rules thus described actually reflected or caused reality. Thus, as Alan Cairns explains, early commentary on the judgments of the Judicial Committee of the Privy Council (JCPC) exhibited a "legal determinism" that understood any decentralizing trends in Canadian public life to flow almost entirely from decisions of the law lords.[7] And as far as the separation of powers was concerned, the legal formalists,[8] wrote Canadian legal theorist W.H.P. Clement, subscribed to a "literary theory" of the constitution which "dwell[ed] upon the division of power between the legislative and executive departments of government ... and ... dilate[d] with quiet enthusiasm upon the 'checks and balances' provided in and by such a division and subdivision of power."[9] In other words, they took seriously the legal formalities of separation.

In time, however, this literal and deterministic understanding of legal formalities was displaced by a focus on empirical realities that were simply not captured by descriptions of the formalities. Given that key institutional actors – such as parties and cabinets – were not even mentioned in the formal constitutional documents, many became convinced "that formal rules are a poor guide to understanding how political power is acquired and exercised."[10] Accordingly, the notion that JCPC decisions had themselves caused decentralization came under fire, it having become impossible to believe that "a few elderly men in London deciding two or three constitutional cases a year precipitated, sustained, and caused the development of Canada in a federalist direction the country would otherwise not have taken."[11] Similarly, to quote Clement again, the "'literary theory,' safeguarding the ark of the constitution with its supposed division of sovereignty into departments, came to be recognized as an incomplete and, in truth, wholly erroneous explanation of the working of the constitution."[12]

With respect to the separation of powers, at least, this shift from formalism to realism and behaviouralism began early. Clement's dismissal of the "literary theory" of separation, for example, was published in 1904, at a time when legal formalism still predominated. Moreover, Clement's realist critique of the separation of powers relied on the even earlier work of Walter Bagehot, who "in his most valuable essays," reports Clement, "attacks with vigor this 'literary theory' with its supposed checks and balances."[13] Indeed, it was Bagehot in 1867 who first popularized the fusion terminology in his influential *The English Constitution*. In his first usage of the term in that work, Bagehot is careful to note "the *nearly* complete fusion" of the executive and legislative branches but drops the qualifier a few pages later.[14] For Bagehot, the formalities (or, as he refers to them, "the dignified parts") of the English constitution obscure the "efficient parts," and his work attempts to explain how the English system operates in fact and not as theory. To this end, he focuses upon the cabinet as the "buckle" that links executive and legislative power and provides England with its "effective secret" for governance.[15] As a reaction to overly formalistic legal theories of English government, Bagehot's analysis can be forgiven for its depreciation of constitutional forms, but, now that his model is conventional wisdom, it is the "nearly" and not the "fusion" that needs emphasis.[16]

The early application of behaviouralism to the separation of powers at the turn of the century was something of an aberration.[17] In most respects, legal formalism remained dominant for much longer. Indeed, the book in which Clement adopted Bagehot's critique of the "literary theory" was in most other respects a highly formalistic tome. By about the mid-1930s, however, there had begun a "general withdrawal of interest in legal phenomena [among political scientists], which lasted "well into the 1960s."[18] Russell observes that this was aided by the disciplinary "separation of constitutional law from political science," which had formerly been pursued by the same people in unified departments. As C. Herman Pritchett notes, "the disciplines of law and political science drifted apart for semantic, philosophical, and practical reasons."[19] Once the study of law had been safely entrusted to "lawyers in their own professional institutions," Russell says, "political scientists were at last free to get on with the empirical study of politics."[20] And they did so with a vengeance. As Donald Smiley's 1967 survey of political science literature shows, the discipline moved "from the institutionalist approach epitomized in R. MacGregor Dawson's *The Government of Canada*, to the behaviouralist concern with individuals and groups in politics."[21] Smiley points to the publication of John Porter's *Vertical Mosaic* (1965), which argued for class as a powerful explanatory variable, as a convenient marker for the ascendance of the behavioural paradigm in Canadian political science. In this new paradigm, "societal" forces (class, region, ethnicity) began to be accorded priority over institutional factors and normative accounts of political theory would be overshadowed by demonstrations of empirical evidence. With its focus on "inputs," the state was conceived from this perspective mainly as the product of society and not as an independent, autonomous agent. Legal determinism had been unequivocally replaced by sociological determinism and behaviourism. This disciplinary turn of mind was highly congenial to Bagehot's fusion doctrine and helped to cement it as a touchstone of the political science orthodoxy.

It was taken for granted by political scientists that this behavioural model of Canadian government would provide a useful counterpoint or "reality check" to the rigid, formal, and legalistic model that would continue to be taught in the nation's law schools. Since the executive's *political* control over the legislature had no *legal* significance, it could safely be assumed that constitutional formalities, like the formal separation of powers, would be actively promoted by the legal community. But the assumption that lawyers would themselves resist the lure of behaviouralism and remain preoccupied with forms and formalities proved to be erroneous as legal practice drifted away from what might be called its "Tocquevillian ideal." Tocqueville understood that lawyers, as a politically influential class, and one occupationally steeped in forms and formalities, could help democracies resist the potentially dangerous depreciation of forms and formalities.[22] "When the American people let themselves be intoxicated by their passions or become so self-indulgent as to be carried away by their ideas, the lawyers make them feel an almost invisible brake that moderates and halts them."[23] While a kernel of the Tocquevillian lawyer persists, it is doubtful that this model characterizes the modern legal profession. Yale Law School Dean Anthony Kronman has written extensively and persuasively about the changes in the legal profession that transformed judging "into a species of office management whose main virtue is efficiency rather than wisdom" and that reduced the ideal of a lawyer-statesman into the mundane legal bureaucrats of today.[24] While legal actors are necessarily aware of legal formalities, there is little evidence of fondness for such formalities; to the contrary, the forms they are supposed to protect are now more often seen as the obstacles to their client's – and therefore their own – success. The modern lawyer's tastes run more towards profitable indeterminacy than an aristocratic appreciation of formality. Accordingly, as James Stoner argues, modern jurists demonstrate "certain impatience with the old forms of the separation of powers ... at least any aspect of those forms that might impede the rational administration of judicial policy."[25]

The depreciation of formalities by the legal community has been accompanied by similar trends in legal scholarship which have reinforced the changes to practice. There are very few defences of formalism in modern legal scholarship, and when formalism is mentioned it is typically as a straw man for one's favoured theory to demolish.[26] The rise of legal realism in the United States in the 1920s and 1930s placed formalism in a negative light that it has yet to shed.[27] Oliver Wendell Holmes, Jr famously derided formalists for their conception of common law as a "brooding omniscience in the sky" instead of the product of human decision making.[28] Successive trends in legal theory have followed legal realism with respect to subordinating legal formalities to some other non-legal objective, whether it be "efficiency" (the organizing principle of the law and economics movement),[29] "correct philosophical first principles" (the centre of Dworkin's "law as integrity"),[30] or gender sensitivity and equality (feminist legal theory), to name some of the more obvious examples. Even those modern legal theories opposed to the idea of non-legal objectives for law have explicitly shared the disdain for legal formalities: the Critical Legal Studies movement[31] is one example and the current fad, legal pragmatism,[32] is yet another. The unpopularity of legal formalism in the legal academy is further evidence that the Tocquevillian hope that lawyers would preserve legal-democratic forms has been lost. With neither legalists nor political scientists preaching the importance of Canadian constitutional forms, it is not surprising that they faded into obscurity.

NEO-INSTITUTIONALISM AND THE AMBIVALENT MODEL

In the political science discipline, a new neo-institutionalist school of thought gradually emerged to argue that the pendulum had swung too far. The realists and behaviouralists were certainly right in rejecting legal determinism, this thinking runs, but they were wrong to ignore or dismiss formalities altogether. If rules do not *determine*, they nevertheless *influence* reality in important ways and must be "brought back in" to achieve a fully satisfying understanding of public life.[33]

Alan Cairns, "the Canadian scholar who has most explicitly drawn out the implications of neo-institutionalism for this country's constitutional politics,"[34] is particularly insightful in exploring the interrelation of legal formalities and on-the-ground political reality. While Cairns is famous for his critique of legal determinism – it was he who refused to believe that "a few elderly men in London" could be so powerful – he has been equally adamant in his opposition to "sociological determinism."[35] If Canadian decentralization could not credibly be attributed to the power of "a few elderly men in London," he argued, neither could societal forces alone provide the explanation. Societal forces are surely important, Cairns conceded, but one cannot responsibly ignore the ways in which decentralization has been encouraged and sustained by the formal institutional division of powers. The state for Cairns is neither the result simply of societal inputs nor a completely independent and autonomous entity but, rather, a socially "embedded state," which profoundly affects society even as it is in turn affected by society. Knopff and Morton tease out the implications of the embedded state for constitutional law: "To a considerable extent modern politicized identities reflect the fragmented structures of the state. Since constitutional law ... influences these structures in important ways, it must be given proper weight in any explanation. The governments that work the constitution may be more important than the constitution itself, but this does not mean the constitution is insignificant ... Constitutional constraints may have little determining power, but neo-institutionalism teaches us to look for influence rather than ultimate causal determination."[36]

If the behaviouralist turn in Canadian political science came unusually early in the form of the fusion doctrine, that doctrine has also been particularly resistant to the neo-institutionalist turn. This is not because neo-institutionalist analyses of legislative-executive interactions have been tried and proven unsatisfactory, but mainly because there have not been many attempts. Yet, if the formal rules of federalism have a significant, though certainly not determining, effect on the social reality of a "federal society," might it not be similarly true that the executive-legislative balance of "partial agency" so clearly envisaged by the formalities of responsible government continues to influence reality in important ways, that it is in fact "fusion" that is "mythical"?

This question can best be approached by way of Harvey Mansfield's gloss on the neo-institutionalist insight, what I will call the "ambivalent model" of institutional behaviour. Mansfield observes that the idea of a partial (and no more than partial) agency of the governmental branches in each other's affairs necessarily involves an "ambivalent" relationship between formal authority and informal practice that is often ignored by modern social science. Mansfield uses "executive power" as his example. Modern liberals are so accustomed to the notion of a "strong executive" – a prime minister or a president that the political universe seems to operate around – that one can easily miss the weakness inherent in the very definition of the "executive" role. As Mansfield points out, *formally* the executive "remains an agent," that is, he "executes" on behalf of someone or something else.[37] In reality, however, we know perfectly well that the executive exercises considerable *informal* discretionary power. Although "formally an agent," writes Mansfield, "the executive is *informally* much stronger than that because his job is not as easy as its harmless title promises."[38] Part of this informal strength, moreover, comes from the fact that the executive shares significantly in, often even dominates, the legislative power.[39] But this does not mean that the formality of weakness is irrelevant or "mythical." Indeed, it is essential to the actual practice of informal strength, for "when [an executive] encounters resistance, and needs to disarm resentment, he can say that he is merely carrying out the will of another – the Congress, the Commanding Officer, the people, the Good Book, the Board, the Company, or any other formal sovereign – even History."[40] In other words, the "formal weakness [actually] enhances his informal strength."[41]

Yet enhancing informal strength by appealing to formal weakness comes at a cost. The formal designation of power is not simply a rhetorical guise to permit the unrestricted exercise of discretionary power. Or rather, the very need rhetorically to justify executive acts as stemming from the legislature's orders tells us something important about the latter's real power. "The strongest power," says Mansfield, "is the one that can *say* it is the strongest and not be contradicted"[42] precisely because it is *formally* the strongest. As Mansfield puts it, "what is said in private may often be more interesting, but what can and cannot be said in public is more important: the latter is the best indicator of who rules."[43]

What is true of the executive is similarly true of the political parties that, under conditions of parliamentary responsible government, help to sustain informal executive dominance. As everyone knows, in situations of majority government at least, party discipline normally ensures that the legislative preferences of the executive will be adopted by the legislature itself. Yet here again, this very considerable power is an informal one, ultimately subject to an important formal weakness. As Mansfield notes, while parties are "now held everywhere to be essential to the law and thus allowed to reflect some of the majesty of law," it remains true that "no party has the legal status of a legislature or an executive, by which its program would count as law or decree."[44] In light of the recent failure of litigation to insist upon legislation consistent with partisan campaign promises, this formal distinction between party platform and the law has rarely been clearer.[45]

In sum, even vast and potent informal power must ultimately yield to direct and incontrovertible exercises of formal power. Informal power (executive domination of the legislature, for example) may well be the primary and regular vehicle for governance, but formal power (legislative control of the executive) both checks and, by providing rhetorical cover for its exercise, sustains informal rule. It is this ultimate ability of the legislature to trump even very powerful executives that keeps the executive's agency in legislative affairs a *partial* agency.

EXECUTIVE FUSION WITH THE LOWER HOUSE?

The obvious rejoinder to this line of argument is that it remains highly unrealistic because it puts so much weight on what is in fact so very rare. True, the legislature *can* override the executive, but since it never (or almost never) *does*, the point is moot and can safely be ignored in any realistic account of how Canadian government actually works. Such a realistic account might indeed be enriched by Mansfield's claim that an executive's appeal to its own formal weakness helps bolster its strength, but certainly not by his corollary claim that such an appeal points to real power in the legislature. This rejoinder is typical of what Mansfield argues is a common pattern in social science: the tendency to behavioralize the formal and then formalize the behavioural. "The first rule of social science," according to Mansfield, "requires a reduction of boastful rhetoric, of ambiguous terms, and of offices defined by their supposed function – in sum, of the formal – to its actual results, its unarguable meaning, and its testable operation."[46] This is behaviouralizing the formal and it entails a depreciation of statistical outliers – that is, rare or unlikely occurrences. The second rule of social science, Mansfield argues, is a reversal of the first: "formalize the behavioural." Given its better match with the substantial reality, the behavioural model is elevated to a kind of formal status, replacing the allegedly mythical formalities. The real model is described by the statistical regularities, and the rare manifestations of the mythical formalities are transformed into quirky exceptions. Mansfield notes that "when the social scientist formulates his pattern or model, he is freed of dependence on accidental fact while free, too, of ambiguous values ... From one side he deflates phony formalities pretending to transcend reality, from the other he condemns 'journalists' who are satisfied with the particulars and do not know the methods of formalizing."[47] As a consequence, social science models frequently miss (and misunderstand) the very real significance of rarely invoked or rarely infringed constitutional limits and powers.

In particular, they tend to miss the fact that a formal power may be rarely exercised precisely because, on good Hobbesian grounds, it is sufficiently clear and powerful that those subject to its constraints generally prefer to avoid its actual implementation by *limiting themselves*. It is true that the prime minister, as leader of the partisan majority in the House, can typically move his agenda through the Parliament with little difficulty.[48] (Even so, only an average of 70 per cent of government bills introduced by the last three Parliaments with majority governments (the 35th, 36th, and 37th) survived the legislative process and received royal assent.[49]) But this regularity can be seen as evidence that the Canadian constitution delivers on the Montesquieuan objective of moderate government at least in part because the formal powers of the legislative assembly put outer limits on just how far even the most power-bedazzled political executive is prepared to go. An able prime minister, (R. MacGregor Dawson) and W.F. Dawson note, will be "sufficiently wise and far-seeing to limit his demands ... to those which will gain the general acceptance of his followers."[50]

To return to Montesquieu's point, imagine a prime minister with truly extremist inclinations in the system of responsible government. Unless this prime minister has the courage and means to overthrow the constitution altogether, he can impose his policy preferences only by persuading Parliament to enact them, the bureaucracy to execute them in the way he prefers, and the courts to uphold them. This might prove difficult. Considering only the support of Parliament, Dawson and Dawson note that, while "general acquiescence [to a prime minister's wishes] can within limits be assumed ... this co-operation is usually given with some reserve, and the possibility of dissatisfaction and even revolt, though it may be remote, is never entirely absent."[51] This possibility of revolt surely moderates whatever extremist or tyrannical desires a prime minister might harbour. In the British context, Scott Gordon argues that, if the prime minister "is a dictator, he is a singularly curious one: unable to determine state policy unilaterally, required to endure unremitting and unrestrained public criticism, and subject to dismissal without a shot being fired."[52] A similar critique might be levelled at Jeffrey Simpson's description of the Canadian prime minister as a "friendly dictator"; "restrained" might be a better qualifier than "friendly."

Evidence for this can be found even in Donald Savoie's *Governing from the Centre*, the book that is most often used to support the proposition that an all-powerful prime minister faces no serious check from Parliament.[53] In this respect, it is striking that Savoie's other major theme – the centre's lack of policy ambition in favour of managing the status quo – is rarely referenced. One might ask why Jean Chrétien, Savoie's most centralizing prime minister, the basis of Simpson's "friendly dictator," is also criticized by Savoie for being "the managerial prime minister." Savoie describes Chrétien's "managerial mindset" as notably eager to "avoid bold initiatives or attempts to lead the country in redefining itself."[54] With respect to its legislative agenda, it is difficult to argue that the Chrétien government took full advantage of its supposed power. Savoie himself, alert to this paradox, argues that it was a function of external limitations, particularly the central bureaucracy's intense desire to avoid media gaffes. However, as Chrétien bemoaned, the management of the caucus is itself a source of media interest: "If I impose a decision, you say I am a dictator, and if I listen to them, the caucus is split."[55] Given its internalization into prime ministerial thinking and planning, it is difficult to conclude that the formal separation plays no part in hemming in executive power.

One might note, in this regard, that although the formal power of the legislature to oppose the prime minister is rarely overtly manifested, even prime ministers with partisan majorities are occasionally reminded of its reality. In Chrétien's case, his final term (2000–04) included two publicly visible examples of such challenges: the addition of sunset clauses to the Anti-Terrorism Bill[56] and the amendments to species-at-risk legislation.[57] One might be tempted to explain away these two cases as nothing more than flashpoints in the long-running rift in the Liberal Party between the prime minister's supporters and those of his successor, Paul Martin – the "journalistic" approach Mansfield derides – but this would fail to recognize that it is the formal power of members of the House of Commons that allowed for the expression of what would otherwise be an informal intra-party struggle. I argue that these successful challenges, made against a prime minister freshly elected (in November 2000) with a 106-seat advantage over the Official Opposition, demonstrate that the centre is not hopelessly beyond any formal controls available to legislators, as fusion proponents suggest.

The first example – the amendments to the Chrétien government's anti-terrorism package – is a powerful one since it is reasonable to assume that the executive hand might be stronger when there is a palpable sense of emergency like that which followed 11 September 2001. The government responded to the heightened threat of terrorism with two pieces of legislation: Bill C-36, primarily addressing the need for additional police powers, and Bill C-42, primarily addressing the need for additional public-safety measures. The latter proved so poorly drafted and unpopular that the government abandoned it in favour of a new Public Safety Bill in the spring of 2005.[58] The former, however, was strongly backed by Prime Minister Chrétien and Justice Minister Anne McLellan. In particular, Chrétien and McLellan insisted that, despite Bill C-36's constitutionally questionable changes to police procedure (such as the use of "preventative arrests"), it was unwise to attach a sunset clause, which would have extinguished the act after a set period and thus required a re-enactment by a future Parliament for the act to remain in force. Prime Minister Chrétien was particularly dismissive of this proposal, declaring that a sunset clause was inappropriate because "we don't know when terrorism will be over."[59] This position became increasingly untenable as academic criticism of Bill C-36 began to mount. A well-publicized conference at the Faculty of Law, University of Toronto, included a strong critique of the legislation by Liberal backbencher and constitutional law professor Irwin Cotler.[60] The inclusion of a sunset clause might have tempered some of this criticism but Chrétien continued to oppose such a measure. At a private caucus meeting in November 2001, Chrétien dressed down his backbench critics and firmly rejected their call for a sunset clause of any sort for C-36. "I think he pretty well closed the door on the sunset clause," leaked one MP, but he added that "I don't think MPs have given up."[61] If the fusion characterization were true, it should have been easy for Chrétien to follow through on his publicly stated commitment and resist the demands of his backbenchers. In reality, however, the centre of government could not simply impose its preference: "Bowing to intense public pressure and *forces within her own caucus*," Justice Minister Anne McLellan "presented a handful of amendments to Bill C-36 that eased most of the concerns of Liberal MPs and the Canadian Alliance."[62] By leading the charge, one newspaper account suggested, Irwin Cotler "set a new benchmark on how far a backbencher can confront his own government and live to tell the tale."[63]

The government's retreat on the sunset clause was echoed in its manoeuvring over the species-at-risk legislation in 2002. In that case, the Chrétien government introduced Bill C-5 to meet Canada's international obligations, promised in 1992, for the preservation of endangered species. Upon consideration of the bill, the House Environment Committee suggested over 100 amendments – mainly addressing the contentious issues of landowner compensation, aboriginal administration of the law, and whether preservation would be mandatory on federal lands – but the cabinet reversed almost every one of the committee's recommendations.[64] The government's strategy was simply to "ram it through the House of Commons" over the committee's objections.[65] This approach alienated backbench Liberals, who generally fell into two camps within the caucus: an environmentalist camp (who argued that the legislation did not go far enough in protecting endangered species) and a group of rural members concerned with the property rights of their constituents. In the months following the committee report, the government attempted to assuage critics by establishing an aboriginal commission to oversee the enforcement of the act (as Liberal backbench MP Rick Laliberte demanded) and by making a binding commitment that specific regulations for landowner compensation would be forthcoming (as demanded by the rural caucus, led by MP Murray Calder).[66] The government was unsure that, even with these major concessions, it would have the unanimous support of the Liberal caucus or even that the act would pass at all, but Environment Minister David Anderson publicly declared that there would be no more changes to the bill.[67] On the eve of the vote, the government blinked and capitulated to the environmentalist members of the caucus by accepting two key amendments (the federal government would protect the species on federal property and cabinet would be given a nine-month deadline to determine whether a species warranted protection).[68] With these changes, the act passed by a 148–85 vote. Chrétien suggested that his role in the process was less dominant than the "friendly dictator" characterization implies: "My caucus – they have views. They are there for that and sometimes one group doesn't agree with the other and it's the beauty of my job: I sit between them all the time and eventually we find a solution."[69] One thing is for sure: in the case of the Species-at-Risk Bill, cabinet did not simply get its way, as the fusion model predicts. In a candid interview months later, Minister Anderson said that "he should have held firm on the endangered species bill" and even though he was "glad it passed" he would not check his "skepticism about some of the proposals ... simply because they were ultimately accepted. It's not because I was persuaded they were all right."[70]

No one would suggest, of course, that the backbench influence over the anti-terrorism legislation or the Species-at-Risk Bill is typical of the Canadian legislative process. These are exceptional cases that prove the rule of executive domination, but they also demonstrate that executive domination of the legislature is itself qualified by the formal power of legislators to reject executive demands. Without the power to check the executive's proposals before they become law, it is doubtful that the backbenchers would have influenced the anti-terrorism and species-at-risk debates as much as they did. As mentioned earlier, a significant number (30 per cent in the last three majority Parliaments) of government bills introduced are never granted royal assent.[71] Even though a presumably large (but unknown) number of these bills are voluntarily abandoned by the government (lost through prorogation and so on), the burden of the legislative process is clear. Any government would surely prefer to govern without the formal requirement that it govern through legislation. The fact that it cannot and does not do so is testament to the formal constitution and the internalization of its moderating demands.

INTERDELEGATION?

A Mansfieldian understanding of ambivalent power also answers Hogg's charge that the seemingly unlimited degree of constitutional interdelegation among the branches proves that there is no general separation of powers in Canada. For Hogg, long-standing precedents that permit the legislature to delegate legislative powers to executive agencies establish that "in Canada there is no requirement that 'legislative' and 'executive' powers be exercised by separate and independent bodies."[72] On closer inspection, however, the very case that Hogg uses to support his contention about the separation of powers shows instead that the *formal* separation must be maintained even if a large degree of *informal* power is indeed delegated.

Hogg argues that the Supreme Court of Canada's 1918 decision on the constitutionality of the War Measures Act in *Re Gray* establishes that there are no limits to the delegation of power between branches or, alternatively, "the courts will not readily imply such limitations."[73] Section 6 of the War Measures Act allowed for the governor-in-council to issue orders having "the force of law" on a broad range of issues including, but not restricted to, "censorship," "appropriation" of property, and "arrest, detention, expulsion and deportation," so long as such measures were necessary during times of "real or apprehended war, invasion or insurrection."[74] If the sweeping powers of the War Measures Act could be lawfully transferred from the legislature to the executive, Hogg argues, then any separation of power according to function is illusory. Once again, however, Hogg discounts any effect of the constitutional formality of separated power. Justice L.P. Duff's opinion in *Gray* speaks to this matter in terms that echo Montesquieu and Madison: "There is no attempt to substitute the executive for parliament in the sense of disturbing the existing balance of constitutional authority by aggrandizing the prerogative at the expense of the legislature. The powers granted could at any time be revoked and anything done under them nullified by parliament, which parliament did not, and for that matter could not, abandon any of its own legislative jurisdiction."[75] Duff argues that "it is a very extravagant description of this enactment to say that it professes (on any construction of it) to delegate to the Governor-in-council the *whole* legislative authority of parliament."[76] Duff's opinion clearly implies that delegation has its limits and that a delegating statute could be unconstitutional (as a violation of the separation of powers) if it did attempt to delegate the entire legislative power. That is not the case with the War Measures Act because, according to Duff, the governor-in-council is a "subordinate body" temporarily acting as "the agent or organ of the legislature."[77] In this respect, the War Measures Act is not much different from the usual Canadian lawmaking process whereby ordinary legislation is drafted and enacted in general terms and followed by the more detailed "regulations" issued by the governor-in-council.[78] Hogg's difficulty with this interpretation of *Gray* is that "it is not easy to imagine the kind of delegation that would be unconstitutional,"[79] but this misses the significant point that any order made by the governor-in-council, even if *practically* final, is *formally* subject to legislative reversal. The fact that this restriction does not require judicial enforcement to achieve its important end – although one should note that Duff "readily implies" it, contrary to Hogg's assertion – does not make it any less of a constitutional imperative.

It should also be noted that Hogg suggests that the lax Canadian approach to delegation is in contrast to the United States, where "the position is otherwise" because of the "separation of power doctrine which is embedded in the federal and state constitutions."[80] Later in the very same paragraph, however, Hogg tells us that, even in the United States, "in practice ... this has not proved to be a serious restraint on the conferral of law-making powers upon administrative agencies or officials" because courts have given a "very attenuated meaning to legislative powers."[81] What then is the difference between the separating powers of the United States and the fused powers of Canada? According to Hogg, in the United States, "there is always the danger that an exceptionally broad and vague delegation might be classified as a delegation of legislative power."[82] Hogg does not tell us why rarely invoked constitutional formalities are significant south of the border but not north of it.

INEFFECTIVE BICAMERALISM?

The same logic that "fuses" the legislature to the executive also implies that the House of Commons is unfettered by the "mere formality" of the unelected Upper House. Just as the all-powerful cabinet can regularly force its agenda through the Commons, so too can it use party discipline (and its power of appointment) to ensure the compliance of the Senate. But, once again, the emphasis on *regular* behaviour underestimates the potential for an infrequently exercised but effective check. When placed under the lens of the ambivalent model, the Senate is shown to exercise more power than purely formal or purely behavioural models of its role would allow.

C.E.S. Franks notes that "most academics and journalists have been satisfied with the accepted image of the Senate as a dusty, obscure Arcadia filled with aged and retired political warhorses" that is "widely criticized for being ineffective and lackadaisical."[83] This is the sort of characterization that one would expect from an empirical analysis of the Senate's performance. Given that it is rarely an obstacle to the passage of government legislation, the Senate can be safely ignored in the ordinary day-to-day grind of Canadian politics. But one should not be lulled into the belief that this behavioural account captures everything about the Upper Chamber's role in the institutional design of the constitution. Formally, of course, the Senate has sweeping powers: all legislation must receive its acquiescence before royal assent and the Senate can even initiate some legislation on its own (provided that such legislation does not spend public funds). The formal power of the Senate is particularly relevant when there has been a partisan change of government such that the incoming government is faced with a Senate membership largely appointed by other parties. As the Brian Mulroney government discovered,[84] a skilled leader of the opposition in the Senate (in that case, Allan MacEachen) can make governing very difficult. (Notice that an informal factor – personal leadership – can invigorate formal power, providing yet another example of the interrelation between the formal and the informal). As Franks describes in detail, the Liberal senators routinely delayed and drew public attention to the government's borrowing bill (Bill C-11, likened by one senator to "a request for a post-dated blank cheque"), the Drug Patent Act, the Goods and Services Tax (GST),[85] a copyright act, and two immigration bills.[86] In each case, the will of Commons ultimately prevailed but the Senate's formal power to reject required the government to take the Senate opposition seriously. The most dramatic display of the Senate's formal power occurred in 1988 when the Senate's refusal to pass legislation implementing the Free Trade Agreement with the United States forced a general election. Having used closure and strict timetabling to force the legislation through the Commons, Prime Minister Mulroney clearly preferred to enact the legislation prior to an election and thus portrayed the Senate obstruction as "hijacking the fundamental rights of the House of Commons."[87] Senate reform advocate Randall White concedes that the Senate "did indeed live up to its highest responsibilities as a body of sober second thought" by granting Canadians an opportunity to vote on an issue of vital national interest that otherwise would never have been submitted for their approval.[88] From the empirical-behaviouralist perspective, one piece of rejected legislation over a period of almost a decade is fairly conclusive evidence of the Senate's political weakness relative to the government. As Mansfield suggests, that single instance can be dismissed as an "accidental fact" (the anecdotal "particulars" more suited to "journalism" in Mansfield's formulation) easily dismissed in the context of the rigorous formalizing of the behavioural.[89] To ignore, however, such a highly significant exercise of formal authority – forcing the government into an election it would otherwise have liked to avoid – would give a false impression of the Senate's actual power.

Accordingly, the Senate is perhaps best understood as an ambivalent institution – formally strong (because of its powers of legislation) and informally weak (primarily because of its unelected membership). The constitutional status of the Canadian Senate echoes the position of the English House of Lords as A.V. Dicey describes it. The House of Lords, Dicey says, has

> admitted the existence of a more or less strong presumption that the House of Commons in general represents the will of the nation, and that the Lords ought, therefore, in general to consent to a Bill passed by the House of Commons, even though their lordships did not approve of the measure. But this presumption may, they have always maintained, be rebutted if any strong ground can be shown for holding that the electors did not really wish such a Bill to become an Act of Parliament. Hence Bill after Bill has been passed by their lordships of which the House of Lords did not in reality approve. It was however absolutely indubitable ... that no Act could be passed by Parliament without obtaining the consent of the House of Lords. Nor could anyone dispute the legal right or power of the House, by refusing such assent, to veto the passing of any Act of which the House might disapprove.[90]

While the Senate *can* use its formidable legislative powers, it only *rarely* uses them because of its substantial informal weaknesses relative to the elected House of Commons. Even its effective use of formal power to precipitate the 1988 election relied upon an appeal to the people to ultimately resolve the issue. A strong institution – both formally and informally – should be able to express its preference into law, but the Senate's preference (against the Free Trade Agreement) was defeated by the re-election of the Conservative government. The Senate could have formally rejected the subsequent legislation but, because of its informally weak position as an unelected body, it respected the result of the election and accepted the government's position. Neither the formal model (which would permit the Senate's continuing resistance to free trade) nor the behavioural model (which could not explain the Senate's resistance in the first place) can accurately explain the Senate's role with respect to the 1988 election as well as the ambivalent model's understanding of the institution as formally strong but informally weak.

CONCLUSION

As the discussion above demonstrates, ambivalence is a common theme in the power relationships between Canadian institutions. In each case, we find broad informal powers matched with formal but often rarely exercised checks. The advantage of such arrangements is that they accommodate the powerful institutions that are often necessary to ensure effective governance but also provide an opportunity for other, seemingly weaker institutions to check the powerful should they fall prey to the temptations of immoderation.

None of this is to suggest that the Canadian doctrine is inherently superior to other possible separation-of-powers arrangements, like the U.S. presidential system or the more aggressively bicameral Australian model. Nor should I be understood as suggesting that Senate reform or executive domination of legislatures are not issues worth addressing in some fashion. Canadians might indeed be better served if senators were to be elected, if the legislature were to undertake greater oversight of the executive, or if party discipline were to be relaxed in order to encourage more assertiveness on the part of backbench MPs (but, I would argue, one must also be aware that further fettering of the executive will reduce its effectiveness). The position taken by this study is simply that the formal boundaries between the legislative and executive and those between the House and Senate provide *some* checks on executive excess.

Beyond their simple existence, it is the ambivalent mode by which these checks operate that is revealing. When we turn to the judiciary over the next three chapters, it is important to realize that judicial-legislative and judicial-executive relations might also take an ambivalent character. Judicial interpretive supremacy, of course, requires the Supreme Court to hold the *whole* interpretive power and its adherents argue that anything less will subordinate the Court in toto to another institution. The more complex arrangements contemplated by the ambivalent model prove this dichotomy false and suggest that coordinate interpretation might be more viable than its detractors believe.

5

The Ambivalent Judicial Role in the Separation of Powers

Contrary to the accepted opinions of some of Canada's foremost constitutional thinkers, the separation of powers continues to play a vital in Canada's constitutional design. Even though the exaggerated claim of executive-legislative fusion has done much to obscure it, the subtle interplay of formal and informal power maintains and animates an effective institutional separation between the legislature and the executive. Viewed through this lens, the fundamental rule of the separation of powers (the power of no branch may be wholly exercised by another) can be easily discerned. Thus far the discussion has focused on the executive-legislative separation in order to prove that the institutional separation can be found even where its opponents suggest it is least likely. It remains to place the judicial branch within this scheme of ambivalent and separated power. That is the task of this chapter.

Unlike the executive-legislative separation, the judicial separation from the representative branches is uncontroversial so long as the separation is characterized as "judicial independence," a notion that receives widespread support from both political scientists and legal scholars. The Supreme Court of Canada itself has relied on the "profound commitment to the constitutional theory of the separation of powers" to support its rulings on judicial independence.[1] As Peter McCormick notes, however, "when the Supreme Court of Canada talks about the separation of powers in the context of judicial independence ... it never connects the idea to 'checks and balances,' a phrase it has never used in any decision."[2] This unwillingness to connect the separation to "checks and balances" results in a judicial conception of the separation of powers that is more akin to the flawed watertight-compartments variant discussed in chapter 3.[3] The more plausible partial-agency model developed throughout that chapter suggests a better approach. It prescribes not only a judicial role protected from politics but a politics shielded, in part, from judicialization. Moreover, it accepts that substantial partial agency is necessary and desirable among all three branches in direct contrast to the watertight separation now asserted in the name of judicial independence (but not, tellingly, in defence of other institutions). To understand this nuanced delineation of roles and powers, it is necessary first to consider the three branches in their most basic functional terms.

THREE BRANCHES, NOT TWO

The ambivalent separation of the judiciary from the other governing powers is part and parcel of the Montesquieuean scheme to divide power. Recall Montesquieu's insistence that "there would be an end of everything, were the same man or the same body, whether of the nobles or of the people, to exercise those three powers, that of enacting laws, that of executing the public resolutions, and of trying the causes of individuals."[4] The third power – "trying the causes of individuals" – is the judicial power. Like the second power – "executing the public resolutions" – the judicial power involves *applying* or *implementing* the laws, and for this reason it had been traditionally understood to be part of the executive power.[5] But, just as liberty is endangered when the powers of "making" and "executing" the laws are wholly conjoined in the same person or institution, so is liberty threatened when those who "execute" the laws (e.g., in the case of criminal investigation and prosecution) simultaneously hold the power of judging whether the law has been appropriately applied (e.g., judging guilt or innocence). Liberty is threatened, in short, not only when legislators directly implement the law but when a single implementer acts simultaneously as police and prosecutor on the one hand and judge and jury on the other. In the modern separation of powers, the first two functions (police and prosecutor) reside in the executive branch and are themselves subject to some degree of separation,[6] while the second two functions (judge and jury) are part of a separate judicial process.

The judiciary must also be separated from the executive because the task of "trying the causes of individuals" includes not only causes or quarrels between individuals (as in the case of civil suits) but also causes pitting individuals against the executive itself. As Blackstone notes, it would be "impossible, as well as improper" for the king to adjudicate such cases.[7] In other words, to the extent that these two "implementing" branches remained joined together, we would confront all the well-worn questions of judging in one's own case, not to mention the huge asymmetry of power between the executive branch of government and the individual. Accordingly, by Montesquieu's time, the judiciary had emerged as the "third branch" of government in liberal separation-of-powers theory. "Again, there is no liberty," says Montesquieu, "if the judicial power be not separated from the legislative and the executive. Were it joined with the legislative, the life and the liberty of the subject would be exposed to arbitrary control; for the judge would be then the legislator. Were it joined to the executive power, the judge might behave with violence and oppression."[8] The difference between the two law-implementing branches (executive and judiciary) will receive further attention below. But first we need additional clarity on what separates the legislative function from both of these implementing branches.

THE SEPARATION OF LAWMAKING AND LAW IMPLEMENTING

The basic distinction between the legislative task of enacting laws and the executive and judicial functions of implementing them is the different levels of abstraction involved. Simply put, legislatures work through generalities whereas executives and courts make more specific judgments. Legislatures are formally required to enact only laws of general application, not edicts targeting particular individuals.[9] It is the difference between permissible legislation that says "university professors must pay tax at twice the rate of other citizens" and impermissible legislation that says "Dennis Baker must pay tax at twice the rate of other citizens." Is this a distinction without a difference, especially if Dennis Baker is a professor? No, because allowing only the first kind of law ensures that the legislative power of the state is not directed against an individual, thus preventing what might be the most egregious and arbitrary infringements to personal liberty, the kinds of infringements dramatically illustrated by the now defunct practice of bills of attainder. Once understood to be a legislative prerogative, attainder bills were commonly used by legislatures to impose punishments (ranging from forfeiture of property to death) directly on particular individuals. For example, the English Parliament once passed an attainder bill that demanded the bishop of Rochester's cook be boiled to death.[10] As T.R.S. Allan notes, "acts of attainder would today be universally condemned as contrary to fundamental principle" and modern constitutionalism denies their operation either by convention (as in England and pre-1982 Canada) or by explicit provision (as in the American constitution and, arguably, by s.11[g] of the Charter).[11]

At bottom, the problem with bills of attainder is that they violate the fundamental rule-of-law principle that like cases be treated alike. This does not mean that the laws must treat all people alike in every respect. The rule of law does not prevent people in higher income brackets (or even professors) from being taxed at a higher rate; it does mean that all people similarly situated with respect to the law in question (e.g., all top income earners or professors) be taxed in the same way. By contrast, the principle of like cases being treated alike is violated if Dennis Baker is singled out for higher taxation *because* he is a professor while other professors continue to be taxed at a lower rate. A *general* law for professors solves this problem.

Indeed, unless like cases are treated alike in this way, it is difficult to speak of law at all.[12] Unlike arbitrary attainders, which come like unpredictable bolts from the blue, laws generally take the form of prospective rules, knowable in advance.[13] This prospective character of law is a profoundly liberty-enhancing cornerstone of the rule of law because it allows individuals to adjust their behaviour in advance, to avoid the prospect of legal punishments or penalties.[14] There is an enormous difference for Dennis Baker between knowing that *all* professors are equally subject to higher taxation and discovering after the fact that only he is being singled out for this treatment. In the first case, he might have decided against graduate school, in the second he can only regret his decision.

The generality of law secures liberty not only by preventing legislators from targeting particular individuals but also by requiring them to live under the general laws they create. Thus, following our examples, if a legislator were to become a university professor, he too would be subject to a higher level of taxation imposed on professors, or if he were to commit an offence for which boiling were the prescribed punishment, he could expect a trip to the pot.

Needless to say, legislators will be less likely to enact unjust laws under which they themselves might suffer.

Unless, of course, legislatures had the power not only to enact general laws but also to apply them, in which case they could again contemplate enacting egregious laws, safe in the knowledge that they could avoid their application. (Or, alternatively, they could enact acceptable general laws to cover corrupt and oppressive implementation). Once again the principle of treating like cases alike would be imperilled. The task of applying general laws to particular situations is thus given to two separate branches: the executive and the judiciary, thereby ensuring that those who make the laws remain subject to the salutary constraint of being subject to those very laws.

In sum, the liberty-protecting purpose of the separation of powers is served in part by limiting legislatures to the enactment of *general* laws and giving the power of applying those laws to *particular* circumstances or individuals to separate branches (the executive and the judiciary). This division of labour is hardly as distinct as all that,[15] as our previous discussion of ambivalent partial agency would suggest, but the complexities and nuances we shall encounter should not obscure the fundamental importance of the basic principle.

SEPARATING EXECUTIVE AND JUDICIAL IMPLEMENTATIONS

If the principle that like cases should be treated alike counsels the separation of (general) lawmaking and (particular) law implementation, it similarly counsels the separation of the implementing function into two distinct branches. This is because the front-line implementing concerns of executive agencies often lead them to de-emphasize treating similar cases alike. The work of an executive agency, says Trevor Allan, is distinguished by "an intrinsic danger of arbitrary treatment" because "whenever it exercises a discretion in the pursuit of public ends, however necessary or desirable, it treats the specific facts of the citizen's case as grounds for coercive action without necessarily assuming any commitment to the similar treatment of other persons in similar circumstances."[16] The rule of law needs a way to counteract and discipline this executive tendency, and it finds it in the supervisory authority of an institution more explicitly designed to emphasize the equal treatment of similar cases: the judiciary. Like the legislature, the courts accept "a comparable constraint of equality or generality."[17] Certainly, courts, like executive agencies, are involved in particular cases or situations, but they seek to judge them "only in accordance with the principles applicable to all, expressing general criteria capable of systematic articulation and open to critical public inspection and debate."[18]

Stated differently, the courts, being "courts of *law*," are limited to applying pre-existing legal standards, whereas the executive must occasionally operate without such standards – hence more "arbitrarily" – because it is "unrealistic to suppose that every important question of public policy could always be determined in advance by the legislature, and agreed upon solutions embodied in general rules."[19] Moreover, as Sir Philip Warwick long ago noted, it would be a "piece of ignorance, to think, because a decision is arbitrary, therefore it is unjust."[20] Nevertheless, an arbitrary decision is more likely to be unjust, and it certainly runs against the grain of the rule of law. Thus, as Gregory Tardi states, the Canadian system of government mandates the "supremacy of legal norms over administrative and political ones, and hence the primacy of legal instruments over all the other ones used in governance."[21] This means, as T.R.S. Allan observes, that the executive "is rightly made subject to the supervision of independent courts,"[22] not least to ensure that any executive interference with liberty is authorized by law.[23]

The founders of the modern separation of powers had precisely the same view. "Laws are a dead letter," says Alexander Hamilton in the *Federalist Papers*, "without courts to expound and define their true meaning and operation."[24] They become a "dead letter without courts" in part because enforcement of the law often requires judicial cooperation. For example, the police may arrest and charge, but legal penalties can be imposed only if a court finds guilt and passes a sentence. Since their cooperation is required, courts can act as a check on executive excess or arbitrariness. As Paul Carrese points out, Hamilton argued that the separate judiciary would protect "particular individuals case by case, as Montesquieu and Blackstone would expect,"[25] that is, by "moderating" the excesses of the other branches.

The executive's subordination to judicial command therefore allows the courts to play a moderating role, consistent with the Montesquiean scheme, by blunting executive discretion. It is telling that one of the few formal exceptions to the executive's subordination, the executive pardon, may be used only to further moderate the application of law (by granting mercy) and not to reverse a judicial acquittal by bestowing a *conviction* on any defendant. It is not arbitrariness per se that must be mitigated but coercive arbitrariness that threatens liberty. Again, the Montesquieuan concern with the immoderation that might result from accumulated power reveals itself to be the centre of the constitutional order. A judicial power that encourages the equality essential to the rule of law may moderate executive power in favour of liberty but there is no reason, in the Montesqeuean scheme, for the judiciary to interfere when the executive itself acts to increase or enhance such liberty. The judicial branch, in other words, holds no monopoly on being a moderating, liberty-enhancing influence and, where it acts to the contrary, it too should be checked.

PARTIAL AGENCY: INTERPRETIVE LAWMAKING

What, more precisely, is the mechanism through which judicial co-operation in the execution of the law exercises its moderating, liberty-enhancing effect? Here we need a closer look at Hamilton's statement that "laws are a dead letter without courts to *expound and define* their true meaning and operation." Note the words emphasized this time: "expound and define." The point is not just that judicial cooperation is required to implement the law. Hamilton is acknowledging the importance of an "interpretive" role for the courts. The task is not the simple mechanical application of clear law to the facts of the case.[26] Indeed, both the facts and the law can be ambiguous, requiring interpretive activity by both executive enforcers and their judicial supervisors. Interpreting the facts, a task common to the two implementing institutions (executive and judiciary), embroils those institutions in a liberty-enhancing system of checks and balances. Interpreting the law is a kind of law*making*, and thus another example of the partial-agency dimension of the separation of powers.

To illustrate the problem of factual ambiguities, consider the case of a speed limit. Here the legal standard is quite clear, but the factual situation may not be. There may be no question that a vehicle was clocked travelling over the limit, but was the radar gun in good working order and had it been properly applied? Was it the accused behind the wheel, or was someone else actually guilty of the offence? Factual ambiguities of this kind are constantly being resolved by the executive officers (in this case the police) charged with applying legal standards, but their understandable emphasis on order and security may lead to biased and mistaken judgments. Thus, an accused who claims factual innocence has the right to present his case in court so that factual ambiguities can be reconsidered by an independent and impartial judge.

In other instances, the factual situation might be quite clear but the law is not. Someone was clearly in possession of a legally prohibited substance, say, but just as clearly believed he was carrying some other, perfectly innocuous product. Does the applicable law establish a "strict liability" offence, under which this individual would be guilty whether or not he "intended" the prohibited action, or does it assume that "mens rea" or "guilty mind" must be present in order to sustain a conviction?[27] The law is ambiguous about this question, and the implementing authorities must make an interpretive judgment.[28]

The interpretive judgments required sometimes involve not only ordinary legislation but also the constitution. Constitutional texts, no less than statutes, require elaboration in order to be applied to any factual case because their language is necessarily general, often vague, and sometimes purely aspirational. Section 7 of the Charter allows violations of one's "life, liberty and security of the person" only if such infringements are consistent with the tenets of "fundamental justice." The invocation of fundamental justice provides precious little guidance for determining, say, whether mens rea is a constitutionally required element for many offences. A cursory knowledge of anglo-American law would surely lead one to conclude that "fundamental justice" does indeed require evidence of a guilty mind for a murder conviction but even that simple application is a contestable interpretive exercise. More complex cases – "felony murder" provisions, for example, which attempt to charge accomplices to a crime (robbery, say) with murder if an intentional death results from the commission of the crime even if the accomplice did not in fact directly kill the victim – require an interpretation not only of the constitutional text but also of the statute in question and the combined application of both interpretations. Whereas the felony murder provision might be best interpreted, absent any constitutional concerns, as not requiring mens rea (for the murder), one's interpretation of the fundamental justice demanded by section 7 could require a mens rea element before the imposition of a stigmatizing murder conviction.[29] Or, alternatively, it might not. Sorting out competing constitutional and statutory demands is a necessary and unavoidable aspect of constitutional law.

Such interpretive puzzles arise, of course, precisely because law must take general form. While the meaning of law phrased in general terms may be quite clear for many situations, factual circumstances inevitably arise that cast its meaning into doubt and raise competing ways of understanding its requirements. It is worrying to leave these interpretive judgments – whether they involve ordinary legislation, the constitution, or both – wholly in the hands of the immediate executive authorities, who might, for example, have an understandable bias in favour of interpretations (both legislative and constitutional) that permit strict liability enforcement of the criminal law. Here again we insist that an accused has the opportunity to defend himself or herself against such interpretations in an independent court of law.

Although factual ambiguity is an important element in applying the law, legal ambiguity is of greater interest for this study because it necessarily involves the partial agency of both the executive and judicial branches in the legislative function of lawmaking (at the levels of both ordinary and constitutional law). Choosing between alternative ways of understanding and applying a law is, after all, an important form of lawmaking or "legislating."[30] An absolute power to interpret might even be considered more powerful than the power to issue law itself; "whoever hath an absolute interpretive authority to interpret any written or spoken laws," according to Benjamin Hoadley's 1717 sermon, "it is he who is truly the lawgiver, to all intents and purposes, and not the person who first spoke or wrote them."[31] The previous chapter explained how the legislature's formal authority over lawmaking is affected by both the formal and the informal influence over its agenda exercised by the political executive or cabinet. To this executive involvement in lawmaking one must now add a dimension of interpretive lawmaking by the various agencies of executive enforcement.

The problem with multiple interpretive judgments of front-line executive agencies, however, is that they may not be consistent enough to satisfy the rule-of-law principle of treating like cases alike. Indeed, to the extent that this is true, the lawmaking character of interpretive judgment is diminished because inconsistent interpretation and application in effect makes the law unknowable to those subject to it. As noted above, rules must be prospectively knowable in order to deserve the status of law. Thus, in the overall liberty-enhancing application of the partial-agency principle, interpretive lawmaking by courts, with their stronger orientation to treating like cases alike, acts as a supervisory check on the interpretive judgments of executive agencies. The executive branch exercises its interpretive discretion first, as it were, as it engages in its various enforcement activities. This discretion may be checked, however, by a subsequent judicial challenge initiated by a citizen demand for his or her "day in court." Since the judicial ruling is explicitly designed with the requirements of generalization in mind, it is more akin to the lawmaking of the legislature.

SEPARATING LEGISLATIVE AND JUDICIAL LAWMAKING: THE CASE-AND-CONTROVERSY CONSTRAINT

That is not to say that judicial lawmaking is *exactly* like that of the legislature. Simply replicating the legislature would be of little advantage. As elsewhere in the complex separation of powers, judicial lawmaking provides another example of partial agency but not complete overlap of powers. Judicial lawmaking is partial for two reasons. First, while legislatures are free to make law entirely de novo, judicial lawmaking is limited to expounding or fleshing out already *existing* law. In a word, judicial lawmaking is "interstitial."[32] Even in the common law realm of "judge-made" law, new developments take their departure from a pre-existing body of case law. Second, the judicial process, including its lawmaking dimension, is triggered and constrained by the need to settle (or "adjudicate") particular or individual "cases and controversies" that arise under the law. As Alan Cairns observes, "courts are not self-starting institutions ... they are called into play by groups and individuals seeking objectives which can be furthered by judicial support."[33] Judges cannot simply take a blank page and write new law, even interstitially. They cannot, for example, simply decide one day to issue an opinion asserting that an otherwise ambiguous criminal prohibition is not a strict liability law but requires mens rea for a finding of guilt, or that if it is indeed a strict liability law, it is unconstitutional under section 7 of the Charter. They must await a concrete case in which an accused charged with the offence raises mens rea as a defence. If the legislature has its power restricted by a requirement of generality, then judicial lawmaking is restricted by a corresponding requirement of particularity.

Only someone directly affected by the law, in other words, has "standing" to raise issues of legal interpretation in court and thus to trigger judicial lawmaking. For similar reasons, courts are reluctant to issue legal interpretations when the concrete case has become "moot" because, for example, the litigant raising the issue has died or the law under which the case arose has been changed by the legislature. In both cases, the court's adversarial procedures cannot be relied upon to arrive at a just settlement because one side may not be as vigorously defended as the other. While the rules of standing and mootness have been considerably relaxed in recent decades, especially as they apply to constitutional cases,[34] the general constraint of concrete cases remains important. As Kent Roach notes, even under Canada's relatively lenient standards, "not just anyone can walk into the Court and start talking about the *Charter*."[35]

The same logic argues against courts issuing purely advisory opinions on legal matters, outside a normal concrete case, when requested to do so by governments. There are, of course, exceptions to this logic. In Canada, for example, governments may "refer" issues to their highest courts of appeal for advisory opinions, but when the JCPC authorized such "reference cases" in 1912, Lord Chancellor Loreburn suggested that "the putting of questions, otherwise than by litigation, to a Court of law" was an unwise and relatively novel addition to judicial duties even if it was intra vires the power of the Canadian government to do so.[36] It is significant, from the perspective of partial agency, that the judicial ability to answer such references is explicitly non-binding on the government and merely advisory. In other words, any judicial lawmaking in a reference case is, at best, informally persuasive and recognized as having no direct formal effect.[37]

For our purposes, two implications of this traditional case-and-controversy logic, as the Americans call it, deserve special attention.[38] First, it is necessary to recognize the inviolability of the judicial settlement as it affects the actual litigants to the case. As Hamilton noted in *Federalist* No. 81, the inability of the elected branches to overturn a specific judicial outcome other than by a new, prospective, and general law is a long-standing feature of English constitutionalism: "It is not true ... that the parliament of Great Britain ... can rectify the exceptionable decisions of their respective courts, in any other sense than might be done by a future legislature of the United States. The [British theory does not authorize] the revisal of a judicial sentence, by a legislative act ... A legislature without exceeding its province cannot reverse a determination once made, in a particular case; though it may prescribe a new rule for future cases."[39] Therefore, from the perspective of the litigants who bring the case to court, the judicial determination is final (in the sense that it is alterable only by other courts). Just as the rule against bills of attainder prohibits the imposition of personal and specific penalties, the legislative and executive branches are prohibited from reopening individual cases to make individual determinations contrary to those found by the judiciary. While the legislature may in fact modify a law after having observed its application to a particular concrete case, that revised legislation does not retroactively apply to the "cause of action" at issue in the decided case.[40] Thus, although the case-and-controversy requirement might be perceived as a limitation on judicial power, it also strengthens judicial power in terms of its real-world effect. Dicey, for one, argues that a court's power over discrete cases actually enhances its power, in contrast to pronouncing on legislation in the abstract: "If anyone thinks this is a distinction without a difference he shows some ignorance of politics, and does not understand how much the authority of a Court is increased by confining its action to purely judicial business."[41] No other institution in the Montesquiean scheme is permitted such direct power over individuals without an opportunity for the other branches to interfere. Indeed, it is for this reason, at least in part, that the "terrible" power to imprison individuals is made not by judges alone (unless the accused consents to such a trial) but only with the acquiescence of a jury made up of ordinary citizens.[42] As we shall see, the power to make inviolable decisions that bind individuals ensures the courts a dominant (and perhaps virtually unbeatable) position in interpretive conflicts over time, but, contrary to the assumptions of some judicial supremacists, it certainly does not preclude such conflicts altogether.

While any interpretive lawmaking undertaken by a judge is binding on the actual parties to the case, it does not necessarily apply beyond the confines of the case. This is the second aspect of the justicability case-and-controversy requirement that is important for our discussion of the courts' interpretive power. In a sense, the legislature and the judiciary share a division of labour regarding generality that suits their comparative institutional advantages: "Legislatures most often make egregious mistakes when they try to rule on single, high-visibility cases for politically expedient purposes ... Courts correspondingly most often make egregious mistakes when they rule in ways that go far beyond what can be confidently inferred from the merits of the actual case or cases at hand."[43] Just as the rule of generality appropriately restricts legislative power, so too does the case-and-controversy requirement inhibit judicial hubris.

In the American context, an open-ended general power for the judiciary to interpret the constitutional text beyond a concrete case was rejected at the 1787 convention. There, Dr William Samuel Johnson proposed adding language to Article III such that it would "authorize the federal judiciary to hear cases arising under 'this Constitution.'"[44] In the ensuing debate ("a precursor to the modern debate over justicability doctrines"), Madison "doubted whether it was not going too far to extend the jurisdiction of the Court generally to cases arising Under the Constitution & whether it ought not be limited to cases of a Judiciary Nature."[45] Johnson's motion failed and, as Madison reports, the delegates agreed that "the right of expounding the Constitution in cases not of this nature ought not be given to [the Judicial] Department."[46] Even Chief Justice Marshall understood that his holding in *Marbury v. Madison* (establishing a judicial power to declare an act of Congress unconstitutional) was limited by the case-and-controversy requirement, which meant that Article III "does not extend the judicial power to every violation of the Constitution which may possibly take place, but to 'a case in law or equity' in which a right under such law is asserted in a court of justice."[47] A court's power to declare laws void, in other words, is coterminous with its power to settle the case before it.

The case-and-controversy limitation suggests a more modest form of judicial review than the judicial supremacist variant. Unlike a "general power of courts to invalidate legislation," one might conceive of judicial review as "a *derivative* discretion in courts to disregard specific enactments whenever they cannot be rendered consistent with constitutional provisions which they presuppose."[48] Presented with the "basic law" of the constitution and a specific legislative provision, the latter is "'impossible to be performed,' in the Blackstonian sense, but the impossibility extends only to the particular circumstances of the litigation immediately before the Court – not to hypothetical circumstances which may give rise to similar cases in the future."[49] From this perspective, "a law which a court refuses to apply in a particular instance nevertheless remains an enforceable statute, until another court sees fit to dispense with it in another particular case, and so on."[50] The distinction between this discrete form of judicial review and its supremacist variant can be discerned in the choice of metaphors that proponents of the rival models use when confronting unconstitutional legislation: where the supremacist talks of "striking down" the law (conjuring the image of a black-robed lumberjack axing the offending statutory tree), a coordinate judge would simply "disregard" the offending law in the course of exercising his or her judicial duties (settling the case before the bench). As Walter Murphy notes, the supremacist demand (requiring all branches "not only to obey [a] ruling but to follow its reasoning in future deliberations") is "a long step from judicial review – the authority of a court, when deciding cases, to refuse to give force to an act of a coordinate branch of government."[51] Both interpretive supremacy and coordinate interpretation include a power of judicial review; the supremacist account simply goes further by unhinging judicial power from its case-specific application.

From a rule-of-law perspective, the case-specific limitation on judicial decisions to the parties is counter-productive because it conflicts with the principle of treating like cases alike.[52] True, a judge who has engaged in interpretive lawmaking is expected to apply the same interpretation to similar cases that come before her, but although her ruling might be of persuasive value to other trial judges, it is not a binding precedent for them; they remain free to "legislate" differently. The resolution of this difficulty, at least within the judiciary, lies in the hierarchy of appeal courts. As the next section shows, however, this resolution takes time, leaving room for a degree of "legal pluralism" in the meantime.

LEGAL PLURALISM AND THE JUDICIAL HIERARCHY

While the lawmaking dimension of the judicial task is present all levels of court, it increases as one climbs the judicial hierarchy. Indeed, there is a strong tradition among appellate courts of accepting only appeals that raise "questions of law" and leaving "questions of fact" to the discretion of the better-situated trial judge (who, after all, was the only judge to hear the evidence first hand). The focus of trial courts is settling the immediate case, and any interpretive lawmaking involved can be understood as simply a necessary but subordinate corollary of the primary task. This is one reason why the law made in this context has traditionally been understood to apply only to the immediate parties of the case, and not beyond, thus generating the possibility of legal pluralism at the level of trial courts.

This pluralism declines as one moves up the appellate hierarchy. While an appeal satisfies a need to ensure procedural fairness to the litigants, it is an appeal court's primary task to help settle interpretive ambiguities (that is, to make law) for all lower courts under its jurisdiction, thereby ensuring the uniform judicial application of legal standards. Its lawmaking role, in short, is no longer merely a necessary corollary; it becomes truly predominant. (At the apex of the hierarchy, the Supreme Court, policy may be made "not as an accidental by-product of its legal function, but because [the Court] believes that certain legal rules will be socially beneficial." [53]) The fact that judges at the same level in the judicial hierarchy are bound only by precedents set by higher courts and not by rulings of other courts at the same level (or different jurisdictions) means that the rule-of-law principle of like cases being treated alike will be violated in any jurisdiction *for a time* – that is, until it is restored by the unifying precedent of a higher court.

This period of legal pluralism is perhaps regrettable from the perspective of strict legal equality (and thus problematic for the particular defendants treated unfairly), but viewed slightly differently, through the lens of legal quality, it appears as a considerable virtue. Legal alternatives that temporarily co-exist provide the appellate courts not only with a variety of options but also with evidence of how each alternative functions in concrete cases.[54] Indeed, this is an advantage the judiciary typically holds over the legislature – "the judgment of courts can come later, after the hope and prophecies expressed in legislation have been tested in the actual workings of our society"[55] – and is therefore a sound advantage within the judicial institution itself. Prudence dictates that it would be unwise to accept, immediately and unconditionally, the first decision made as the correct one. Judicial mistakes can, of course, occur at any time (in the first, second, or nth decision), but allowing the issue to "ripen," in Alexander Bickel's evocative phrasing, helps bring all relevant dimensions into view and thus minimizes those errors.[56] For this reason, higher appellate courts and virtually all modern supreme courts have the discretion to choose the cases that they will hear. By restraining themselves from hearing a case, appellate judges can manage the time dimension of legal pluralism to minimize judicial errors.

These virtues of legal pluralism are threatened by the claim that the judiciary is the *exclusive* interpreter of the constitution. If the judicial branch is the only institution qualified to interpret the constitution, as some supremacists suppose, then it logically follows that all interpretive conflicts over the constitution must occur within the judicial branch itself (that is, only within judicial fora). Since this argument is an extension rather than a necessary component of judicial interpretive supremacy,[57] I refer to it as the claim for "judicial insularity." From this perspective, non-judicial institutions may express their disagreement with judicial interpretations only through appeals to courts higher on the judicial hierarchy (because, again, only courts, and not other institutions, can interpret). In the meantime, this logic runs, non-judicial institutions continue to be bound by the *initial* or latest judicial interpretation even though future decisions might be pending.

Taken to its logical conclusion, this call for judicial insularity would lead "governments to suspend their enforcement of a law on the say so of a single trial-level judge."[58] In fact, this now routinely occurs in cases of constitutional invalidity. A prime example is the 1989 Alberta seat-belt controversy. In 1989 a trial judge's invalidation of the province's mandatory seat-belt law prompted the Alberta government to announce that it was suspending all prosecutions until its appeal was granted. "What was significant," Knopff and Morton write, "was the government's assumption that a single judge in a single case could suspend the law's operation and that only other judges could restore it."[59]

A similar result occurred in the wake of the trial judgment in *R. v. Sharpe*. At the trial level, Judge Duncan Shaw found the Criminal Code provisions prohibiting the possession of child pornography to infringe unconstitutionally the freedom of expression of the accused. The British Columbia government appealed the case but, in the meantime, it also suspended all prosecutions of similar cases. While this decision might be justified on the grounds of legal uniformity, there is little evidence that the government considered anything but uncritical obedience to judicial command. If the government had persisted under its own interpretation of the law and pursued the cases before it, the appeal courts would have had the benefit of multiple trial court judgments before them. Instead of this outcome, we are left with Judge Shaw, a single trial judge, effectively making general law for the entire province simply because of the assumption that executive actors may not hold interpretive judgments that have not (yet) been endorsed by a judicial actor.

This assumption of judicial insularity makes little sense.[60] Given that same-level judges (for example, trial judges) are not bound to follow each other's precedents, it seems illogical to require the executive to abandon its own judgment on the word of one judge when another might readily accept it. If we prize alternate trial-court judgments for providing useful data to contextualize appellate decision making, then executive recalcitrance in the face of an opposing trial judgment should be encouraged instead of disallowed. It is, of course, within the discretion of the attorney general to accept a trial-court judgment as definitive and cease all prosecutions, but this too is an executive judgment, requiring some degree of interpretation, and thus need not be understood simply as executive obedience to judicial command.

Not only do proponents of judicial insularity insist that the executive branch submit to the authority of lower courts (pursuing reversals only through the appeals process), they sometimes demand that legislative discretion must also be restricted by these preliminary judgments. In this view, a lower-court finding of unconstitutionality means that the legislature cannot pass any new legislation that conflicts with the announced judicial rule without (in the case of the Charter) using the section 33 override. In other words, once a court – any court – decides a Charter issue, the government has three options: it may acquiesce to the constitutional principles announced by the decision, formally declare that its response is extra-constitutional (that is, it is legislating "notwithstanding" the judicial ruling), or begin the laborious process of constitutional amendment. Responding to a lower-court ruling with ordinary legislation that does not contain a notwithstanding clause is, from this perspective, something that "our Constitution doesn't permit."[61]

This was the conclusion of Sujit Choudhry and 133 (self-described) "constitutional experts" in a public letter addressed to Stephen Harper, then leader of the Official Opposition. In the aftermath of the Supreme Court reference declaring same-sex marriage legal but not necessarily compulsory,[62] Harper advocated new legislation that would retain the traditional definition of marriage and potentially create new legal categories for same-sex couples. According to Choudhry and his colleagues, such legislation is constitutionally impermissible, absent a notwithstanding declaration, because it would conflict with lower-court rulings that did require same-sex marriages as a matter of constitutional law: "Even though the Supreme Court of Canada did not address this issue in the recent same-sex marriage reference, courts in British Columbia, Saskatchewan, Manitoba, Newfoundland, Ontario, Quebec, Nova Scotia and the Yukon are now unanimously of the view that a definition of marriage that excludes same-sex couples is unconstitutional. The consensus of constitutional experts is that these decisions are correct ... The truth is, there is only one way to accomplish your goal: invoke the notwithstanding clause."[63] In other words, a series of lower-court judgments on discrete cases immediately bind Parliament's discretion to enact new laws. There is clearly no room for interpretive disagreement with the lower court: "You should either invoke the use of the notwithstanding clause ...," Choudhry's letter concludes, "or concede that same-sex marriage is now part of Canada's legal landscape."[64] This is a somewhat staggering result, especially since, as Harper himself noted, "we have a long history of introducing legislation contrary to lower-court decisions."[65] To his credit, one law professor, Alan Brudner of the University of Toronto, did write in Harper's defence on constitutional grounds (while disagreeing with him on the policy itself).[66] Commenting on Choudhry's letter, Brudner notes that no one can know with certainty how the Supreme Court would treat a legislative restatement of the traditional definition of marriage. Brudner points out that, "of course, the betting odds lie heavily against such [legislation], but the legal experts claimed to be stating the law, not predicting judicial behaviour."[67]

By making Parliament subordinate to an extrapolation of lower-court judgments, Choudhry and his colleagues have stretched the judicial-insularity argument beyond the point of credibility. The flaw in their argument can be demonstrated by substituting the notwithstanding clause with its logical corollary, the formal process of constitutional amendment. Both the notwithstanding clause and formal amendment concede the correctness of the judicial interpretation of the constitutional text and allow governments and legislatures either to ignore the text (in the case of the notwithstanding clause) or to change the text itself (in the case of amendment). In terms of their capacity to respond to "correct" judicial interpretations, then, the two powers are identical. Yet Choudhry and his colleagues fail to mention the possibility of constitutional amendment as a course of action Harper might take. To do so, of course, would highlight the excessive weight they have given to the lower-court opinions. A pre-emptive constitutional amendment to overturn a lower-court interpretation that the Supreme Court specifically avoided endorsing would surely strike most reasonable observers as overkill. From this perspective, using normal legislative measures to continue the constitutional dialogue, at least until the Supreme Court rules, appears to be a viable and prudent policy.

Once the Supreme Court rules, however, the argument for judicial insularity and the argument for judicial supremacy become indistinguishable. If the necessity of using the notwithstanding clause or formal amendment was premature with respect to lower- court rulings, then it gains strength when the Supreme Court issues a definitive ruling. Surely now, the supremacists insist, the time for legal pluralism is over. If the interpretive conflict has ended, and if the government wishes to proceed with its own contrary interpretation, it must override or change the constitution itself. From this perspective, lesser forms of interpretive resistance – such as Parliament's enactment of the *O'Connor* dissenting opinion or the textual retort to *Morales* – are no longer permissible. This more challenging claim is the subject of the next chapter.

6

Legal Pluralism after the Supreme Court Decides

The differences between coordinate and supremacist interpretive approaches come into starkest relief once the Supreme Court rules. Even those interpretive supremacists who accept interpretive participation by the executive and legislature as the case climbs the judicial hierarchy now insist that a ruling of the Supreme Court settles any interpretive ambiguity and ends all inter-institutional dialogue over the meaning of the constitution short of the formal overrides provided by section 33 and constitutional amendment.[1] From this perspective, the finality of the Supreme Court becomes the logical lodestar: interpretive disputes require a definitive resolution, and, if neither section 33 nor constitutional amendment is used to provide such resolution, then the Supreme Court's interpretation must do the job. Otherwise the constitution becomes dangerously indeterminate. It is this perspective that explains the widespread and vehement opposition to the Court's acceptance of legislative interpretive participation in *Mills* and *Hall*. In those cases, the Court allowed Parliament to upset the judicially arrived at settlement of a constitutional controversy through the ordinary means of a statutory enactment. If all decisions of the Court are open to legislative reversal, then the effectiveness of judicial review is greatly threatened. This concern was addressed in chapter 2 where it was argued that the minority and textual retorts provided only a limited and structured form of legislative participation in the interpretive process.

More generally, proponents of coordinate interpretation wonder why the "time dimension" of legal pluralism must end with the Supreme Court decision. Final courts of appeal, they insist, can be wrong, sometimes spectacularly wrong, as in the infamous U.S.

decisions of *Dred Scott v. Sandford* (where the Court held that slaves were not citizens but property) and *Lochner v. New York* (where the Court held that legislation prohibiting the overworking of employees beyond ten hours a day and sixty hours a week unconstitutionally infringed economic liberty). Why, in such cases, must the representative branches jump immediately to the onerous process of constitutional amendment or a misleading "notwithstanding" declaration to correct the mistake of as few as five (or, in Canada, even four or three) Supreme Court judges? Or, to put it the other way around, why should a simple majority of judges immediately trigger the supermajoritarian response of amendment or the politically charged (and temporary) response of section 33? For coordinate theorists, in other words, it is often perfectly reasonable for a legislature to test the Supreme Court's resolve and conviction in its own judgment by persisting for a time longer with its contrary legislative interpretation. After all, if the Supreme Court is sufficiently confident in its judgment to persist in it, its interpretation will ultimately prevail because, without judicial cooperation in applying the law to concrete cases, legislative efforts become, in Hamilton's words, a "dead letter." In other words, a confident Supreme Court can eventually require the legislative branches to resort to the formal overrides, but, in the coordinate perspective, there is no need to engage those mechanisms immediately.

Indeed, there are solid advantages to extending the time dimension of legal pluralism for a period after a Supreme Court decision. Even if the Supreme Court adheres to its initial interpretation and thus ultimately prevails over a competing legislative interpretation, the latter can help ensure that the Court's interpretation is truly an *institutional* choice and not merely the preference of one particular Supreme Court bench in one particular case. While legal scholars might decry "relitigation" of the same issue as a waste of judicial resources,[2] the fact that the original case and any potential sequels are separated by a period of time means that it is possible that some of the practical (that is, non-legal) elements of the issue have changed.[3] Such changes might include turnover in the Court's membership, shifting public opinion, additional information, and/or simply changes in circumstance. By requiring the judicial interpretation to be supported by more than a single panel in a single case, a recalcitrant legislature helps separate enduring legal-constitutional principle from what might be transitory preferences of personality.

In this fashion, the legislature can play a limited but important role in the interpretive process even when its interpretation is not adopted as constitutional canon. When the legislature does succeed in persuading the Court to change its mind, as happened in *Mills* and, in part, in *Hall*, that, too, contributes to a more solid and enduring constitutional resolution. The alleged cost in constitutional indeterminacy claimed by supremacists is much overblown, as the next section of this chapter shows; the rest of the chapter then fleshes out the many advantages of extending coordinate legal pluralism for a period after an initial Supreme Court judgment.

THE LEGAL CERTAINTY SECURED BY A SUPREME COURT RULING

The argument for interpretive supremacy offers a false choice between absolute judicial interpretive authority and radical constitutional indeterminacy. The stakes are far more subtle, since even the strongest forms of coordinate interpretation accept judicial authority over particular cases. It is therefore important at the outset to clarify what is meant when a Supreme Court ruling is proposed as "definitive." If continuing legal pluralism (that is, post-Supreme Court ruling) means the wholesale abandonment of all legal certainty, even for the parties involved, then it is surely intolerable since "our sense of justice requires that appeals to higher courts be permitted in order to prevent miscarriages of justice ... but the process must, at some point, be brought to an end, and an ultimate judicial authority is established in order to accomplish this."[4] Never-ending legal disputes (like Dickens's *Jarndyce v. Jarndyce*) will force despairing disputants to turn to other means of dispute resolution (perhaps even violence) and our system of law will be critically undermined.

The institutional coordinacy contemplated by separation-of-powers theorists, however, avoids this pitfall by relying on the case-and-controversy logic embedded within the separation doctrine to ensure sufficient legal certainty. In addition to the settlement imposed upon the litigants to the case at bar (and recalling the immunity of such settlements from any legislative or executive interference), the high court ruling binds all subordinate courts since no lower court is allowed to ignore a Supreme Court interpretation in favour of its own.[5] All future similarly situated litigants are therefore reasonably assured of a judicial outcome consistent with the original Supreme Court ruling. It is even possible, under this approach, for the Supreme Court to issue a prospective remedy for the individual litigants in a particular case who might not be satisfied by the political process initiated by a delayed declaration of invalidity.[6] To the extent that judicial cooperation is required for the law to have legal effect, the impact of the judicial interpretation is decisive on this case-by-case basis.

The Court's power over discrete cases thus ensures the effectiveness of judicial review even under a system of coordinate constitutionalism. Since judges, no less than any other official or citizen, are required to obey the constitution, fidelity to the judicial understanding of the constitution obligates them to refrain from applying what is (from their perspective) an unconstitutional law to the dispute they are trying. While this "disregarding" of a law is different from "striking down," it is nevertheless a significant power. As the final interface between law and citizen, the courts hold immense direct power over litigants and thus their interpretation of the law (constitutional or otherwise) is unlikely to be ignored. This is evident even with statutory law, where the legislature is supposedly supreme, since the judicial power over discrete cases is final; as law professor Hamish Gray observes, since "the effectiveness of Parliament's enactments will depend wholly on the application and enforcement of those enactments by judges ... parliamentary sovereignty rests with the courts."[7] Similarly, with constitutional law, the Court can undermine the efficacy of a contrary legislative interpretation of the constitution simply by insisting upon the original judicial interpretation and denying the legislative sequel any legal force (as the U.S. Supreme Court did in *Flores* and *Dickerson*). Legislatures can continue to enact general laws consistent with their interpretation of the constitution, this view holds, but if their laws are susceptible to being overturned by the judiciary upon every application, it might be a waste of legislative resources to persist in such an ineffectual manner over time. This control of the legal effect of any law ensures that, as a practical matter, the Supreme Court has the de facto final word on many matters of constitutional importance.[8]

The case-by-case level of legal certainty is not, however, sufficient for interpretive supremacists. They demand an additional degree of legal certainty by insisting that the Court's de facto influence over constitutional meaning be made de jure (formalizing the informal, in Mansfield's terms). Not only is the Court's ruling immediately binding on all subordinate courts but, according to the supremacist, it must prevail with similar immediacy over all coordinate institutions as well. In other words, interpretive supremacists reject the case-and-controversy restriction on judicial power in favour of an immediate and broad application of the Supreme Court's decision. What cannot be tolerated, in this view, is for the legislature to persist with its own interpretation of the constitution through the enactment of ordinary laws.

COORDINACY ALLOWS FOR LEGAL PLURALISM TO CONTINUE

The coordinate approach to constitutional interpretation accepts ordinary-law responses as a viable means of moderating judicial power. One might argue that, given the Supreme Court's absolute control over the legal effect of statutes on litigants, legislative interpretations of the constitution are rather pointless. Yet, to the contrary, such statutory expressions of dissent might be effective in the sense that they (1) ensure that the judicial interpretation is restricted to specific cases-and-controversies and (2) serve as "constitutional hints" from the other branches to prompt the Court to rethink its own interpretation.[9] The first is particularly important when the non-judicial branches attempt to mitigate (what to them is a clear) judicial error in interpretation by confining it as much as possible. The second is especially potent when a judicial reversal might be imminent, as in the case where the Court is closely split or where it may have strayed too far from the clear wording of the constitutional text. Each provides a compelling rationale for allowing a degree of institutional legal pluralism to persist after the Supreme Court rules.

CONFINING ERRONEOUS JUDICIAL INTERPRETATIONS: THE *DRED SCOTT* SCENARIO

Even when the Supreme Court speaks with an unqualified and unified voice, there is a compelling argument in favour of extending the time dimension of legal pluralism: it allows for additional opportunities to mitigate judicial mistakes in interpretation. The time-dimension virtues of coordinate constitutional thinking in this sense are best articulated and defended by Abraham Lincoln in his response to the *Dred Scott* ruling.[10] Even before the ruling was announced, the U.S. Supreme Court and its defenders insisted that the Court's unique position (its "high and independent character") empowered it to "decide and settle a controversy which has long and seriously agitated the county," namely slavery.[11] Such was the presumed authority of the Court that one of its members, Justice John Catron, wrote to then-President James Buchanan admonishing him that it would be "improper to express any opinion on the subject."[12] In contrast to the assertion that the Court is the final and exclusive authority on constitutional matters, Lincoln proposed that even Supreme Court decisions might be legitimately resisted by the non-judicial branches if circumstances warranted. This was no mere abstract point for Lincoln, who made it the foundation for both his unsuccessful run for the Senate and, later, his successful campaign for the presidency. Faced with the *Dred Scott* ruling, one of the ugliest and most vile judicial opinions ever issued, Lincoln could have simply rejected the Court's authority and engaged in public judge bashing.[13] As a lawyer and a strong defender of the rule of law, however, Lincoln preferred a more constitutionally sound approach and proposed a sophisticated coordinate response to the Court's opinion. Lincoln's position ably summarizes the key points of the coordinate approach and is therefore worth quoting at length:

> I do not forget the position, assumed by some, that constitutional questions are to be decided by the Supreme Court; nor do I deny that such decisions must be binding, in any case, upon the parties to a suit, as to the object of that suit, while they are entitled to very high respect and considerations in all parallel cases by all other departments of the government. And while it is obviously possible that such decision may be erroneous in any given case, still the evil effect following it, being limited to that particular case, with the chance that it may be overruled and never become precedent for other cases, can better be borne than could the evils of a different practice.
>
> At the same time, the candid citizen must confess that if the policy of the government, upon vital questions affecting the whole people, is to be irrevocably fixed by decisions of the Supreme Court, the instant they are made, in ordinary litigation between parties in personal actions, the people will have ceased

to be their own rulers, having to that extent practically resigned their government into the hands of that eminent tribunal. Nor is there in this view any assault upon the court or the judges. It is a duty from which they may not shrink to decide cases properly brought before them, and it is no fault of theirs if others seek to turn their decisions to political purposes.[14]

Critics of judicial power occasionally quote the "people will have ceased to be their own rulers" portion as an appeal to democratic sentiment but, without the remainder of the text, the subtleties of Lincoln's approach are lost.[15] In Lincoln's response to *Dred Scott*, one can find a fully developed model of coordinate constitutional interpretation.

As an initial matter, it is significant that Lincoln accepts the fundamental premise of judicial review by conceding that "constitutional questions are to be decided by the Supreme Court." This is not as obvious as the modern defender of the judicial power might assume. Given the context (the period immediately preceding the Civil War) and the issue (the Missouri Compromise in particular, slavery in general), Lincoln could have plausibly argued that the *Dred Scott* Court had inappropriately ruled on a "political question" beyond its jurisdiction.[16] To do so, however, would reject the Madisonian idea that coordinate interpretation demands "inextricably nested relationships" between the governing institutions. Since the Court would be excluded from the interpretive process altogether, the "political questions" doctrine would have simply substituted unilateral legislative interpretive power for judicial supremacy instead of the complex cooperation mandated by the coordinate approach. Rather than simply insisting on a political interpretation entirely divorced from judicial reasoning, then, Lincoln calls for the Court's interpretive judgment to be afforded "high respect and consideration in all parallel cases by all other departments of the government." Despite whatever reservations Lincoln expresses about the *exclusive* authority of the Court to decide constitutional questions, he is clearly encouraging the Court to play a leading role in interpretative controversies. Indeed, it is "a duty from which they may not shrink."

Despite the leading role of the Court, Lincoln argues that democratic self-government is inconsistent with the notion that important matters of policy may be "irrevocably fixed by the decisions of the Supreme Court, the instant they are made, in ordinary litigation." Lincoln's language – "irrevocably fixed," "the instant they are made" – returns to the time dimension of legal pluralism. Lincoln argues that important political disputes cannot be instantly and authoritatively resolved by any single institution. This means not that constitutional principles are forever indeterminate but simply that time and flexibility are necessary to crystallize institutional decisions into enduring constitutional principles. When interpretive decisions are widely accepted over a considerable length of time (and, as Lincoln proposed, routinely endorsed by the electorate), a "gradual accretion of constitutional doctrine," as Bickel calls it, emerges to be ultimately accepted as a binding inter-institutional rule.[17] But, until that crystallization, interpretive pluralism in constitutional affairs must be permitted to allow each institution to fulfil its constitutional obligations as it understands them.

This interpretive pluralism is itself limited, however, by the accepted separation of institutional functions. In the case of the judiciary, it is well accepted, as Lincoln concedes, that its authority to bind the parties to a resolution of a particular case must not be unsettled by other branches ("such decisions must be binding, in any case, upon the parties to a suit"). Whatever restrictions are placed on the Court's power to settle constitutional questions, the decision of the Court is final and authoritative for the actual litigants to the suit. Yet, since that discrete settlement is the act of a single unchecked institutional decision maker, it is prone to the very immoderation that the Montesquiean scheme seeks to mitigate. For this reason, it is important that this dangerous immoderation be restricted to the discrete case and controversy and not immediately applied across all institutional boundaries as a matter of formal rule. The case-and-controversy restraint is especially important in the constitutional context since the consequences of any immoderation can be particularly far-reaching.

The containment of a mistaken judicial interpretation of the constitution is Lincoln's key concern. As even the most ardent defender of judicial power must concede, it is "obviously possible that [a] decision may be erroneous in any given case." Faced with such a decision, the non-judicial branches should act to limit "the evil effect following it" by aggressively limiting the judicially announced interpretation to its "particular case" in the hopes that "it may be overruled and never become precedent for other cases." Lincoln therefore relies heavily upon the case-and-controversy logic to separate the inviolable judicial power over discrete cases from the informal judicial influence over general policy. Interpretive mistakes must, regrettably, be respected in the former sense but must be vigorously corrected in the latter.

In the *Dred Scott* context, Lincoln is not suggesting that the fugitive slave Scott himself can be set free by executive or legislative fiat. Instead, Lincoln argues that the particular dispute between Scott and his master does not resolve the issue of escaped slaves on free soil or the constitutional status of slaves as "men," or the constitutionality of slavery in general. Even though the Court may have taken positions on these issues to arrive at its decision, the decision is binding only on the parties involved in the case and it is not necessary for the other branches to be bound by the Court's broader foundation for its decision. This was dramatically illustrated by an incident that occurred during Lincoln's presidency. When a commercial schooner was seized because it was captained by a black man, Lincoln's attorney general, Edward Bates, was forced to reconcile the reasoning in *Dred Scott* (which declared blacks to be non-citizens to justify its decision) with existing naval law, which permitted only citizens to command a ship flying the American flag.[18] Bates ignored the holding in *Dred Scott* and ruled that birthplace, and not race, determined one's citizenship.[19] Our modern tendency to assume that constitutional interpretation is the sole domain of the courts was not shared by Lincoln's contemporaries – one Washington newspaper predicted that Bates's independent executive judgment, along with a similar decision on equal pay for black soldiers, "will henceforth stand as landmarks of constitutional interpretation."[20] The decisions of his attorney general clearly followed Lincoln's insistence that the acceptance of the particular judicial outcome does not commit one to the entire constitutional vision articulated by the Court; even if Scott himself must be bound, the executive and legislature can and should resist the Court's restrictive definition of "citizen."[21]

Here again the time dimension of constitutional legal pluralism is explicit. Lincoln proposed to ignore *Dred Scott*, not as applied to poor Dred Scott himself, but in its broader policy implications. When he is accused by his political opponent Stephen Douglas of "resisting" *Dred Scott*, Lincoln answers that he "[does] not resist it. If I wanted to take Dred Scot from his master, I would be interfering with property ... But I am doing no such thing as that; all that I am doing is refusing to obey it as a political rule."[22] Now, if the judicial system as a whole, including the Supreme Court, persisted with the *Dred Scott* precedent, the judiciary would eventually win out (in the absence of a formal constitutional amendment) because every future Dred Scott would suffer the same defeat in every case that could justiciably come before the courts. Executive and legislative resistance could, however, slow this process down and force the courts to continually issue decisions reaffirming its position over what might become a lengthy period of time and with the participation of a greater number of judges. Surely this is what Tocqueville had in mind when he observed that, after a judicial determination of unconstitutionality, "the law thus censured is not abolished; its moral force is diminished but its physical effect is not suspended. It is only gradually, under repeated judicial blows, that it finally succumbs."[23]

"CONSTITUTIONAL HINTS": PROVOKING JUDICIAL RECONSIDERATION

Obviously, any attempt to confine an erroneous judicial interpretation means that at least one of the non-judicial branches holds an interpretation that it considers correct and with which it hopes to persuade the Court. Lincoln's strategy for dealing with *Dred Scott* was to force the Court to issue "repeated judicial blows" and, in the meantime, assert an alternative interpretation to challenge the Court's resolve. On *Dred Scott*, Lincoln remarked that "when a question comes up upon another [similarly situated] person, it will be so decided again, unless the court decides in another way, unless the court overrules its decision ... Well, we mean to do what we can to have the court decide the other way."[24] Judicial independence means that executives and legislators cannot direct judges to rule in a certain way (this would also violate the rule of partial agency, illustrating that the principle of judicial independence is itself embedded in the separation of powers), but there is nothing to prevent them from trying to influence judicial doctrine in an informal manner. Executives and legislatures "doing what they can to have the court decide the other way" is precisely what the non-judicial branches did successfully in *O'Connor-Mills* and attempted to do in the *Morales-Hall* sequence.

During the extended period of constitutional legal pluralism after a Supreme Court ruling, it is necessary for each institution to assert its interpretation constantly, using its own institutional powers, and persist until its political will diminishes or an accommodation can be reached. U.S. Senator John Breckenridge vividly described the process of interpretive conflict possible in a coordinate system: "Although ... the courts may take upon them to give decisions which impeach the constitutionality of a law, and thereby, for a time, obstruct its operations ... I contend that such a law is not the less obligatory because the organ through which it is to be executed has refused its aid. A pertinacious adherence of both departments to their opinions, would soon bring the question to issue, in whom the sovereign power of legislation resided, and whose construction of the law-making power should prevail."[25]

Coordinate interpretation rejects the constitutional superiority of any institution in favour of a contest in the context of legal pluralism in which any institution's interpretation, asserted with "pertinacious adherence," might prevail. Admittedly, during this period, the judicial power to decide conflicts directly between litigants amounts to a practical hegemony over constitutional interpretation. Since the legislature possesses no correlative power to apply its interpretation and executive interpretations remain subject to judicial supervision (under the rule of law), a persistent judiciary is likely to win any interpretive battle, even if it must do so one case at a time. The adjective is significant, however, since the judiciary must be *persistent* to be successful.

Nowadays, when non-judicial institutions demonstrate a "pertinacious adherence" to their own interpretations, the action is routinely condemned as "non-compliance." American political scientists Devins and Fisher argue that this term is a loaded one that implies an assault on the rule of law when such assertions might be better understood as appropriately furthering inter-institutional disagreement. "Is noncompliance contemptuous of the judicial process?" they ask. "Not necessarily; *it depends on the ruling*. If the Court misjudges its power and inflates its institutional position, it cannot expect acquiescence from the public and other branches of government."[26] In other words, the authority of the Court is dependent upon its particular ruling and not upon an abstract rule of institutional superiority.

Would varying judicial authority on a case-by-case basis undermine judicial authority altogether? Note that, in the passage above,

Breckenridge concludes that an interpretive contest would ultimately yield to the institution "in whom the sovereign power of legislation resided" and thus suggests that the representative branches would typically win out over their judicial peers. President Franklin Roosevelt was of a similar opinion and noted that "the lay rank and file can take cheer from the historic fact that every effort to construe the Constitution as a lawyer's contract rather than a layman's charter has ultimately failed. Whenever legalistic interpretation has clashed with contemporary sense on great questions of broad national policy, ultimately the people and the Congress have had their way."[27] In Roosevelt's assessment, Congress "ultimately" wins interpretive disputes. This may be so, but if it is true, it is only because, as elected representatives, members of Congress more quickly adjust to public opinion while the courts, purposely insulated from such pressures, are slower to arrive at the same position. Moreover, Roosevelt seems to assume that the interpretive position of each institution (and that of "the people") is held static throughout the period of constitutional pluralism. A more realistic appraisal would recognize that a persuasive judicial decision can have a dramatic effect on public opinion and legislative inclinations and that a strong statutory rejection of the Court's interpretation, backed by popular sentiment, might cause the Court to reconsider its position when the statutory sequel comes before it. In both the *Mills* and *Hall* cases, we have seen constitutional interpretations emerge that were in all likelihood not the favoured interpretation of any one branch but rather a compromise acceptable to all the branches.

The judicial acceptance of the legislation in *Mills* and (at least the substance of the legislation) in *Hall* suggests that statutory interpretations of the constitution are not as pointless as the judicial supremacist might assume. In such cases, the statutes serve as a hint from the legislature that tests the resolve of the Court for its own interpretation.[28] Clearly, in order to achieve this effect, such statutes must be unconstitutional from the perspective of the Court's existing jurisprudence. Since they suggest that the Court's interpretation immediately binds the other institutions of government, judicial supremacists insist that any such hints are constitutionally impermissible. The coordinate approach, on the other hand, treats such statutes as part of an evolving process of interpretive development in which the Supreme Court's opinion on a discrete case is but one data point.

The hostility to this more fluid account of constitutional interpretation was vividly demonstrated by the letter – already discussed in the previous chapter – by 134 lawyers in reaction to the Conservative Party's 2005 opposition motion to reinstate the traditional definition of marriage through ordinary legislation in response to judicial rulings requiring same-sex marriage.[29] According to the judicial supremacist view of these lawyers, a legislature that passes an ordinary law contradicting a constitutional interpretation of the judicial branch is acting lawlessly, inviting legal anarchy, and, in the words of Sujit Choudhry, one of the authors of the letter, "wear[ing] down the gears of the Constitution."[30] Choudhry claims that Harper's position is based on "assumptions that our Constitution doesn't permit," namely, the understanding that the non-judicial institutions cannot respond to judicial decisions with ordinary laws unless they invoke the notwithstanding clause.[31] The federal minister of justice, Irwin Cotler, agreed with Choudhry's letter and suggested that "Harper appears to be living in a kind of legal Disneyland, as if you can wave a magic wand and thereby override the Constitution and the courts."[32] This position ossified to the point that, two years later, it would be the only "intellectually honourable" and "legally correct" position.[33] Jeffrey Simpson explained that "the law is what the courts say it is. Period. There's nothing Parliament can do, except what Parliament will not do – use the notwithstanding clause."[34]

In *Mills* (and to some extent *Hall*), however, we have seen ordinary-law interventions having a dramatic effect on the interpretive process. While legislative and executive challenges to the Court's interpretive authority are also limited by the separation of powers (that is, they cannot unsettle the Court's judgment in the discrete case and they cannot compel judges to apply the executive or legislative interpretation in future cases), they are accepted as legitimate political interventions aimed at shifting the interpretive debate away from the Court's preferred interpretation. Given the *Mills* and *Hall* precedents, Harper's ordinary-law response to the same-sex marriage cases could reasonably be expected to alter the legal trajectory of the emerging jurisprudence on the issue. When pressed on this possibility, Choudhry concedes that "nothing prevents Parliament from enacting an obviously unconstitutional definition of marriage."[35] It is therefore entirely possible that new legislation on marriage – particularly if it introduced elements (civil unions and so on) not at issue in the earlier cases – could provoke a similar change in the judicial interpretation, just as Harper claimed. Choudhry's only answer to this possibility is his remark that "at some point, the process would wear down the gears of the Constitution."[36] More than any other, this comment demonstrates the fundamental discomfort that many lawyers and legal academics have with non-judicial checks and balances. From the standpoint of the separation of powers, such inter-institutional conflict is necessary for moderation and essential to the proper operation of the constitution. Far from "wearing down the gears," inter-institutional conflict invigorates and animates the constitutional design by giving institutional form to legitimate political disagreement over constitutional meaning. Only from the perspective of judicial supremacy, where the gears smoothly crush parliamentary choices into judicial obedience, does Choudhry's warning make sense. If one views the judiciary as the exclusive and authoritative voice of the constitution, then legislative enactments that are "clearly unconstitutional" are nothing more than awkward and burdensome obstacles that unjustifiably delay the enactment of judicial preferences. The popularity of this view among the legal elite suggests that the Canadian system of checks and balances is widely misunderstood by those who should understand it best.

INADEQUACY OF THE FORMAL MEANS TO CONTEST A SUPREME COURT INTERPRETATION

Choudhry's letter argues that Harper's ordinary-law strategy is impermissible because there are formal means available to the legislature to respond to judicial decisions it opposes. This follows the supremacist logic that the only means of contesting a Supreme Court's interpretation is through formal constitutional amendment or, where applicable, invocation of the notwithstanding clause. An interpretive power construed in this fashion, however, would create a stark asymmetry: a judicial interpretation – perhaps amounting to a judicial amendment of the constitution – can be made by a simple majority of a nine-judge court; it can be formally overruled only by an exceedingly supermajoritarian process or with the high costs of using the notwithstanding clause. Ultimately, of course, these remedies are indeed the only way to overcome a settled and firm judicial interpretation, but it remains unclear why this must be the case immediately upon an initial Supreme Court opinion on a subject. Why, for example, jump immediately to the difficult process of constitutional amendment to overrule a narrow Supreme Court majority if, given obvious disagreement on the Court itself, the majority might reconsider and change its mind? Unlike the ordinary-law responses, the formal amending power and the notwithstanding clause are poor vehicles for this limited form of inter-institutional interaction because they are unlikely to be invoked in response to a single judicial interpretation and thus are unable to provide the moderating influence our Montesquiean design requires.

The star-crossed attempts to amend the constitution through the Meech Lake and Charlottetown accords, and the subsequent unwillingness of political actors to engage in further megaconstitutional politics, suggest that formal constitutional amendment is far too remote to deter undue judicial creativity.[37] Moreover, with one notable exception, constitutional amendments have rarely been used in Canada to overturn specific judicial interpretations.[38] While province-specific constitutional amendments have been made under section 43 in recent years, these micro-amendments are not available for curbing Charter rights and are very limited in scope. [39] Although formal amendments remain technically possible, they hardly pose a threat to even the most imaginative acts of judicial interpretation.

Similarly, the notwithstanding clause is ill-suited for advancing alternatives to specific judicial interpretations. In fact, the text of section 33 implies that its usage means that the legislature concedes that the Court's interpretation of the text is correct but that the legislation should operate "notwithstanding" this correct interpretation. As such, it is hardly the best instrument for advancing legitimate and sincere legislative interpretations of the constitution.[40] This textual difficulty, combined with the negative sentiments garnered through the clause's association with the Quebec sovereigntist movement,[41] means that a grossly disproportionate price must be paid for any exercise of section 33 to counter a judicial interpretation. The practical unavailability of section 33 – and one legal commentator has even gone so far as to suggest that this section "cannot legitimately be exercised against the Charter's entitlements or the judiciary's power of review"[42] – means that the legislative override is also unlikely to inhibit interpretive overreaching by the Court.[43] Christopher Manfredi argues that the Court has observed the reluctance of the representative branches to invoke section 33 and that this has resulted in an increase in the Court's "willingness to impose future policy constraints on legislative actors."[44] Whereas the 1988 *Morgentaler* decision invalidated Canada's abortion law on narrow and technical grounds, inviting legislators to enact a new procedurally valid law aimed at the same substantial end, the Court's 1998 *Vriend* decision on homosexual equality dispensed with any notion of future legislation in favour of a judicially rewritten statute (using the extraordinary remedy of "reading-in," as discussed in chapter 7).[45] In other words, as section 33 became less and less of a plausible check, the Court responded exactly as Montesquieu would have expected: it began to take the separation-of-power constraint less seriously as an obstacle to its preferred policy.

The formal checks of constitutional amendment and the notwithstanding clause are therefore insufficient to perform the moderation-inducing, liberty-enhancing role that the Montesquiean scheme requires. The failure of the formal checks suggests that alternative (and perhaps informal) checks are required to deliver on the promise of the separation of power. As discussed in chapter 1, the desideratum of additional checks is particularly heightened in cases where the Supreme Court is narrowly divided on the constitutional issue or where the Court is clearly adding to the constitutional text. In such cases, one could argue that the need for some moderating influence on judicial power should attenuate the excessively burdensome process required for formal constitutional change. But judicial supremacists resist the idea that ordinary-law responses can modify the constitutional interpretations of the Court even in these compelling circumstances.

CRITERIA FOR LIMITED COORDINATE RESPONSES

A modest form of coordinate interpretation, however, can reconcile the Court's role as the leading constitutional interpreter with a limited legislative role in shaping constitutional rights. Such an approach offers clear criteria for judging whether non-judicial participation in constitutional interpretation is a legitimate exercise of partial agency. I propose that statutory interference with the interpretive power of the judiciary is consistent with the separation of powers if (1) the legislative response does not interfere with the formal judicial power of settling the case before the bench, (2) it preserves the Court's leading (but informal) role in settling constitutional controversies, and (3) there is a compelling reason to believe that legislative participation will enhance the outcome of constitutional settlements. Both the minority and textual retorts meet these three criteria.

The Court's Formal Power of Adjudicating the Concrete Dispute Is Preserved

The minority and textual retorts do not affect the parties to the original case. Although his case would be ultimately diverted out of the criminal justice system in favour of an aboriginal healing circle,[46] Bishop Hubert O'Connor's right to a new trial using the more lenient rules for the production of the victim's therapeutic records, as mandated by the Court, was never in question. (The accused in the sequel case, Brian Mills, was found not guilty of sexual offences despite the higher threshold for obtaining the victim's third-party therapeutic records.[47]) It is worthwhile to note that both regimes governing the production of records, despite the differing prescriptions for balance between the rights of the accused and the rights of the victim, leave the final decision on production to the trial judge. Similarly, the new bail hearing for Maximo Morales was heard under the rules declared by Lamer's decision in the original case and not under the newly legislated rules at issue in *Hall*. (Morales's new bail hearing was moot because he was ultimately kept in custody for another outstanding criminal charge.) In each case, the distinction between the Court's formal power to decide concrete cases and Parliament's power to enact laws of general application was respected.

The Court Remains the Primary Interpretive Agent

Both the minority and textual retorts allow the Court to take the leading role in resolving constitutional controversies and restrict the legislature to an essentially corrective role. In the case of the minority retort, Parliament is selecting only from the options the Court has raised. It is hard to imagine a more limited parliamentary check to judicial power since the effectiveness of the retort is strictly linked to the legal uncertainty the Court contributes to with its internal disagreement. If there is a clear legal consensus on the issue, then the minority retort is useless; the effect of the legislative intervention therefore is entirely within the power of the Court (as a whole) to prevent. If there is a sharp disagreement about the proper legal result, then Parliament is well positioned to assist the Court by democratically endorsing one of the multiple Court-identified legal options. Used in this fashion, the minority retort might increase legal certainty, contrary to the conventional critique of coordinacy, by providing democratic weight to what might otherwise be a weak judicial precedent. Regardless of its capacity to add certainty, the legislative involvement is minimal and reactive whereas the Court's primary role in constitutional affairs is preserved.

The textual retort appears to be a more intrusive form of legislative participation but it too is effective only at the margins of judicial power. It is true that the textual retort allows for a parliamentary interpretation of the constitution that may be wholly independent of the interpretation advanced by the Court. The non-judicial interpretation contemplated, however, is largely confined to the language found in the constitutional text and is not a free-floating or expanded notion of what the constitution might mean. In this way, the textual retort acts as a legislative check that ensures that the Court acts as an interpretive (and not legislative) body in resolving constitutional controversies. To put it in Mansfeldian terms, the Court is granted an *informal* power to build upon constitutional provisions (even if it appears close to "legislating") in order to apply them, but, against this *informal* judicial expansion of the text, the legislature may respond with the very text that the Court is *formally* required to interpret. Permitting a parliamentary appeal to the text neatly reflects the traditional liberal ambivalence towards power: neither the legislature nor the court rules, rather it is the text that dominates.

Constitutional supremacy, in this view, secures a leading but not determinative role for the judiciary. Justice Owen Roberts of the U.S. Supreme Court once suggested that constitutional review is a simple matter. It is only necessary, he argued, to "lay the article of the Constitution … beside the statute … [and] decide whether the latter squares with the former."[48] Although it lacks hermeneutic sophistication, Roberts's approach demonstrates the continuing importance of textualism to a constitutional democracy. After all of the (admittedly necessary) work of interpretation and discretion, if, in the final analysis, a judicial ruling cannot plausibly be said to meet Roberts's test, then one has reason to doubt the legitimacy of the chain of interpretative logic that led to such a perverse result. Thus, even allowing for "living tree" or "purposive" interpretations of the document, the text itself must remain the central focus of the adjudicative process and the textual retort helps sustain that centrality. Laying the textual retort beside the constitution, as Roberts suggests, proves the validity of the former since it largely replicates the latter. Faced with such legislation, the Court should be reminded that, although it takes the lead in interpreting the constitution, its power remains strictly *interpretive* and not, in any formal sense, legislative. From this perspective, the textual retort is entirely consistent with the separation of powers properly understood.

A Compelling Reason for Legislative Involvement in the Interpretive Controversy

In chapter 2, I argued that a general defence of legislative participation could be made on the grounds of democratic equality (decisions that affect all are best made by all) as refined through representative means. Legislative involvement in the interpretive exercise has the obvious advantage of leaving the ultimate decision in these close cases to an electorally accountable institution (the people must not "cease to be their own rulers"), but, in addition to enhancing democratic accountability, legislative participation can also encourage positive democratic habits generally.

As Morton and Knopff have suggested, "liberal democracy works only when majorities rather than minorities rule and when it is obvious to all that ruling majorities are themselves coalitions of minorities in a pluralistic society."[49] Using the language of "rights," judicial decisions rhetorically suggest that the Court's decision is final and anyone who disagrees with it is "wrong" or, at best, "misguided." Legislative decisions, in comparison, are tentative and subject to reversal by a future government.[50] Instead of being summarily dismissed, citizens on the losing side of a legislative determination are invited to seek out new coalitions and build support for their perspective. In the judicial context, such overt campaigning for the reversal of a decision is frowned upon and, if it occurs at all, it is done covertly. By increasing legislative participation, the minority and textual retorts provide a valuable incentive for the public deliberation that would otherwise be short-circuited by judicial supremacy.

The constitutional legal pluralism introduced by the minority retort is akin to the legal pluralism that would have been welcomed as useful prior to the Supreme Court's decision. If *O'Connor* had not been challenged by the legislation at issue in *Mills*, it is uncertain when (or even whether) the Court would have revisited its original decision on therapeutic records. The litigation resulting from the legislative sequel provided an opportunity to incorporate new evidence on the workings of the *O'Connor* regime. Catherine Kane of the Justice Department notes that "present knowledge regarding the varying procedures that are being followed by courts ... had advanced by 1997. The Department had been holding extensive public hearings on the impacts of [*O'Connor*] thereby giving policy makers a better idea of the practical impacts of the changes."[51] The lengthy legislative process ensures the time necessary to consider fully the operation and impact of the original decision.

While the above comments could support legislative participation in any interpretive controversy, the minority and textual retorts offer particularly compelling reasons to permit parliamentary interventions. In the case of the minority retort, the close judicial result is indicative of an issue where strict legal analysis has failed and therefore the input of non-judicial actors is legitimate. While it is certainly appropriate for members of the Court to venture an opinion on the issue before them, it is a different matter entirely to suggest that those preferences must be determinative even in the face of parliamentary opposition. As Graham Garton of the Justice Department notes, *Mills* is best understood as "an endorsement of Parliament's authority to set policies that reflect Canadian realities, even if those policies don't adhere strictly to prior decisions of the Court."[52] It is difficult to argue that the regime set up by the *O'Connor* majority is a better legal opinion or more consistent with the constitution than the one favoured by the minority; they simply differ on the appropriate balance between an accused's right to a full answer and the victim's right to privacy. No amount of legal reasoning is going to provide the answer to what is inherently a *political* decision about how to reconcile these two important rights. From this perspective, the notion that one judge's preference should outweigh the declared will of Parliament is highly suspect. As I argued in chapter 1, the "switch-over" judges in *Mills* may have recognized this point and changed their vote as an act of deference to Parliament. The sharp judicial disagreement in the original case provides a compelling justification for the minority retort since the disagreement on the Court signals legal indeterminacy on a matter of politics that is best settled by the representative institutions.

In the case of the textual retort, the special justification for legislative participation comes from the nature of the statute itself, which mimics the constitutional text. Its direct link to the text makes the textual retort less an independent legislative interpretation and more a reminder to the Court of its strictly interpretive role in lawmaking. Even the most expansive views of judicial authority hang upon some notion that judicial power is inherently *interpretive*. The "living tree" metaphor, for example, conceives of the constitution as "an instrument capable of adapting with the times by way of a process of evolutionary interpretation, *within the natural limits of the text*, which 'accommodates and addresses the realities of modern life.'"[53] If even the minimal legislative participation of the textual retort is rejected, then there is no workable means to check a Court that has abandoned its interpretive role in favour of unrestricted legislating.

"Constitutional rights," Devins and Fisher argue, "are better protected by a political process that involves all three branches, the states, and the public."[54] Interpretive contests conducted on the basis of "give and take and mutual respect" allow "all parts of government to expose weaknesses, hold excess in check, and gradually forge a consensus on constitutional values."[55] While these constitutional values are gradually forged, constitutional pluralism reigns through "an open process" with "many points of entry and opportunities for reconsideration."[56] Writing in 2004, Devins and Fisher tap into the vein of constitutional thinking that extends back to Locke and Montesquieu, through Madison and Lincoln, to arrive at this attractive understanding of judicial review and its limits. For Canadians to ignore this alternative to the stark assertions of judicial supremacy is tragic.

7

Judicial Remedies and the Separation of Power

While partial agency permits – and even encourages – substantial *informal* involvement of one branch in matters formally allocated to another, it requires any such inter-branch interference to remain partial in the sense that the exercise of informal powers may ultimately be overruled by the formal authority. Parliaments, we have seen, may be executive-dominated to a considerable extent, but there is no fusion of executive and legislative powers as long as the "trained seals" on the backbenches retain the formal power to reject the government's proposals. The minority and textual retorts follow this pattern by incorporating legislative participation into the interpretive process but continuing to leave the ultimate determination of specific cases to the judicial branch. Similarly, the considerable judicial involvement in the policy process remains partial agency so long as courts do not fully subsume the formal legislative and executive powers, particularly the legislative power to approve spending and the executive power to implement the law (including judge-made law). Just as executive-dominated legislatures would become fully fused – in violation of the letter and spirit of the separation of powers – if backbenchers were somehow deprived of their formal powers to rebel and unseat the government, so would judicial control over executive and legislative power exceed the bounds of partial agency if the non-judicial branches were stripped of their ability to resist the judicial exercise of their formally assigned powers. This chapter argues that the Supreme Court's recent jurisprudence regarding its own remedial authority has exceeded this boundary by allowing courts directly and formally to wield legislative and executive power.

Expanding the Court's remedial powers is especially significant because formal limits on judicial remedies have traditionally been understood as important mitigating factors for the counter-majoritarian character of judicial power. In a well-known passage of *Federalist* No. 79, Alexander Hamilton argues that judicial power poses no serious threat to democratic decision making because, as the "least dangerous" branch, courts have "no influence over either the sword or the purse; no direction either of the strength or of the wealth of society; and can take no active resolution whatever. It may truly be said to have neither FORCE nor WILL, but merely judgment; and must ultimately depend upon the aid of the executive arm for the efficacious exercise of this faculty."[1] The concern that an unchecked Supreme Court could impose its policy preferences upon the representative branches is unfounded, Hamilton explains, because the implementation of any judicial decision remains wholly dependent on the actions of the executive and legislative branches. In other words, just as the executive and legislative branches require judicial cooperation in the effective application of law to particular cases, so too does the judiciary require the cooperation of the executive "sword" and legislative "purse" to implement its policy principles beyond the confines of the particular case. Unless, of course, the judiciary manages to seize the power of sword and purse, which is exactly what judicial interpretive supremacy allows it to do. If, as the supremacists suggest, the courts possess an authoritative and exclusive power to interpret the constitution, then they also have the collateral ability to adjust constitutional limits on their remedial powers as they see fit, in violation of the Madisonian injunction that no branch "can pretend to an exclusive or superior right of settling the boundaries between their respective powers."[2] This chapter contends that the Canadian Supreme Court, relying on the claim of constitutional interpretive supremacy, has indeed usurped the executive and legislative powers, including the executive sword and legislative purse.

THE JUDICIAL CONSTRUCTION OF SECTION 24(1)

The constitutional power to fashion judicial remedies is governed by section 24(1), which permits courts "of competent jurisdiction" to provide remedies they consider "appropriate and just in the circumstances." As Justice W.R. McIntyre recognized, "it is difficult to imagine language which could give the court a wider and less fettered discretion" than the wording of section 24.[3] Even this broad grant of power, however, must yield to constitutional limits. For example, it is generally accepted that a section 24(1) remedy cannot require a provincial government to exercise a federal power.[4] Federalism, in other words, acts as a constitutional constraint on Charter remedies. This result follows from section 52(1), which declares the constitution to be the "supreme law of Canada" and thus paramount over judicially created remedies. Simply put, the broad remedial powers of the courts must themselves be constitutional.

What then might be said of the constitutional separation of powers as a limit on judicial remedies? The Court has acknowledged that its section 24 remedies must "respect the relationships with and separation of functions among the legislature, the executive and the judiciary."[5] It is equally clear, however, that the Court treats the separation of powers as a second-order constitutional principle at best and not nearly as certain as those imposed by federalism concerns. This is demonstrated by the Court's insistence on characterizing the separation-of-powers principle as part of a broader "dialogue" metaphor and its declaration that "judicial restraint and metaphors such as 'dialogue' must not be elevated to the level of strict constitutional rules to which the words of s. 24 can be subordinated."[6] Since separation-of-powers concerns fail to reach the level of "strict constitutional rules," the Court's logic runs, the court-designed remedies of section 24 take precedence.

On its face, however, the remedial power found in section 24(1) is limited by the separation of powers because it explicitly connects the Court's power to issue remedies with the case-and-controversy requirement discussed in chapter 5. The strong remedial power ("such remedy [that is] appropriate and just") assigned to "a court of competent jurisdiction" may be applied only to a discrete party and a discrete legal cause of action ("*Anyone* whose rights and freedoms ... *have been infringed* ... may apply ... to obtain such remedy ... [that is] appropriate and just *in the circumstance*' [emphasis added]). This wording is in keeping with the traditional understanding of the courts as arbitrators of concrete disputes.[7] That is what Justice McIntyre had in mind when he followed his description of section 24 (the "wide and less fettered discretion" quotation cited above) with a less-noted remark that "the *Charter* was not intended to turn the Canadian legal system upside down" and "what is required rather is that it be fitted into the existing scheme of Canadian legal procedure."[8] One must also keep in mind that section 31 of the Charter states that "nothing in this Charter extends the legislative powers of any body or authority," including the courts. In other words, section 24 reflects and codifies traditional judicial powers and does nothing to enhance the court's power over cases that are not immediately before the bench.

The case-specific character of section 24 is in sharp contrast to the more abstract supremacy clause (s.52). Section 52 declares all laws that violate the constitution to be void and of no force or effect. Unlike section 24, the section 52 declaration does apply to every law at all times and not just those immediately before the Court. The catch, of course, is that section 52 does not charge any particular institution with the task of voiding laws on the grounds of unconstitutionality. Given that the Charter framers were well aware of the long-running controversy over judicial review in the United States, it is striking that they would not explicitly assign this interpretive power to the judiciary if that were their intention. Yet, even though section 52 omits any mention of the judicial branch, legal scholars insist that it means the courts are the ultimate arbiters of constitutional validity. Hogg, for example, argues that "since it inevitably falls to the courts to determine whether a law is inconsistent with the Charter, s. 52(1) provides an explicit basis for judicial review of legislation in Canada."[9] Aside from its questionable use of the word "explicit," Hogg's argument is somewhat circular – courts are the arbiters of constitutional consistency because they are "inevitably" the arbiters – and, more important, Hogg's reading of section 52 does not support an *exclusive* power to determine the constitutionality of laws. In fact, the ambiguity of *who* declares laws unconstitutional suggests that no institution may claim exclusive authority to enforce the section 52 declaration and thus constitutional supremacy requires the interpretive power to be ambivalent in the sense that all institutions can claim *some* informal authority over it. In keeping with this coordinate construction, section 52 can be understood as requiring each institution to exercise its own institutional powers in accordance with its own understanding of the constitution.

One might object at this point that the coordinate approach supports the Court's remedial jurisprudence since it would allow the judicial branch to exercise its remedial powers according to its own interpretation of the constitution. Here, once again, the partiality of the inter-branch agency must be stressed. In order for the institutional separation to be maintained, the branches must be constitutionally independent. Therefore, judicial remedies must remain, in some plausible sense, "judicial." As Chief Justice McLachlin recognized (in the context of a controversy over the competence of a justice of the peace to find a Charter breach), "s.24 should not be read so broadly that it endows courts and tribunals with powers that they were never intended to exercise."[10] Just as the coordinate constitutional approach would not permit the legislature to adjudicate discrete cases simply because legislators might purport to find this to be part of their constitutional power to legislate, the judicial branch is restricted to *judicial* formal powers and, as we shall see in the controversial cases below, the Court itself admits that it is exercising legislative and executive powers through its expanded remedies. Again, such informal agency is acceptable – even encouraged – so long as it is partial in the sense that it allows the assigned branch the formal opportunity to resist the informal influence. As I demonstrate below, this is not the case with the Court's modern remedial jurisprudence.

This is not to say, as some critics suggest, that advocates of coordinate constitutionalism "just don't want courts to play any role in our constitutional democracy."[11] Kent Roach might think that "judges' decisions mean zip unless they're implemented," but the coordinate approach appreciates some of the more subtle features of judicial power.[12] The cumulative result of sections 24 and 52 from the coordinate perspective is a grant of formal power to the courts with respect to the individual litigants before them but only an informal power to declare laws unconstitutional for all branches. The judiciary's formal authority under section 24(1) allows it to grant injunctive or pecuniary relief to the litigants as the court sees fit and protects this remedy from being altered, amended, or challenged by any other institution. However, the broader declarations made under section 52(1) are informal in the sense that they should not immediately and directly bind other institutional agents. It is, of course, open to other institutions to agree with the court's reasons and accept its judgment that the law is unconstitutional, but any such influence is, by definition, informal. Even if the Supreme Court's advice on constitutionality is routinely accepted, and there are reasons to hope that it would be, that would not transform informal into formal authority (no more so than the executive's dominance over the legislature invalidates the legislature's formal ability to hem the executive). The executive and legislative branches are free, under this conception, to operate under *their* understanding of what is constitutional (thus exercising *their* section 52[1] powers). In other words, the legislative and executive effects of the Court's constitutional rulings are necessarily the responsibility of the legislature and the executive. In this arrangement, judicial decisions surely mean more than Roach's "zip" but they are not as definitive as the judicial supremacists might wish.

SEIZING THE LAW: THE JUDICIAL ASSUMPTION OF LEGISLATIVE POWER

As discussed in chapter 5, judicial power necessarily implies a degree of legislative power. Indeed, a central concept of the common law is that judge-made law may effectively fill in the gaps and lacunae left by never fully comprehensive legislative schemes. This is a prime example of judicial partial agency over the legislator: whatever the judicial exercise of the legislative power is, the legislature can formally respond with new legislation that supersedes any judicial lawmaking. With the Charter, however, courts have used their remedial powers of severance and "reading-in" to legislate in a fashion that "bypassed the legislative process altogether" and thus denied the legislature its formal chance to approve or disapprove of the judicial amendment (unless it repeals the legislation altogether).[13]

This remedial power to legislate is not an inescapable consequence of the Charter's mandate of constitutional supremacy. An early Charter decision by the Nova Scotia Supreme Court found that the province's Family Benefits Act infringed the equality guarantee in section 15 by granting benefits to single mothers but not single fathers.[14] Faced with this constitutional defect, the court considered whether it should strike down the legislation entirely or simply read-in the excluded group (single fathers) so that they could enjoy share in the benefits. Judge Merlin Nunn refused "to assume the role of legislator" by redrafting the legislation and instead declared the invalid act, in its entirety, to be of "no force or effect."[15] This defensible approach was expressly disavowed by the Supreme Court of Canada, however, because its "ironic" result was thought to run counter to the basic purposes of the Charter.[16]

Expanded remedial options – including the legislative reading-in – were endorsed by the Supreme Court of Canada in *Schachter v.*

Canada. For the *Schachter* Court, the technique of reading-in is simply an extension of a much broader form of judicial pruning that assists, not thwarts, legislative intent. In that decision, Chief Justice Lamer, writing for a majority of the Court, equates reading-in with "severance," a remedial technique that addresses a constitutional defect by invalidating only the offending portion of the legislation and lets the remainder of the act stand. As Lamer notes, the severance technique was devised to serve the end of judicial restraint: "Severance is used by the courts so as to interfere with the laws adopted by the legislature as little as possible."[17] This minimal-interference rationale has subsequently been transformed, somewhat perversely, into a justification for the wholesale rewriting of statutes. Both severance and reading-in, according to Lamer, rely upon a basic assumption that the Court is in a position to make: that is, the "assumption that the legislature would have passed the constitutionally sound part of the scheme without the unsound part."[18] Given a separation of powers that places great significance on the existence of formal opportunities for institutional disagreement, this is a highly problematic assumption for one institution to make for another. Lamer admits that there "is no easy formula" for determining whether a legislature would have passed the judicially amended legislation but suggests that the courts can follow "the twin guiding principles" which are "respect for the role of the legislature and the purposes of the *Charter*."[19] It is not difficult to see which of Lamer's "twin principles" will prevail in the judicial mind: respect for the legislature will inevitably take a backseat to the Charter, whose "purpose" is knowable only to judges. Unless the Court is willing to take the legislature's understanding of the Charter's purposes seriously, essentially denying the Court its interpretive supremacy, then Lamer's principles may indeed be reduced to an "easy formula": judicial control over legislation.

As the *Vriend* case illustrates, it is the judicial supremacist approach that the Court follows. Delwin Vriend, a lab coordinator, had been fired by King's College in Edmonton for violating the college's policy on sexual orientation. Since the college's administrative policy was, from the perspective of the Charter, private action, Vriend filed a complaint under the Alberta Individual's Rights Protection Act (IRPA) but was rejected by Alberta's Human Rights Commission because the IRPA did not include sexual orientation as a prohibited form of discrimination.[20] Despite frequent calls by interest groups for the addition of such a provision, and recommendations of the Human Rights Commission itself, the Alberta legislature had repeatedly rejected amending the IRPA to include sexual orientation as a protected ground.[21] Supported by an array of gay and lesbian interest groups, Vriend applied to the courts to challenge the IRPA as an unconstitutional infringement of his equality rights as guaranteed by section 15 of the Charter. The Court accepted Vriend's argument and read-in sexual orientation to the IRPA's list of prohibited grounds of discrimination.

It is important to recognize the broad scope of the Court's order and the extent to which it goes beyond the factual case presented by Vriend. By reading-in sexual orientation to key definitional sections of the IRPA, the Court made it unconstitutional to discriminate, for virtually any private or public purpose, on the grounds of sexual orientation. If one can conceive of potential judicial responses to Vriend as a continuum, then this would be a polar "legislative" option. At the other "judicial" end of the continuum, the Court could have addressed Delwin Vriend's case in its particulars, perhaps forcing the Human Rights Commission to order his reinstatement at the college or, more likely, awarding him damages for his unjust termination. Between these judicial and legislative poles, a middle-ground position might have been to read-in sexual orientation only to the employment provision (s.6) and leave other applications to future cases. One might hope that a Court mindful of the formal limits of its power would tend towards the judicial and not legislative ends of the continuum, but the *Vriend* Court showed no such restraint in adopting the most legislative remedial option available. It is true that the Court's definitive judgment reduces the need for more litigation to expand the ruling's reach, but it is unclear, from a separation-of-power standpoint, why the burden of further litigation is not simply an attendant cost of judicial power (indeed, the requirement that judicial power be exercised on a case-by-case basis is meant to be an internal check on judicial overreach and an essential, pragmatic "check and balance"; see chapter 5). By adopting the most legislative remedy available, the *Vriend* Court demonstrated a lack of appreciation for the formal limits of its judicial power.

Had the Court wished to further inter-institutional dialogue, as it claimed to be doing, *Vriend* presented an obvious opportunity for it to demonstrate remedial restraint with a suspension of its ruling. The majority's justification for reading-in focuses on results; if the legislature, in the event of an invalidation, would have eventually enacted the judicially imposed amendment, then the Court can save considerable time and effort by simply creating constitutionally valid revised legislation immediately. From this perspective, however, the legislative process is viewed as a mere formality that might be safely ignored. This denigration of the legislative process runs counter to the conception of it suggested by the separation of powers; the formal requirement that statutes be passed by the legislature ensures at least a minimal degree of public consultation, open debate, and pressure towards mutual accommodation that is not necessarily characteristic of the judicial process. In this respect, the *Vriend* remedy is emphatically not partial. The *Schachter* rules for reading-in attempt to make this remedial power *seem* partial (that is, by permitting only discrete minor changes that are consistent with the general intent of the legislature), but, *on the point of controversy*, the Court assumes unchecked legislative authority. On the question of whether the IRPA protects against discrimination on the grounds of sexual orientation, the Court's affirmative answer is directly coded into law with no opportunity for the legislature to reject or modify the judicial exercise of legislative power.

The bypassing of the legislature is justified, the Court and its supporters suggest, because the judiciary is only "carrying out the will of another" by making good on the legislature's intent and thus acting in accord with the partial-agency model. Kent Roach, for example, claims that the Court "uses [reading-in] only when it concludes that both the *Charter* and the intent of the legislature will be better served by judicial amendment."[22] In *The Supreme Court on Trial*, Roach approves of the *Vriend* remedy because the majority simply "assigned the burden of legislative inertia" in "a sensible and principled fashion."[23] Roach concludes that, from this perspective, it is Justice Major's preferred alternative – a delayed declaration – which is the "drastic remedy."[24] This is a bit of rhetorical nonsense since the only way a delayed declaration could be considered a more drastic remedy than an immediate reading-in is if the legislature failed to answer the Court with new legislation, thus forcing a future court decision to declare the entire act unconstitutional. But, if one predicts that the legislature would be so hostile to such amendments, then it is inappropriate, in Roach's own view, to read-in since "the intent of the legislature" would *not* be "better served by judicial amendment."

Whether or not the Court possess the ability to make the assessment of legislative intent accurately (an open and significant question), the Court's approach, like Roach's, is problematic because it suggests that judicial interventions can perfect statutes that contain mistakes or that may have been deliberately compromised to ensure passage through the legislative process. As Manfredi notes, "the underlying message of [*Vriend*] is that legislatures sometimes fail to understand how to achieve their own objectives, and that courts can correct this failure with a bit of remedial intervention."[25] This judicial desire to perfect is particularly troubling in the context of ameliorative legislation. In such cases, executives and legislatures may attempt to address social ills by piecemeal programs offering only limited relief. Given scarce resources and the possibility of unintended consequences, this incremental approach is often a reasonable means of action. Unilateral judicial expansion of such programs can unsettle legislative bargains, introduce unintended consequences that the cautious legislature sought to minimize, and use resources without regard to their replenishment. Each of these dangers can be mitigated, of course, if the courts hew closely to the case-and-controversy limitation on their power but they are magnified when courts exercise broad legislative powers.

SEIZING THE PURSE: JUDICIAL POWER OVER PUBLIC SPENDING

In budgetary terms, the judicial expansion of the IRPA in *Vriend* was relatively cost-free since it imposed obligations on private (or quasi-private) actors rather than directly spending public funds. If judicially imposed remedies that tend towards the legislative pole were restricted to only cost-neutral measures, then this would be a significant restraint on the Court's agency over legislative power (given that, as the Canadian founders clearly understood, the capacity to the make the law is severely hampered without control of the public purse). Such a rule would respect the clear assignments of power regarding public funds established in the BNA Act. As discussed in chapter 3, the power of the purse in liberal democracies has always been a legislative prerogative but this does not mean that the executive plays no role. To the contrary, the partnership of the legislative and executive branches over the power of the purse, based on a separation of their functions, is explicitly set out in sections 53 and 54 of the BNA Act. Working together, these sections arrange for shared control over finance: the Commons may reject the cabinet's budget but it may not initiate its own; cabinet can offer a synoptic plan but cannot proceed without approval from the legislature. These mutually reinforcing checks are undermined when the Court not only exercises its inescapable power of interpreting the constitution in order to adjudicate a concrete dispute, but also seizes the power of the purse in order to remedy a finding of unconstitutionality. While the Court has recently signalled that this power will be exercised with restraint in order to respect legislative prerogatives (in the 2004 cases of *Auton v. British Columbia [Attorney General]* and *Newfoundland [Treasury Board] v. N.A.P.E.*), it has refused to rule out further court-ordered expansions to ameliorative social-benefit programs designed to provide only limited relief.

In *Eldridge v. British Columbia (Attorney General)*, the laudable public health-care system was judicially expanded to include specific benefits for disabled patients. The Court found that the section 15 equality guarantee of the Charter includes a right to "effective communication" for deaf patients in the delivery of health services.[26] The Court ruled that "the appropriate and just remedy" for British Columbia's failure to supply sign-language interpreters was not only "to grant a declaration that this failure is unconstitutional" but also "to direct the government of British Columbia to administer the *Medical and Health Care Services Act* ... and the *Hospital Insurance Act* in a manner consistent with the requirements of s. 15(1)."[27] While the Court affords some legislative deference in terms of remedial options, Justice La Forest notes that "it is probably fair to surmise that sign language interpretation will be required in most cases."[28] In other words, the government is ordered to supply sign-language interpreters as part of its health-care budget. This judicial circumvention of sections 53 and 54 means that the Court's spending does not require popular approval and avoids difficult questions of policy trade-offs.

In a cost-free world – the abstract, case-specific environment the Court is presented with – everyone would agree to supply hospitals with sign-language interpreters since there would be no reason to do otherwise. The real world is not cost-free, however, a fact that the Court blithely discounts by noting that "financial considerations alone may not justify *Charter* infringements."[29] The real-world issue is not whether interpreters are a justifiable public good but whether they can be afforded given the potentially painful trade-offs between goods that can be purchased with scarce public funds. Even for deaf patients, interpreters do little good if they are signing "you will have to wait six months for an MRI." Because it makes its decisions across all policy fields, the executive is far better placed to see and evaluate these trade-offs than a Court focused upon a single complainant. Given that granting a benefit is always easier than taking one away or denying it, the Court's unifocal approach necessarily favours additional spending and, crucially, does so without the burden of responsibility. Essentially, the Court gets to play Santa Clause while leaving others to be the Taxman.

In the Court's defence, *Eldridge* can be characterized as nothing more than a judicial demand for governments to "take special measures to ensure that disadvantaged groups are able to benefit equally from government services."[30] Technically, the Court's actual remedy supports this interpretation since the Court suspended its declaration of invalidity for six months to allow for the government to remedy the unequal treatment of deaf patients. According to the Court, the government has a choice: it can provide health care in an egalitarian fashion or it can decide not to provide service at all. Yet, despite the Court's rhetoric of deference – "It is not this Court's role to dictate how this is to be accomplished"[31] – the decision to fund (non-negotiable from the Court's perspective) is the end of the real policy debate. No one seriously believes that Canadian governments will completely abandon public health care. In practice, everything must be made to accommodate the judicially privileged budgetary demand.

The Court's remedial action is analogous to the familiar process of attaching riders to major legislation in the United States. It is common in the American budgetary process, with its "multiple cracks" structure, for individual legislators to attach specific pet spending projects to large appropriation bills, safe in the knowledge that other political actors (who will often have their own preferences attached) will not jeopardize the entire bill.[32] This is precisely the form of decentralized log-rolling with public funds that section 54 is meant to ensure against. In *Eldridge*, the Court's confidence that universal health care will be maintained in British Columbia allows it to "tinker at the margins" by spending public funds as it sees fit while supposedly denying itself the final word on the subject. This technique must be exercised cautiously to avoid provoking a repeal of the underlying legislation.

Perhaps conscious of the policy result of *Schachter* – where the judicial extension of maternity benefits to adoptive parents led to a reduced period of leave for all parents[33] – the *Eldridge* Court carefully notes that the cost of providing interpreters is (in its opinion) "only $150,000."[34] The Court's figure fails to include funding that flows from the decision's precedential value, which is noteworthy because the decision has already been used once by courts (to extend government benefits to cover the additional costs of chronic-pain sufferers) and may be used at the Court's discretion to benefit any future litigants it deems worthy.

In *Nova Scotia (Workers' Compensation Board) v. Martin*, the Court upheld an equality challenge to Nova Scotia's Workers' Compensation Act on the grounds that it impermissibly diverted chronic-pain sufferers to an alternate regulatory scheme. This alternate scheme – the Functional Restoration (Multi-Faceted Pain Services) Program Regulations – substituted a four-week remedial program in lieu of the benefits normally available to injured workers. The Nova Scotia scheme was found unconstitutional because it imposed "differential treatment" upon a disadvantaged class (chronic-pain sufferers are deemed an analogous class to those identified in s.15[1]). The government's objective of preventing fraudulent claims is insufficient, in the Court's opinion, to limit benefits "on their presumed characteristics as a group" and unfairly "ignores the needs of those workers who, despite treatment, remain permanently disabled by chronic pain."[35] Despite evidence that the Accident Fund (set up by the act) has "accumulated considerable unfunded liability," the government may not, according to the Court, restrict benefits for repeat claimants. The constitutional requirement of treating all compensation claims equally in this respect means that reforms that emphasize benefits for "one-off" injuries are impermissible. The Supreme Court's expansion of the ameliorative Workers' Compensation Act is, in effect, a legislative amendment that spends the resources the government has responsibly collected.

However, even if one finds, as the Court did in *Eldridge*, that a judicially mandated benefit is relatively cheap, the Court's eagerness for cost-effective improvements to the health-care system remains misguided. The proper arena for considering such reforms is the regular executive-legislative process. The Court, of course, assumes that an unsuccessful policy outcome is evidence of procedural unfairness towards vulnerable minorities. Given the reality of scarce resources, however, ameliorative programs cannot be unlimited, and only elected representatives, as the recognized agents of the entire citizenry, can legitimize the often harsh, seemingly arbitrary but altogether necessary limits of these laudable programs. These limits, of course, need not be permanent and proponents of extending such programs can seek future legislative revisions to accommodate their concerns. Absent specific evidence of procedural unfairness, the statutory dimensions of ameliorative programs should be respected.

By giving itself the authority to expand benefits, the Court has accumulated legislative and executive power over the public purse. Its new "unified" power over public finance means that the Court can hear a complaint (its traditional judicial power), propose a spending remedy (exclusively an executive power under s.54), and shield that remedy from legislative scrutiny (thwarting the purpose of s.53). The Court's power is resolutely undivided – a single institution has complete control over this (admittedly discrete) policy issue in a manner precisely proscribed by the constitution. Consider the perspective of an interest group seeking access to public spending. The centralized power to initiate legislation (s.54) means there are only a few high-level access points for lobbying and, even with access, the interest group will be competing against many others for executive attention. Ministerial and/or bureaucratic support does not mean automatic policy success since the proposal will still need to survive legislative scrutiny. Even with an executive-controlled legislature, the process requires considerable time and careful effort. However, if the interest group can frame its demand as a "right," then the burdens and pay-offs dramatically shift. Despite the high costs of litigation, a judicial remedy is worth obtaining because it offers an indisputable, permanent, and almost immediately effective claim on public funds. Given the contrast with a temporary legislative victory, it is inevitable that more groups will use the courts to achieve their preferred policy outcomes. Allowing such a judicial short-circuit over the onerous requirement of sections 53 and 54 undermines the core fiscal tenet of responsible government.

As suggested above, the coordinate construction of section 24(1) provides plenty of scope for judicial remedies but requires that they take a *judicial* form, that is, they should be akin to traditional adjudicative remedies. Courts have always been able to direct public funds by awarding damages when the government is the defendant.[36] Pecuniary Charter damages, however, have been limited as a result of the rule denying combined sections 24(1) and 52 remedies.[37] This rule, which exists solely to protect executive officials acting in good faith, should not apply when (1) it is the policy itself, not the official's conduct, that fails to meet judicial standards and (2) when the alternative remedy is *more* intrusive of another branch's domain (if, for example, the alternative is a fully realized, judicially imposed legislative program). So, in the *Eldridge* case, the Court might have awarded monetary damages for denial of effective care to deaf patients on a case-by-case basis; that is, Eldridge herself might have been awarded damages for the failure of the B.C. government to provide maternity care that includes effective communication (or perhaps the government could have been required to reimburse Eldridge for an interpreter she might have hired). While there may be difficulties in ascertaining the amount of these damages, or even if there was damage realized at all, this problem is magnified – not avoided – when the Court implements a remedial-benefits scheme (costs are indeterminate[38] and damage need not be established). Faced with the possibility of more complainants successfully using the precedent, the government may, of course, decide that the enactment of a universal scheme is the best solution to avoid future judicial losses. Or it may not, and choose to continue paying out on a case-by-case basis (the burden of litigation may, in fact, prevent cases where the realized damage of the infringement is minimal or not easily proved). Or perhaps the government might attempt to mitigate the damages it knows it will incur by not legislating a comprehensive scheme (by, for example, employing a small number of interpreters to be used only where the damage might be probable and immense). Under this approach, the legislature cannot ignore the judicial interpretation of what the constitution requires but it retains its formal prerogative over the legislative power. Unlike the actual remedy in *Eldridge*, judicial power would not be extended beyond its traditional limits to include future complainants and future damages (issues not related to the case at bar), thus minimizing the scope for judicial legislating. This piecemeal damages approach has been experimented with (notably by the trial judge in *Auton*[39]) but has not been endorsed by the Supreme Court or accepted generally by the legal community.

Indeed, supporters of judicial power reject the notion that the authority of the Supreme Court is confined to a specific case. Kent Roach has been particularly critical of the notion that *Eldridge*-like decisions should be limited and instead prefers the immediate nationwide application of any Supreme Court ruling: "Even though British Columbia was the only direct party to the case, it is untenable to think that general constitutional law issues decided by the Supreme Court of Canada must be re-litigated on a province-by-province basis ... Such an expensive and costly approach would make remedies illusory for disadvantaged groups affected by the Court's decisions."[40] Roach is correct that such an approach would be costly (in terms of relitigation), but one might suggest that this is the cost of the separation of powers (or, perhaps, the cost of politics generally). It would be cost-effective, for example, to have one national government make all law for the country but the extra cost of eleven separate legislative jurisdictions is paid to allow for federalism. Inter-institutional relations between courts and legislatures should be no different. Needless to say, governments and courts, conscious of these high costs, are likely to seek compromises in all but the most contentious of cases. When it comes to these most controversial cases, is it not possible that inter-institutional disagreement is worth paying for?

When it comes to *Eldridge*, however, Roach is unwilling to tolerate any legislative disagreement with the Court's decision. He has criticized both the B.C. government's initial response (setting up a twenty-four-hour toll-free voice and TTY line within the six-month delayed-declaration period) and its ultimate response ten months later (extended service to include interpreters upon request for physician and hospital visits). With respect to the other provinces, Roach finds that "governmental responses to *Eldridge* have been more uneven and less positive."[41] Roach notes that Ontario has essentially relitigated under the cheaper human-rights commission process. The *Eldridge* response suggests that "it may not be safe to assume that governments that are not direct parties to a dispute will promptly, voluntarily and in good faith comply."[42] Roach concludes that, where there are "national implications," a "recalcitrant province that has refused to comply with clearly applicable precedent from the Supreme Court has proven itself ... 'unworthy of trust.'"[43] A legislature that seeks to exercise its formal authority over the legislative power, in the face of judicial agency, is for Roach illegitimate. Once more Roach belies his own enthusiasm for dialogue between courts and legislatures by portraying executives and legislatures to be "unworthy of the trust" necessary to be a responsible interpreter of the constitution; when it comes to interpretive matters, judicial supremacy, and not the separation of power, is his constitutional lodestar.

SEIZING THE SWORD: THE JUDICIAL ASSUMPTION OF EXECUTIVE POWER

In its *Doucet-Boudreau* ruling, the Supreme Court seized the "sword" of executive power in an unprecedented and dramatic fashion. Traditionally, the executive had the power to implement law, including court-made law. While section 9 of the BNA Act established executive power, such power was necessarily partial since it purported to execute the will of another institution – the legislature with respect to statutory law and the judiciary with respect to the common law. Once a legal case was concluded, giving effect to the legal ruling or order was a matter for executive actors. True, this gave non-judicial actors some role in shaping the actual impact of a law or legal ruling, but that is an inherent aspect of the partial agency of the branches in each other's affairs that underlies healthy checks and balances. Nor did this mean that the judiciary had no comeback to a perceived executive failure to implement its order properly, but that comeback depended on litigants bringing a new case. *Doucet-Boudreau* overcame this traditional constraint on judicial power by permitting a court to maintain continuing supervision of its order in the same case. The case arose under section 23 of the Charter, which includes a minority-language education right that the Supreme Court has interpreted (in *Mahe v. Alberta*) to require specific programs and facilities for the minority-language group where "numbers warrant." The trial judge ordered five Nova Scotia school districts to remedy their breach of this right by building, before a specified deadline, the homogeneous French-language secondary schools necessary to serve their francophone communities. The Supreme Court decided that a judge who finds an unjustified violation of section 23 has the power to retain jurisdiction in order to hear status reports detailing efforts at compliance (and, presumably, issue new orders in response to those reports),[44] as the trial judge in the instant case had ordered. As the *Doucet-Boudreau* majority recognizes, this remedy gives the supervising judge "functions that are principally assigned to the executive," though apparently it only "touches" on those functions.[45]

Does the judicial remedy employed in *Doucet-Boudreau* simply "touch" on executive power? In Madisonian terms, does it remain an appropriate example of the partial agency required by checks and balances? Consider the actual role played by Nova Scotia trial judge Arthur LeBlanc in his retention of jurisdiction in *Doucet-Boudreau*. In the reporting sessions, he resolved issues "concerning, among other things, the type of construction of these school facilities, whether they would be new school facilities or the renovation of existing buildings, submissions with respect to other school facilities which were not part of the original application, and extending to such minute detail as, for example, the type of ventilation system which would be included in the school facilities."[46] Justice Edward Flinn of the Nova Scotia Court of Appeal concluded that "in conducting these reporting sessions, the trial judge was acting more in the capacity of an administrator than as a judge."[47] The Supreme Court disagreed and suggested that these orders do not "depart unduly or unnecessarily from their role of adjudicating disputes."[48] Given the range and detail of the trial judge's supervision, however, it is difficult to accept the remedy as simply "touching" on executive power. It remains to determine whether it nevertheless qualifies as partial agency.

While the *Doucet-Boudreau* assumption of executive power raises key questions of institutional competence – are courts better than bureaucrats at evaluating ventilation systems? – the more relevant consideration for this study is its departure from that part of the separation of powers captured by the traditional common law notion that a judge's role ends with judgment (*functus officio*). By overcoming the *functus officio* norm, the *Doucet-Boudreau* remedy eases the restraint inherent in the requirement that judicial power be exercised collectively. Even the most ardent social-science positivists, who insist that judicial decision making is explained by personal preference, concede that a degree of restraint emerges from the fact that judicial power is institutional and not personal.[49] Thus, whatever the individual preference of an appellate court judge, he or she requires the support of colleagues in order to make that preference law. This logic applies more broadly to the judiciary as a whole. If the decision is based on objective reasoning instead of personal preference (to the extent possible), then one would expect every judge to reach the same result in any given case. Since law is (to some degree) undeniably subjective, such mechanical jurisprudence is impossible (and probably undesirable). Given this inherent uncertainty, judicial power is entrusted to a *body* of men and women. From this perspective, the *functus officio* rule makes considerable sense. Once a decision is made, the judge's power is finished. Therefore, any residue of personal preference is subjected first to the decisions of elected actors (who may decide to ignore or respond creatively to the decision) and then, in event of non- or partial compliance, to a *new* judge. The retention of jurisdiction in *Doucet-Boudreau* undermines this restraint and increases the potential impact of a judge's personal policy preference.

Given the existence of an appeal, this may appear a minor point. Individual preference, after all, will surely be restrained by appellate court judges. Yet there is something odd about a remedy that seeks to avoid relitigation (the primary justification for the retention of jurisdiction) but relies upon the possibility of further litigation for its legitimacy. Even in a transaction cost-free universe, moreover, the retention of jurisdiction still increases the *relative* power of the individual judge with respect to the judicial power as a whole. One might object that this is an internal matter for the judiciary, rather than a question of inter-branch separation, but the danger of unifying executive and judicial power is surely exacerbated by this increase in personal power. Unified power wielded by a single institution is dangerous enough; wielded by a single judge it is even more problematic.

Within the discrete sphere of minority-language education policy, the accumulation of power Montesquieu feared is manifest. The judiciary legislates by interpreting section 23 to require linguistic minority "management and control" of facilities,[50] applies it to the litigants by resolving a dispute (finding a constitutional violation in *Doucet-Boudreau*), and assumes a governing role over compliance (the continuing supervisory role established by the remedy). There is no role for other branches to obstruct, modify, or respond other than simple compliance with judicial preferences. This arguably goes well beyond the kind of partial agency in another branch's affairs that our constitutional system requires.

For some jurists, this concern is outweighed by the benefits of such an effective remedy. Dissenting from his Court's invalidation of the remedy, Justice Gerald Freeman of the Nova Scotia Court of Appeal says that the reporting remedy "appears to be a pragmatic approach to getting the job done expeditiously."[51] According to Freeman, "the danger of oppressive judicial intervention is very real" but not a concern in this case because the trial judge made "correct" decisions.[52] Even if Freeman is right and these particular judgments are correct, the establishment of such an intrusive remedy as a precedent cannot be ignored. Once the separation is breached in this fashion, the judicial branch may be tempted to use its enhanced remedial power whenever the constitutional separation interferes with the imposition of its policy preferences. It should be noted that, in the case at bar in *Doucet-Boudreau*, the novel retention remedy was pre-emptive – imposed in the "unlikely" event that the government defied trial judge LeBlanc's orders.[53] Given that, "by and large," the executive and its agencies "have complied with the courts' orders even where they have been issued as mere declarations,"[54] the pre-emptive resort to judicial management clearly indicates that the formal delineation between judicial and executive authority is not taken very seriously.

When it comes to this separation, the *Doucet-Boudreau* majority simply argues that "determining the boundaries of the court's proper role ... cannot be reduced to a simple test or formula; it will vary according to ... the context of each case."[55] The absence of any test or doctrine is itself a striking rebuke to the principle of separated powers. Since judging the variance necessary to accommodate a given context is assumed to be a matter wholly within the Court's discretion, this directly contradicts the Madisonian understanding of what counts as appropriate partial agency. Madison is quite clear that it is no longer *partial* agency when one branch has the exclusive power to define the constitutional powers of the other branches: "The several departments being perfectly coordinate by the terms of their common commission, none of them, it is evident, can pretend to an exclusive or superior right of settling the boundaries between their respective powers."[56] This notion of separated but coordinate powers has been rejected by the *Doucet-Boudreau* majority and its academic supporters.

In their minority opinion in *Doucet-Boudreau*, justices Louis LeBel, Marie Deschamps, John Major, and Ian Binnie explicitly base their rejection of the retention remedy on the separation of powers, "a cornerstone of our constitutional regime." "Awareness of the critical importance of effectively enforcing constitutional rights," LeBel and Deschamps write, must be consonant with "an understanding of the proper role of courts and of the organizing principles of the legal and political order of our country."[57] The dissenters note that Court has employed separation-of-power rhetoric in cases of judicial independence but now appears reluctant to see that it has "an obverse side as well which equally reflects the appropriate position of the judiciary within the Canadian legal system."[58] In this case, "when the trial judge attempted to oversee the implementation of his order, he ... assumed jurisdiction over a sphere traditionally outside the province of the judiciary."[59] LeBel and Deschamps advance an understanding of the separation of power akin to the partial-agency model detailed in this study; they find an institutional separation that is not watertight but that nonetheless prescribes basic (and mutually reinforcing) limits on each institution's power. For LeBel and Deschamps, inter-branch exercises of partial agency must respect the formal constitutional status of each institution: "Just as the legislature should, after a judicial finding of a *Charter* breach, retain independence in writing its legislative response, the executive should after a judicial finding of breach, retain autonomy in administering government policy that conforms with the *Charter*."[60] In other words, the judiciary must allow for those quintessential Montesquieuean opportunities for each branch to check the others, which means that the retention of jurisdiction by the judicial branch subverts the constitutional design by denying the executive its chance to moderate policy through its own exercise of power.

A particularly revealing attack by Marilyn Pilkington on the position held by the *Doucet-Boudreau* minority leaves no doubt that the legal community's acceptance of intrusive remedies and concomitant disdain for coordinate interpretation is, at least in part, a result of a confused understanding of the separation of powers as entrenched in the Canadian constitution. Pilkington accuses the dissenters as not being "entirely clear what the separation entails" because they refer to both the "balance that has been struck between our three branches of government" and the fact that "the executive is inextricably tied to the legislative branch."[61] For Pilkington, "these statements contradict each other," but, as I have endeavoured to show, the Canadian constitution allows for substantial partial agency between constitutionally separated institutions (and thus there is no contradiction between the minority's two statements, as Pilkington alleges). Pilkington adds that "in asserting a strict separation of powers between the executive, legislative, and judicial branches of government, the dissenters are appropriating a concept based on the American constitution and using it to limit the scope of judicial remedies, as advocated by some Charter critics who argue that courts are usurping government's ability to govern."[62] The dissenters (and "some Charter critics") are, in Pilkington's view, wrongly imposing a "strict" American principle on the Canadian fused system. By this point in this study, one hopes that her errors regarding Canada's institutional separation are obvious. Partial agency – which is as much a part of English constitutionalism as American (and which therefore is fundamentally Canadian) – by definition excludes a strict separation and this is emphatically not what the *Doucet-Boudreau* dissenters nor this author are suggesting. If one accepts, however, that even partial agency has its limits (that is, it is *partial)*, then the scope of judicial remedies must also be limited in that regard. If the mistaken conventional wisdom surrounding Canada's institutional separation has ossified to the extent that the judiciary can directly exercise legislative and executive power without correction, then we can expect more aggressive (and more confused) remedial jurisprudence in the future.

CONCLUSION

Some Final Words about the "Final Say"

When controversies over rights erupt, there is a temptation to reduce political disagreement to a simple matter of "trumps."[1] This tendency is epitomized by what I refer to as the "final say" question of judicial politics. One recent poll, commissioned by the Institute for Research on Public Policy (IRPC), asked: "In your opinion should the courts or Parliament have the final decision related to rights issues?"[2] This stark framing suggests only two viable options: either Parliament trumps the courts or the courts trump Parliament. While a majority (54 per cent) of respondents favoured the courts, a significant minority (31.2 per cent) supported Parliament, but the answer most closely approximating the approach I propose in this study – "unsure" – garnered a measly 14.8 per cent. "Unsure," I submit, is the correct answer because the scope of one's final say and the extent of the rights issue are highly ambiguous.

There are actually three possible positions on the questions of final say when it comes to the interpretation of the constitution: (1) the judicial power to interpret is subordinate to the interpretive power of Parliament; (2) the judicial power to interpret is superior to that of Parliament; or (3) the judicial power is coordinate with the parliamentary power. The first two positions can both be described as "supremacist" since they suggest that the relationship between the judiciary and the representative branches can flow in only one direction – one institution is supreme and its interpretive decisions are binding on the other(s). The third, non-supremacist alternative corresponds most closely to the "unsure" answer to the IRPC poll. Though it was strongly outpolled by the two supremacist approaches, it deserved to be the winner. It has been the purpose of this study to rehabilitate the Canadian coordinate model as both a more nuanced reflection of reality and the basis for superior institutional prescription. Let us begin this concluding overview by recapitulating how both supremacist positions reduce robust and complex relationships to a single simple rule of institutional supremacy.

TWO VARIETIES OF SUPREMACY

The first position – judicial subordination to Parliament – is not as foreign as it may seem at first blush. After all, as Larry Kramer notes (and as discussed in chapter 2), such a system – the traditional English model – is hardly "fanciful" and "one is hard put to point to another system, even in the modern era, that has worked longer or better."[3] Pre-1982 Canada, of course, is another example of a constitutional system where enactments of the appropriate federal or provincial parliaments were supreme in the sense that they could not be set aside by any other institution,[4] including the courts. Jeffrey Goldsworthy argues that this system provides a compelling answer to the question of a final say: "What is at stake is the location of ultimate decision-making authority – the right to the 'final word' – in a legal system. If the judges were to repudiate the doctrine of parliamentary supremacy, by refusing to allow Parliament to infringe unwritten rights, they would be claiming that ultimate authority for themselves. In settling disagreements about what fundamental rights people have, and whether particular legislation is consistent with them, the judges' word rather than Parliament's would be final."[5]

In truth, parliamentary supremacy in constitutional affairs has never been as absolute as theorists like Goldsworthy suggest. There is, of course, Coke's claim in *Dr. Bonham's Case* that even acts of Parliament are "void" if they are "against common right and reason, or repugnant, or impossible to be performed."[6] Echoing Coke, modern English legal scholars like T.R.S. Allan and Eric Barendt argue that English courts can mitigate (and even set aside) legislation or administrative action considered to be rights-infringing on the grounds of the "rule of law" (for Allan) or the "separation of powers" (for Barendt).[7] Similarly, in pre-1982 Canada, we have seen instances where the "rule of law" and the "implied bill of rights" have been advanced to protect individual rights.[8] Moreover, the untrammelled authority of the judicial branch to resolve concrete cases for particular litigants (as discussed in chapter 5) means that parliamentary supremacy is checked at the precise interface where abstract law acquires its practical force. As Hamish Gray suggests, since "the effectiveness of Parliament's enactments will depend wholly on the application and enforcement of those enactments by judges ... parliamentary sovereignty rests with the courts."[9]

Even if parliamentary supremacy was an adequate description of institutional priority in constitutional interpretation prior to 1982, it is difficult to argue that it remains so post-1982. The combined operation of sections 52(1) and 24(1) of the Charter clearly entitles judges to set aside a law, for the purposes of settling the case before them, if they believe the law is unconstitutional in order to achieve a result "appropriate and just in the circumstance." In the pre-1982 setting, judges may have worked around or mitigated laws they viewed as unconstitutional but, post-1982, judges may dispense with the veneer of obeying parliamentary will and simply avoid applying the law to the case at hand. At a minimum, the Constitution Act, 1982 legitimizes a form of judicial review that need not be concealed by subterfuge and obfuscation.

For some, this legitimization of judicial review ineluctably leads to the second supremacist option: judicial interpretive supremacy. Jamie Cameron, for example, frames the debate by declaring that "either the Constitution is supreme or not" and by deriding anything less than judicial interpretive supremacy as an "emasculation of [the Court's] authority to interpret the *Charter*."[10] Invoking the perspective of the final say, Justice Binnie claims that "if the 'political branches' are to be the 'final arbitrator' of compliance with the *Charter* of their 'policy initiatives,' the enactment of the Charter affords no real protection at all to the rights holders whom the Charter, according to its text, was intended to benefit. Charter rights and freedoms, on this reading, would offer rights without a remedy."[11] Leaving aside the questionable assertion that constitutional rights matter only if they have *judicial* remedies, Binnie's approach, like Cameron's, illustrates the all-or-nothing nature of the supremacist mind. If the Charter does not mandate judicial interpretive supremacy, they seem to be arguing, then the Charter is useless.

As Frederick DeCoste describes, proponents of this position emphasize the transformative effect of the Charter on our constitutional narrative, claiming that the Charter "ended one regime, parliamentary supremacy, and ushered in another, constitutional supremacy, and ... that, through this foundational change, the judicial branch became charged – as trustees, arbiter, and interpreter – with safeguarding constitutional rights from legislative and executive encroachment."[12] Assuming such a "regime change" in 1982 is problematic, however, because many vestiges of parliamentary supremacy are embedded in the new regime of constitutional supremacy. Constitutional supremacy, in other words, cannot simply be translated as judicial supremacy. After all, the Charter contains explicit provisions limiting entrenched rights (s.1) and even a parliamentary override (s.33). As the dialogue theorists are eager to point out, these provisions enable the representative branches to respond to the judicial decisions and, even if only in a limited non-interpretive sense, allow them the final say. Just as parliamentary supremacy is hard to square with the text of the Charter, so too is the judicial supremacy variant poorly suited to Canadian constitutionalism.

The two supremacies are, in fact, inextricably linked. The supremacist vision of Parliament – whose final say is exercised de facto by the dominant executive – begets the supremacist vision of the judiciary, because the latter seems to provide the only realistic check and balance to what is understood as fused parliamentary power. A strong Charter-empowered judiciary, in other words, is the only means of counter-balancing an executive that would otherwise be unchecked. As I argued in chapter 4, executive domination of legislatures may be a problem warranting attention, but one must be careful to recognize that the formal distinction between the cabinet and the legislature – denied by fusion enthusiasts – provides *some* check on executive excess. In truth, the executive cannot be said to control the *whole* legislative power. The fact that the executive is formally limited has two consequences for the purposes of this study. First, it supports the claim that Canada's separation of powers demands that no institution wholly possess the power formally assigned to another. Secondly, it means that the dominant executive does not in fact wholly possess legislative power – that is, the executive is not as all-powerful as the proponents of a strong judicial check suppose and therefore not in need of an unchecked judiciary.

The emphasis on an overawing *judicial* check, to the exclusion of any other kind, reduces the separation of powers between the fused Parliament and the independent judiciary to what Craig Forcese and Aaron Freeman refer to as the "trip switch in Canadian constitutional law."[13] According to Forcese and Freeman, the switch indicates where "parliamentary supremacy gives way to 'constitutional' supremacy":

On one side, Parliament is supreme and the courts must simply interpret and carry out Parliament's dictates expressed in Acts of Parliament. On the other side, Parliament strays beyond its constitutional jurisdiction and must be subordinated to the Constitution. On this uncomfortable side, courts do two things: first, they are arbiters of where that switch is, by interpreting the Constitution and, sometimes, discerning even binding unwritten constitutional principles by which Parliament must abide; and, second, they decide whether a given statute of Parliament trips the switch. Once it is triggered, Canadian democracy becomes a system of *de facto* judicial supremacy.[14]

Canada, in other words, is trapped between two supposed supremacies. Such an outcome is incongruent with the subtle checks and balances we observe in other parts of the constitution.

The issue of the Charter's co-existence with the rest of the constitutional design was directly spoken to in the 1990 Federal Court of Appeal case of *Southam Inc. v. Canada (Attorney General)*.[15] In that case, Chief Justice Iacobucci (as he then was) took issue with trial judge Barry Strayer's suggestion that "the adoption of the *Charter* fundamentally altered the nature of the Canadian Constitution such that it is no longer 'similar in Principle to that of the United Kingdom.'"[16] "Accepting as we must that the adoption of the *Charter* transformed to a considerable extent our former system of Parliamentary supremacy into our current one of constitutional supremacy," Iacobucci declared, "so it seems to me that the British system of constitutional government will continue to co-exist alongside the *Charter*."[17] If we understand the "British system of constitutional government" not as a regime of unchecked parliamentary supremacy but, rather, as one incorporating ambivalent checks and balances, then we should attempt to understand the Charter as a component of that system rather than as an external supreme check, as the "trip switch" approach would have us believe.

From a Montesquiean perspective, with its recognition of the human tendencies towards immoderation and the accumulation of power, such a trip switch provides little obstacle for a Court intent on pursuing its policy preferences, especially since such a Court is both the arbiter of where that switch is and whether it is triggered. The judicially controlled trip switch is particularly problematic for executives and legislators who believe that the court's interpretation of the constitution is incorrect. If the Court calls its decision constitutional – putting the decision on its side of the switch – then the judicial interpretation must be immediately adopted by the representative branches as their own. Essentially, Canada's non-judicial institutions are required to exercise their constitutional powers and fulfil their constitutional duties according to an interpretation they consider erroneous. In his critique of the dialogue theory, Grant Huscroft argues that "once it is acknowledged that decisions of the Court may be wrong, it is incumbent upon the authors to make the case for the requirement that the other branches of government must follow the Court's decisions."[18] The dialogue theorists, like interpretive supremacists generally, "fail to do so."[19]

WHEN ALL INSTITUTIONS ARE "NOT QUITE SUPREME"

The dialogue theorists respond to this argument by simply asserting that "the decisions of the executive and legislature have no claim to finality," but, as Huscroft notes, coordinate constitutionalists make no such claim on behalf of the finality of the representative branches ("this a response to an argument that no one makes"[20]). Hogg and his co-authors go so far as to assert that Canadian coordinate theorists are, at base, simply proponents of legislative supremacy.[21] To the contrary, this study demonstrates that coordinate interpretation, properly understood, rejects the very notion that a single institution must be supreme in favour of a more robust understanding of institutional relations that appreciates the interplay of formal and informal powers. When it comes to the interpretation of the constitution, I argue, these formal and informal dimensions should not be overlooked.

The complex institutional arrangements described in this study belie the simple supremacist models that pervade conventional constitutional wisdom in Canada. While it is obviously foolish to believe that legislatures have as much influence over public policy as the executive, as a purely formal understanding of the constitution might suggest, behavioural models of fusion, which dismiss constitutional forms to conclude that the executive can always have its way over the legislature, are equally misleading. The supremacist models have trouble reconciling formal and informal power because they have but one dimension ("which institution is superior")

Conclusion

to capture relationships that are multidimensional. Thus, constitutional supremacy must either be judicial or parliamentary supremacy. In other words, supremacist models miss the reality of the often subtle checks and balances elsewhere in the institutional design.

Only the coordinate approach, with its incorporation of formal and informal power, allows for constitutional supremacy with *no concomitant institutional supremacy*. From this perspective, the Constitution Act, 1982 is best understood as elevating the judiciary from a subordinate constitutional branch (supremacist position 1) to a co-equal branch capable of asserting itself independently, without the additional step of judicial superiority (supremacist position 2). This arrangement requires the idea of partial agency because it permits interdependence between the branches while also ensuring each branch's independence. In the case of constitutional interpretation, it allows for a more complete picture of the judicial interpretive power: a power that is formally weak (applying only to discrete cases and not determinative for other branches) but informally strong (often persuading the other branches, if only because its power over discrete cases will be controlling on a case-by-case basis). One can therefore expect the judicial interpretation to inform and perhaps even control the constitutional understandings of the representative branches. This agency over the interpretive forays of non-judicial branches is strictly *partial*, however. Should the legislature wish to confine a judicial error in interpretation and/or send a constitutional hint to the Court suggesting a preferred interpretation (that is, the situations contemplated in chapter 6), it may continue legitimately to hold and to act upon an interpretation that is contrary to the Court's. This interpretive pluralism, thought by most to be uncontroversial in the period prior to a Supreme Court ruling, continues to be justifiable even after the Supreme Court has ruled. Non-judicial actors need not patiently wait for the Court to reconsider its judgment; they have an active and legitimate means – statutory enactment – to provoke such rethinking and test the Court's resolve.

The capacity of the representative branches to make such statutory challenges is threatened, however, by the process Mansfield alerts us to – the tendency to formalize the behavioural. Since even the coordinate account accepts that the judicial branch takes a leading role in constitutional controversies, with only occasional legislative or executive participation, one can easily become accustomed to the notion that the judiciary is the appropriate venue for deciding interpretive controversies. This is reasonable until the desire to formalize the "reality" of judicial supremacy strikes. It is then that the infrequent but significant exceptions risk being stripped of their formal legitimacy. I submit that this process is well under way in Canada with respect to the judiciary's power to interpret the constitution. As Grant Huscroft observes, "judicial exclusivity in interpreting the *Charter* is not only well established as a constitutional norm, but ... it has become an important consideration in the political process."[22]

Unless the partiality of the Court's interpretive power is explicitly recognized, the "constitutional norm" of judicial supremacy threatens to become constitutional law. In a recent case, justices Louis LeBel and Marshall Rothstein suggested as much when they declared that "in our system, the Supreme Court has the final word on the interpretation of the Constitution."[23] This book argues that such blanket statements of interpretive supremacy are mistaken and ill-suited for Canada's ambivalent arrangement of institutions. My argument is, in essence, an appeal to our history and the logic of our constitutional design. Ultimately it is Canadians who will have to judge the Court's attempt to claim the final say.

Notes

INTRODUCTION

1 Bickel, *Least Dangerous Branch*; See also Friedman, "The History of the Countermajoritarian Difficulty."
2 Ely, *Democracy and Distrust*.
3 Bickel, *Least Dangerous Branch*; Sunstein, *One Case at a Time*. Others, like American legal scholar Lawrence Tribe, simply reject the "futile search for legitimacy" (*Constitutional Choices*, 3).
4 These approaches are not necessarily mutually exclusive. As we shall see, the second approach may require a degree of judicial self-restraint in order to avoid interpretive finality. For the moment, however, this distinction is analytically useful.
5 This famous comment is attributed to former U.S. chief justice Charles Evans Hughes. Huscroft notes that Hughes's remark was extemporaneous and made before he was chief justice (and while running for governor of New York). Huscroft recounts some of the use (and misuse) of this quotation by Canadian legal authorities in "'Thank God We're Here,'" 249–50.
6 In Canada, Supreme Court judges have promoted this view: "You cannot entrench rights in the constitution without some agency to monitor compliance ... because of its independence, relative impartiality and security of tenure the judiciary was the obvious choice" (Hon. Bertha Wilson, "We Didn't Volunteer," in Howe and Russell, eds., *Judicial Power and Canadian Democracy*, 75); the interpretation of the constitution is "left by a tradition of necessity to the judicial branch" (Estey J., *Law Society of Upper Canada v. Skapinker* [1984] 1 S.C.R. 357 at para 11).

7 *Marbury v. Madison* 5 U.S. (1 Cranch) 137. The use and misuse of Chief Justice Marshall's *Marbury* opinion is chronicled in Clinton, *Marbury v. Madsion and Judicial Review*. As Clinton notes, the decision itself is perhaps best understood as advancing judicial *equality* in interpretation, not interpretive supremacy. On the matter of constitution authority, Marshall clearly states that "it is apparent, that the framers of the constitution contemplated that instrument, as a rule for the government of courts, *as well as of the legislature*" (emphasis added by Clinton) (Clinton, *Marbury*, 14). Nevertheless, the notion that *Marbury* stands for an unanswerable judicial power to interpret the constitution has become deeply ingrained since 1958. The Supreme Court of Canada has accepted this judicial supremacist version of *Marbury* in *Skapinker* at para 12 (Estey J.).

8 *Cooper v. Aaron* 358 U.S. 1 (1958): *Marbury v. Madison* stands for the "basic principle that the federal judiciary is supreme in the exposition of the law of the Constitution" (19).

9 Wolfe, *The Rise of Modern Judicial Review*, 261.

10 Hogg, Thornton, and Wright, "*Charter* Dialogue Revisited," 35–6. In their view, the interpretation of the Charter merely extends the practice of judicial review on federalism grounds. In the federalism case, however, the Court is actually playing a role that is best described as "partial agency" (see below) by assigning power to another institutional actor rather than deciding the substantive outcome itself. While the courts may, of course, achieve the substantive outcome they prefer by assigning it to a level of government that agrees with its choices, the courts are limited by the fact that they require a representative institution as a partner to achieve their desired end. This is dramatically different from the Charter context where a court may act against all representative institutions and impose its own preferences independently.

11 Hogg, Thornton, and Wright argue that Canadian proponents of coordinate interpretation are "drawn" to the notion that controversies over constitutional "interpretation should be settled for all government branches (not just one branch) by the legislative branch of government" (ibid., 38n.133). The "version" of coordinate interpretation employed by this study is the "departmental" approach that Hogg et al. suggest is unknown in Canadian scholarship.

12 Burt, *Constitution in Conflict*, 68–9.

13 Agresto, *The Supreme Court and Constitutional Democracy*.

14 Burt, *Constitution in Conflict*.

15 Tushnet, *Taking the Constitution away from the Courts*.

16 Nagel, *Constitutional Cultures*.
17 Kramer, *The People Themselves*.
18 Murphy, "Who Shall Interpret?"
19 Paulsen, "The Most Dangerous Branch."
20 Eisgruber, "The Most Competent Branches."
21 Devins and Fisher, *The Democratic Constitution*.
22 Manfredi, *Judicial Power*.
23 Huscroft, "Constitutionalism from the Top Down," 101: "There should be no doubt that it is appropriate for the government to disagree with the Court's interpretation of the Charter and to act accordingly. The executive and legislature are duty bound to act in accordance with the constitution, and the constitution is not simply whatever the Court says it is."
24 Manfredi's former student James Kelly claims to endorse "coordinate constitutionalism" but his treatment of cases such as *Sauvé II* suggests otherwise. See Kelly's characterization of the Sauvé sequence in *Governing with the Charter*, 163. Anticipating this criticism, Kelly argues that a "few extremely activist decisions do not demonstrate a general pattern of subordinate constitutionalism" (136).
25 Hogg and Bushell (Thornton), "The Charter Dialogue"; Manfredi and Kelly, "Six Degrees of Dialogue"; Roach, *Supreme Court on Trial*.
26 While some dialogue enthusiasts, such as Kent Roach, have always been in favour of judicial interpretive supremacy (*Supreme Court on Trial*, 249–50), it has been unclear whether the original authors of the dialogue theory, Hogg and Bushell, approved of such interpretive supremacy. Given their claim that their theory meant that "the critique of the *Charter* based on democratic legitimacy cannot be sustained" (Hogg and Bushell, "The Charter Dialogue," 105), one might think that their idea of legislative participation would not be limited to non-interpretive matters. Yet, in a 2007 article, Hogg and Bushell (with new co-author Wade Wright) wrote that their "position is that final authority to interpret the *Charter* rests properly with the judiciary (or, to put it differently, that judicial interpretation of the *Charter* is authoritative)" (Hogg et al., "*Charter* Dialogue Revisited," 31). On this point, see Huscroft, "Constitutionalism from the Top Down," 92–3.
27 Hogg et al., "Charter Dialogue Revisited," 31.
28 Christopher P. Manfredi is one of the few Canadian academics to endorse a truly coordinate approach (Manfredi, *Judicial Power*, 23). Even those who advocate coordinate constitutionalism (Kelly, *Governing with the Charter*) and oppose judicial supremacy in general (Kent

Roach, *Supreme Court on Trial*) resist any challenge to judicial interpretive supremacy.
29 [1999] 3 S.C.R. 668 [*Mills*].
30 [1995] 4 S.C.R. 411 [*O'Connor*].
31 Hogg et al., "*Charter* Dialogue Revisited," 50.
32 Roach, *Supreme Court on Trial*, 280; Roach criticizes the Court for accepting the "in your face" *O'Connor* retort in "Dialogic Judicial Review and Its Critics," in Huscroft and Brodie, eds., *Constitutionalism in the Charter Era*, 50.
33 [2002] 3 S.C.R. 309 [*Hall*].
34 [1992] 3 S.C.R. 711 [*Morales*].
35 *Hall* at para 127 (Iacobucci, J.). See also Coughlan, "Half-Full Glasses," 310.
36 Hogg, *Constitutional Law*, 7–24. Hogg's comment has been approvingly quoted by the Supreme Court of Canada in *Re Residential Tenancies Act, 1979* [1981] 1 S.C.R. 714 at 728 (Dickson J); *Sobeys Stores Ltd. v. Yeomans and Labour Standards Tribunal (N.S.)*, [1989] 1 S.C.R. 238 (Wilson J.); *Douglas/Kwantlen Faculty Assn. v. Douglas College* [1990] 3 S.C.R. 570 at 601 (La Forest J.); *MacMillan Bloedel Ltd. v. Simpson* [1995] 4 S.C.R. 725 at para 52 (McLachlin J., dissenting).
37 Kelly, *Governing with the Charter*, 81.
38 Monahan, *Constitutional Law*, 96.
39 Hogg, *Constitutional Law*, 7–24.
40 J.A. Strayer, *Westergard-Thorpe et al. v. Attorney General of Canada et al.; Jones et al. v. The Queen et al.*, 183 D.L.R. (4th) 458 at para 28.
41 Pilkington, "Enforcing the Charter," 85.
42 Even those who accept a principle of separated powers in the Canadian constitution characterize it as "an emerging and poorly understood facet ... [that] has only recently received formal recognition": Sossin, "The Ambivalence of Executive Power," in Craig and Tomkins, eds., *The Executive and Public Law*, 57.
43 Forsey, "The Courts and the Conventions of the Constitution," 22. Emphasis added.
44 Peter McCormick notes that, while the Supreme Court has used the term "separation of power," "it never connects the idea to 'checks and balances,' a phrase it has never used in any decision." "New Questions about an Old Concept," 857.
45 Hogg, *Constitutional Law*, 14–15.
46 Ibid., 7–25; The Constitution Act, 1867 (U.K.) is reproduced in R.S.C. 1985, appendix II, no. 5. Hereinafter the Constitution Act, 1867 will be

referred to as the British North America Act (BNA Act) for the reasons described by Romney, *Getting It Wrong: How Canadians Forgot Their Past and Imperiled Confederation*, 276.
47 Greene, et al., *Final Appeal*, 6.
48 Sossin, "The Ambivalence of Executive Power," 52.
49 Allan, *Law, Liberty, and Justice*, 8.
50 In his study of the *Vriend* decision, Frederick DeCoste argues that the Supreme Court's approach to the separation of powers is based on the notion that "the tension which defines the separation of powers is displaced by joint sovereignty as between the legislative/executive branch and the judicial branch" ("The Separation of State Powers in Liberal Polity," 244). Thus, "in the Court's version of the doctrine, the legislative branch is portrayed as despotic while the judicial branch is portrayed as an aristocracy of final resort ... Whereas legislative sovereignty is willful, judicial sovereignty is moral" (244–5).
51 Kent Roach, *Supreme Court on Trial*, and "Sharpening the Dialogue Debate," 190.
52 Vile, *Constitutionalism and the Separation of Powers*.
53 Alexander Hamilton, John Jay, and James Madison, *The Federalist*, No. 47 (attributed to Madison), 309.
54 Monahan, *Constitutional Law*, 97.
55 Hogg, *Constitutional Law*, 14–15.
56 White, *Cabinets and First Ministers*, 14.
57 Kelly, *Governing with the Charter*, 11.
58 Flanagan, "Liberal Tactics," A19.
59 Roach, "Sharpening the Dialogue Debate," 190.
60 Mansfield, *The Taming of the Prince* and *America's Constitutional Soul*.
61 Cooper, "Limitations and Ambiguities," in Gibson, ed., *Fixing Canadian Democracy*.
62 *A.G. (Ontario, et al.) v. A.G. (Dominion of Canada)* 3 D.L.R. 509 at 515 (J.C.P.C.) (Loreburn, L.C.). See chapter 5.
63 See Chapter 4.
64 See Chapter 4.
65 Dicey, *Introduction to the Study of the Constitution*, 103. Dicey's comment relates to the courts' interpretive role in federalism disputes.
66 Ibid., 92.
67 [1992] 2 S.C.R. 679 [*Schachter*].
68 [1998] 1 S.C.R. 493 [*Vriend*].
69 [2003] 3 S.C.R. 3 [*Doucet-Boudreau*].
70 *Eldridge v. British Columbia (Attorney General)* [1997] 3 S.C.R. 624.

CHAPTER ONE

1. (1997) 521 U.S. 507 [*Flores*].
2. (1990) 494 U.S. 872 [*Smith*].
3. (2000) 120 S. Ct. 2326 [*Dickerson*].
4. (1966) 384 U.S. 436 [*Miranda*].
5. *Graves v. New York* (1939) 306 U.S. 466, 491–2 (Frankfurter J. concurring). As Erik Luna notes, Frankfurter's views had evolved from the time when he made the blunt statement that "the Supreme Court is the Constitution." Frankfurter, "The United States Supreme Court," 240. Luna, "Constitutional Road Maps," 1173.
6. Cameron, "Dialogue and Hierarchy," 1068.
7. Sujit Choudhry takes this position. Makin, "Harper Blasted on Gay Marriage," A1.
8. This issue continues to generate controversy in both the United States and Canada. The latest statement of the U.S. Supreme Court is *Gonzales v. O Centro Espitita Beneficente Uniao Do Vegetal* (21 February 2006), no. 04–1084 [*Vegetal*]. The most recent statement in Canadian law on this subject is *Multani v. Commission scolaire Marguerite-Bourgeoys* 2006 SCC 6.
9. *Sherbert v. Verner* (1963) 374 U.S. 398 [*Sherbert*].
10. This set of facts, in essence, was the case before the court in *Sherbert*.
11. Scalia's opinion for the Court was joined by Chief Justice Rhenquist and justices Byron White, John Paul Stevens, and Anthony Kennedy. O'Connor concurred in a separate opinion which applied the *Sherbert* "compelling interest" test but found that the law met its burden. Justice Harry Blackmum, joined by justices Thurgood Marshall and William Brennan, dissented, finding that the law did not meet the compelling state interest test.
12. *Smith*, 878.
13. Tushnet, *Taking the Constitution away from the Courts*, 4.
14. Section 5 explicitly grants Congress the "power to enforce, by appropriate legislation, the provisions of [the Fourteenth Amendment]." The Fourteenth Amendment guarantees all Americans "the equal protection of the laws." See Laycock, "Federalism as a Structural Threat to Liberty." It is this feature of the RFRA's enactment that allows the Court to reinterpret *Flores* in *Vegetal* as invalidating the RFRA only as it applies to state laws (thus effectively reviving the RFRA for the purposes of *federal* legislation).
15. On the politics behind the RFRA, see Berg, "What Hath Congress Wrought?"

16 139 Cong. Rec. H8713–15 (3 November 1993); 139 Cong. Rec. S14,470–1 (27 October 1993). President Bill Clinton signed the bill into law (the widespread congressional support, of course, indicates that the bill might have been veto-proof in any event).
17 *Flores*, 529.
18 Ibid.
19 Ibid., 536.
20 McConnell, "Institutions and Interpretation," 165.
21 Ibid., 163.
22 Kahn, "Institutional Norms and Supreme Court Decision-Making," in Clayton and Gillman, eds., *Supreme Court Decision-Making*, 194.
23 O'Connor clearly states in *Flores* that "Congress lacks the ability independently to define or expand the scope of constitutional rights by statute" even though *Smith* was "wrongly decided" (545). At the same time, she does suggests that judicial reconsideration is warranted in light of Congress's "legitimate concerns ... that *Smith* improperly restricted religious liberty" (545). In terms of federal legislation, the Court has since effectively reversed *Flores* in *Vegetal*. The Court in *Vegetal* retroactively confined *Flores* to state laws and validated the RFRA's constitutionality with respect to federal legislation. Chief Justice John Roberts, writing for the Court, avoids any discussion of the separation-of-powers reasoning in *Flores* and simply limits *Flores* to a brief footnote (at 8n.1).
24 On this issue, the majority consisted of Chief Justices Antonio Lamer and justices John Sopinka, Peter Cory, Frank Iacobucci, and John Major. Dissenting on this issue were justices Gérard La Forest, Claire L'Heureux-Dubé, Charles Gonthier, and Beverley McLachlin.
25 *O'Connor* at para 156 (L'Heureux-Dubé J., dissenting on this issue).
26 Manfredi, *Judicial Power*, 180, 182–3. Manfredi and Kelly, "Dialogue, Deference and Restraint," 334–5. See also Cameron, "Dialogue and Hierarchy," 1056–7.
27 Feldthusen, "Access to the Private Therapeutic Records," 562.
28 *Mills*, 708.
29 It is difficult to reconcile Iacobucci and Major's change in position with Christopher Manfredi's conclusion that "if any dialogue occurred in *Mills*, it was an internal one among the justices about which *O'Connor* regime should prevail" (*Judicial Power*, 180). Internal dialogue surely took place, but it was, of course, occasioned by Parliament's "minority retort," and it seems likely that Parliament's disagreement with their original position had some impact on Iacobucci and Major's change of mind.

30 Hogg and Bushell, "*Charter* Dialogue."
31 *Mills*, 712.
32 Ibid., 688. Judicial interpretive supremacists have a particularly hard time accepting this portion of the judgment. See, e.g., Cameron, "Dialogue and Hierarchy," 1058–63 (especially, "either the Constitution is supreme or it is not" [1062]).
33 *R. v. Mills*, 56 Alta. L.R. (3d) 277 (Q.B.) (Belzil J.).
34 *Mills*, 713; Hiebert claims that, in *Mills*, the Court accepted Parliament's reassertion of control over the rules of disclosure (*Charter Conflicts*, 115–16). Manfredi disputes this characterization and notes that the "Court did not defer to legislative judgment in *Mills*, but merely affirmed a policy that four of its own members had constructed in 1995" (*Judicial Power*, 180) (see also Kelly, *Governing with the Charter*, 110). Both Hiebert and Manfredi fail to consider that *Mills* is actually an example of *shared* interpretive power – the ultimate outcome would not have been arrived at if either the legislative or judicial branch had simply acted in isolation. Just as an independent legislative judgment was hewed by the O'Connor minority (as Manfredi suggests), the judicial minority could not prevail without the support of the legislature (and thus Parliament did reassert *some* authority over disclosure, as Hiebert suggests).
35 Roach includes *Flores* as an example of unwarranted judicial supremacy (Roach, *Supreme Court on Trial*, 27, 301n.49).
36 Ibid., 243, 280–1; also see generally Roach, "Constitutional and Common Law Dialogues." *Mills* has also been criticized for abandoning the rights of the accused. Dennis Edney, counsel for Brian Mills, opines that "'under Bill C-46 you get nothing. It was a cowardly response by the Supreme Court of Canada to public pressure and special interest groups" (The FREDA Centre for Research on Violence against Women and Children, http://www.harbour.sfu.ca/freda/c46/c46chron.htm).
37 Roach, *Supreme Court on Trial*, 280; Roach criticizes the Court for accepting the "in your face" *O'Connor* retort in "Dialogic Judicial Review and Its Critics," 50.
38 Roach, *Supreme Court on Trial*, 278, 287–8.
39 Similarly, Jamie Cameron argues that the decision in *Mills* is wrong because it allows "institutional confrontation" to be undertaken with ordinary legislation when it "should be channeled through s.33's mechanism for overriding the Charter." Cameron, "Dialogue and Hierarchy," 1057.
40 Roach, "Constitutional and Common Law Dialogues," 528–9.
41 *Re: Remuneration of Judges* [1997] 3 S.C.R. 3 at para. 180–1.

42 *Sauvé v. Canada (Attorney General)* [1993] 2 S.C.R. 438; *Savué v. Canada (Chief Electoral Officer)*[2002] SCC 68 [*Sauvé II*]; See also Knopff and Morton, *Charter Politics*, 292–331.
43 The single challenge to voting exclusions on age-discrimination grounds failed in *Fitzgerald v. Alberta*, 2004 ABCA 184.
44 The difference can be appreciated by considering an un-Mirandized repeat offender. Having been frequently arrested (and Mirandized), the suspect is undoubtedly aware of his right to remain silent and to exclude his confession might be considered an unjust technicality. Also see *Dickerson*, 2338.
45 *Miranda*, 467.
46 Ibid. The Court explicitly affirmed *Miranda*'s subconstitutional status in *Michigan v. Tucker*, (1974) 417 U.S. 433, where it said that *Miranda* rights are "not themselves rights protected by the Constitution" (444).
47 *Miranda*, 467.
48 18 U.S.C. s.3501.
49 Ibid.
50 The execution of the provision is a source of some controversy. Cassell suggests that all justice departments *did* enforce the law until the Clinton administration abandoned it. The record is unclear because it is difficult to separate instances where the department was attempting to limit *Miranda* (through subsequent judicial actions) or relying on 3501. Given the success the executive had in creating exclusions to the *Miranda* rule, it is possible that 3501 was seen as superfluous. See *Michigan v. Tucker* and David Sonenshein, "*Miranda* and the Burger Court," 407–8.
51 Reid, "*United States v. Dickerson*," 1348.
52 Cassell's efforts are summarized on his website under "Time to Overhaul *Miranda*?" (http://www.law.utah.edu/faculty/websites/cassellp/time2.gif).
53 The legislation was invoked by a majority of United States Court of Appeals for the 4th Circuit over the objections of the Justice Department. Only an amicus brief, from the Washington Legal Centre and Safe Streets, argued that section 3501 should be employed. The amicus brief can be found at http://www.law.utah.edu/faculty/websites/cassellp/meritsbrief.html. Given the decision of the Justice Department not to proceed with the case against Dickerson, some scholars, such as Erwin Chemerinsky, argue that the case never should have been decided by the Court. See Chemerinsky, "The Court Should Have Remained Silent."

54 *Dickerson*, 2329 (Rehnquist C.J.). Michael Dorf and Barry Friedman argue that *Dickerson* leaves open some degree of inter-institutional participation in the defining of rights despite being "on its face ... a strong statement of judicial supremacy in constitutional interpretation" ("Shared Constitutional Interpretation," 62).
55 *Dickerson*, 2333 (Rehnquist C.J.).
56 Ibid., 2336 (Rehnquist C.J.). On the nature of "prophylactic" constitutional rules, see Strauss, "The Ubiquity of Prophylactic Rules" and "Miranda, the Constitution and the Congress." See also Berman, "Constitutional Decision Rules."
57 Justice Clarence Thomas joined Scalia's dissent.
58 *Dickerson*, 2337 (Scalia J.).
59 Ibid.
60 Ibid.
61 Ibid., 2342 (Scalia J.).
62 Ibid., 2337 (Scalia J.).
63 Bradley, "Behind the *Dickerson* Decision," 81.
64 Ibid.
65 There was a pragmatic solution to the case avoided by the Court. Since the legislation was over thirty years old and never applied during that time, the legitimacy of the statute as representative of the current Congress is questionable. The Court might have required Congress to repass the statute today under something like the doctrine of desuetude. Such an approach would, however, be inconsistent with the general American treatment of statutes. The majority briefly noted that *stare decisis* prevents the overruling of *Miranda* (*Dickerson*, 2336), but one senses that the Rehnquist Court was loath to suggest that any decision dating back to the Warren Court is untouchable.
66 The Sixteenth Amendment itself was a response to a judicial ruling (*Pollock v. Farmers' Loan and Trust Co.* [1895] 158 U.S. 601) that invalidated the 1894 income tax enacted by Congress. Despite the unequivocal language of the Sixteenth Amendment, the Court ruled that federal judges are exempted from income tax as a consequence of Article III, section I. See *Evans v. Gore* (1920) 253 U.S. 245. *Evans* was itself overruled in *O'Malley v. Woodrough* (1939) 307 U.S. 277. These cases are summarized in Segal and Spaeth, *The Supreme Court and the Attitudinal Model Revisited*, 5–6.
67 *Dickerson*, 2347 (Scalia J., dissenting).
68 Manfredi, "The Day Dialogue Died."
69 The federal government initially left the granting and denial of bail for all offences entirely within the scope of judicial discretion. Rules for

granting or denying bail remained unwritten from 1896 until they were codified in the 1972 Bail Reform Act.
70 In addition to *Morales* and *Hall*, see *R. v. Bray* [1983] 2 C.C.C. (3d) 325 (Ont. C.A.); *R. v. Pearson* [1992] 3 S.C.R. 665.
71 *Morales*, 714 (Lamer C.J.).
72 *Morales*, 732 (Lamer C.J.).
73 Ibid., 737 (Lamer C.J.).
74 Ibid., 751 (Gonthier J.).
75 Ibid.
76 Ibid., 751–2 (Gonthier J.).
77 *Hall* at para 70 (Iacobucci J.).
78 Trotter, *The Law of Bail in Canada*, 145–6; cited in *Hall* at para 105 (Iacobucci J.).
79 Coughlan, "Half-Full Glasses," 310.
80 *Hall* at para 5 (McLachlin C.J.).
81 McLachlin was joined by justices L'Heureux-Dubé, Gonthier, Michel Bastarache, and Ian Binnie.
82 *Hall* at para 33 (McLachlin C.J.).
83 *Morales*, 751 (Gonthier J.).
84 *Irwin Toy v. Quebec* [1989] 1 S.C.R. 927 at 983.
85 Ibid.
86 *Hall* at para 18 (McLachlin C.J.).
87 F. Bobiasz, testifying for the Department of Justice before the Standing Senate Committee on Legal and Constitutional Affairs, Issue no. 60, 2nd Sess., 35th Parl., 21 April 1997, 60:30; *Hall* at para 18 (McLachlin C.J.).
88 *Hall* at para 32 (McLachlin C.J.).
89 Mitchell, "Developments in Constitutional Law,"143; *R. v. Nova Scotia Pharmaceutical Society* [1992] 2 S.C.R. 606.
90 *Hall* at para 33 (McLachlin C.J.).
91 Ibid.
92 Ibid. at para 36 (McLachlin C.J.).
93 Iacobucci was joined by justices John Major, Louise Arbour, and Louis Le Bel.
94 *Hall* at para 127 (Iacobucci J.).
95 Mathen, "Dissent and Judicial Authority," 328.
96 *Hall* at para 43 (McLachlin C.J.).
97 Ibid. at para 127 (Iacobucci J.).
98 Ibid. at para 104 (Iacobucci J.).
99 Ibid.
100 An exception is Stephen Coughlan, who bemoans the fact that *Hall* proves that "some individual advances in *Charter* protection are later

lost." Coughlan, "Half-Full Glasses," 310. On the other hand, the invalidation, according to Eric Siebenmorgen of the Ontario Ministry of the Attorney General, is unlikely to have much impact "as a practical matter" since judges rarely resort to the broader language excised. Schmitz, "Tertiary Ground for Denying Bail Upheld by Supreme Court," 8.
101 Mitchell, "Developments in Constitutional Law," 144.
102 Tibbetts, "Public Fear Overrides Right to Bail," A6.
103 Roach argues that *Dickerson* could have been avoided if the U.S. constitution contained an override like the notwithstanding clause but, given that it does not, he "prefers the type of judicial supremacy that motivated the Court's decision in *Dickerson*" over "legislative supremacy" (Roach, "Dialogue or Defiance," 367). Cameron, "Dialogue and Hierarchy," 1062n.84.
104 Manfredi, "The Life of a Metaphor."
105 *Sauvé II* at para 17 (McLachlin C.J.).
106 Ibid.
107 Nagel, *Constitutional Cultures*, 116.
108 Kelly finds an "emergence of coordinate constitutionalism in Canada, as the cabinet and the Supreme Court have shared responsibility for the Charter and its interpretation" (*Governing with the Charter*, 16) but demonstrates his supremacist sympathies when he discusses *Sauvé II*: "Parliament's decision to disenfranchise certain prisoners is an example of a politically motivated policy decision that lacked a constitutional basis because there is no ambiguity in the interpretation of the *Charter*'s democratic rights" (163). The sharply divided Court in *Sauvé II* (5–4), to say nothing of the "strategic" *Sauvé I* decision, suggests there is a great deal of ambiguity and reasonable disagreement about the interpretation of the right to vote. Kelly pretends otherwise in order to portray the Court's stark judicial supremacist behaviour in *Sauvé II* as a justifiable exception to the otherwise "emergent coordinate constitutionalism" he observes.
109 Roach, "Constitutional and Common Law Dialogues." The creators of the "dialogue metaphor" now explicitly endorse judicial interpretive supremacy (Hogg et al., "Dialogue Revisited": "Our position is that the final authority to interpret the *Charter* rests properly with the judiciary" [31]).

CHAPTER TWO

1 Huscroft, "Thank God We're Here," 255.
2 Justice Binnie takes a different tact and argues that, if the drafters of the constitution wanted a limited judiciary, they "should have said

so" (Makin, "Senior U.S., Canadian Judges Spar over Judicial Activism," A2). It is surely more difficult to argue that an omission supports a positive formal power than to claim – as I do – that where the constitution is silent, the power is assigned ambivalently and is strictly informal.
3 "Respecting Democratic Roles," speech to the Conference on "The Law and Parliament," Ottawa, Ontario, 22 November 2004.
4 Ibid.
5 Hogg, *Constitutional Law*, 37–2 (emphasis added). There is a viable defence of this statement in that it refers to "judicial review" and not "judicial interpretive supremacy." To the extent that Hogg means that courts now posses the authority to exercise judicial power in accordance with their understanding of the constitution, his statement in incontestable. The context suggests, however, that Hogg means that the judicial interpretation should be binding on all other state actors.
6 Wilson, "We Didn't Volunteer," 75.
7 Ibid.
8 Andrew Jackson, presidential message vetoing the bill to re-charter the Bank of the United States, 10 July 1832, in H.S. Commanger, ed., *Documents of American History* vol. 1 (1963): 272.
9 Nagel, "Disagreement and Interpretation," 32.
10 Kramer, *The People Themselves*, 106; Kramer includes Louis Fisher (*Constitutional Dialogues*) and Sylvia Snowiss (*Judicial Review and the Law of the Constitution*) in this camp.
11 Vicini, "Meese Scoured for Saying High Court Rulings Not Law of Land," A17. Cited by Devins and Fisher, *Democratic Constitution*, 27.
12 Cameron, "Dialogue and Hierarchy," 1068.
13 Alexander and Schauer, "On Extrajudicial Constitutional Interpretation."
14 Ibid., 1379.
15 Kramer, *The People Themselves*, 285.
16 Levinson, *Constitutional Faith*, 29.
17 Ibid.
18 Tushnet, "Two Versions of Judicial Supremacy," 954.
19 Robert Nagel sharply rebukes Alexander and Schauer for assuming that the Court effectively settles constitutional disputes. Nagel wonders "how anyone who has lived through a significant part of the modern period of tumultuous judicial creativity could treat the relative stability of judicial interpretations as self-evident is baffling." Nagel, "Judicial Supremacy and the Settlement Function," 857.
20 Tushnet, *Taking the Constitution away from the Courts*, 28.
21 See Whittington, "Extrajudicial Constitutional Interpretation," 804.
22 Tushnet, *Taking the Constitution away from the Courts*, 29–30.

23 Kramer, *The People Themselves*, 32.
24 Choudhry and Hunter, "Measuring Judicial Activism," and Manfredi and Kelly, "Misrepresenting the Supreme Court's Record?"
25 Michael Conant notes that 5–4 cases are "the strongest examples of unsettled law" and suggest that the "epistemic indeterminacy" they create undermines the conception of law as reliable knowledge. Conant, *Constitutional Structure*, 5.
26 U.S. Chief Justice Hughes wrote that dissents appeal "to the brooding spirit of the law, to the intelligence of a future day, when a later decision may possibly correct the error into which the dissenting judge believes the Court to have been betrayed." Charles Evans Hughes, *The Supreme Court of the United States*.
27 Section 33 applies only to sections 2 and 7 through 15 of the Charter. While this covers most Charter cases, it would not provide protection for legislation responding to decisions like *Sauvé II* (interpreting the right to vote in s.3).
28 Jeremy Waldron, "Some Models of Dialogue between Judges and Legislators," in Huscroft and Brodie, eds., *Constitutionalism in the Charter Era*, 36–7; Manfredi, *Judicial Power*, 192–4.
29 Wilson, "We Didn't Volunteer," 75.
30 C.f. Roach, "Dialogic Judicial Review and Its Critics," 61: "When the override is used to reverse a court decision, it is likely that people will realize that the legislature is not really overriding the relevant Charter right, but rather the court's interpretation of the right." One of Roach's colleagues at the Faculty of Law, University of Toronto, Lorraine Weinrib, disagrees, arguing that "the clause amounts to a red flag to government members, opposition parties, co-ordinate governments, the media and international onlookers," and, in the case of the Albertan government's flirtation with using the provision to cap payments to victims of forced sterilization, Weinrib notes that "many protested as much against the peremptory negation of constitutional rights as against the specific policy" (Weinrib, "The Loophole That Holds the Charter Together").
31 Whittington, "Extrajudicial Constitutional Interpretation," 817.
32 Alexander and Schauer, "On Extrajudicial Constitutional Interpretation," 1371.
33 According to Justice David Souter, this would not constitute a "trial": *Nixon v. United States* 506 U.S. 224 (1993) at 254 (Souter J., concurring). Souter was considering whether a Senate impeachment trial that consisted of a coin flip would attract judicial review. Justice John Paul

Stevens responded by saying, "Respect for a coordinate Branch of the Government forecloses any ... improbable hypotheticals" (at 238 [Stevens J., concurring]). See Tushnet, *Taking the Constitution away from the Courts*, 105.

34 Waldron, *Dignity of Legislation*.
35 Ibid., 148.
36 This does not necessarily mean that there is no "correct" answer. It simply means that objective truth or rightness is not legally determinative. If the objectively "wrong" side is the majority, it will be legally right.
37 If it is simply a matter of numbers, there would be some reason to believe that the institution composed of the greater number of members would be more likely to devise the best policy (thus the hundreds of parliamentarians would fare better than the nine members of the Court). Also see Surowiecki, *The Wisdom of Crowds*.
38 Mayhew, *Congress: The Electoral Connection*, 5.
39 Waldron, *Dignity of Legislation*, 1-2.
40 Roach, "Constitutional and Common Law Dialogues," 529.
41 Ronald Dworkin, one of America's pre-eminent legal theorists, offers this comparison in *Freedom's Law*: the political process is "dominated by political alliances that formed around a single issue and use the familiar tactics of pressure groups to bribe or blackmail legislators into voting as they wish" to arrive at a "political compromise that gives all powerful groups enough of what they want to prevent their disaffection," and so fortunately "we have an institution that calls some issues from the background of power politics to the forum of principle. It holds out the promise that the deepest, most fundamental conflicts between individual and society will once, someplace, finally, become questions of justice. I do not call that religion or prophecy. I call it law" (Dworkin, *Freedom's Law*, 344-5, 71). Whittington notes Dworkin's suspect comparison in "Extrajudicial Constitutional Interpretation," 811.
42 Whittington notes that non-judicial institutions are often guided by principle as much as courts are: "Political debates on matters of constitutional principle are common, and form the background against which judicial decisions themselves are made. The Court is not alone in making principled decisions about constitutional values. It is choosing sides in pre-existing debates." Whittington, "Extrajudicial Constitutional Interpretation," 819.
43 Cameron also suggests that the retort undermines the institutional "symmetry of respect." Cameron, "Dialogue and Hierarchy," 1059.

44 Speaking of the legislative sequel to *Flores*, Robert Nagel notes that the "RFRA represented partial legislative deference to judicial precedent." Nagel, "Judicial Supremacy and the Settlement Function," 857.
45 Baer, "Striking the Balance in Sexual Assault Trials."
46 Roach, "Dialogic Judicial Review and Its Critics," 91.
47 Roach, "Uses and Audiences of Preambles"; Hiebert, *Charter Conflicts*, 105.
48 Hiebert, *Charter Conflicts*.
49 Waldron, *Dignity of Legislation*, 9–11.
50 Komesar, "Slow Learning in Constitutional Analysis," 218.
51 See also Murphy, "'Who Shall Interpret,'" 401.
52 Devins and Fisher, *The Democratic Constitution*, 18.
53 *Canada (Attorney General) v. Hislop* [2007] 1 S.C.R. 429 at para 103 (LeBel and Rothstein JJ.). This endorsement of coordinacy is qualified by the additional statement that "in our system, the Supreme Court has the final word on the interpretation of the Constitution" (at para 111).
54 [1987] 2 S.C.R. 636.
55 Roach, *Supreme Court on Trial*, 183.
56 [1995] 3 S.C.R. 199.
57 Roach, *Supreme Court on Trial*, 186.
58 Komesar, *Imperfect Alternatives*, 201.
59 *Rodriguez v. British Columbia (Attorney General)* [1993] 3 S.C.R. 519; *United States v. Burns*, [2001] 1 S.C.R. 283, 2001 SCC 7.
60 Morton and Knopff, *The Charter Revolution*. See also Brodie, *Friends of the Court*.
61 Komesar, *Imperfect Alternatives*, 201.
62 Alexander and Schauer, "On Extrajudicial Constitutional Interpretation," 1378n.80.
63 Tushnet, "Two Versions of Judicial Supremacy," 955.
64 Waldron, *Law and Disagreement*, 297.
65 Ibid.
66 Ibid.
67 Ibid., 298.
68 Bessette, *The Mild Voice of Reason*.
69 Ajzenstat, "Reconciling Parliament and Rights." Montesquieu, whose work is focused upon in the next chapter, similarly thought that the *form* law takes would work to ensure the goodness of its content. See Pangle, *Montesquieu's Philosophy of Liberalism*, 111–12.
70 Canada Evidence Act, R.S.C. 1970, c. E-10.

71 Bill C-61, the Young Offenders Act, was introduced on 16 February 1981 and given royal assent in July 1982. Therefore, the genesis and drafting of the bill can be described accurately as "pre-Charter" even if its official enactment came shortly after the Charter arrived. Young Offenders Act, 1980–81–82–83, (Can.), c.110; Young Offenders Act, R.S.C., 1985, c. Y-1.
72 R.S.O. 1990, c. H.19.
73 Hogg, *Constitutional Law*, 31–3; John White disagrees and suggests that Canada's record is marred by too many instances of "political passion directed at conspicuous minorities" ("Not Standing for Notwithstanding," in Charlton and Barker, eds., *Crosscurrents*, 66). Azjenstat, "Reconciling Parliament and Rights," 658.
74 Hogg, *Constitutional Law*, 31–3.
75 Roach, *Supreme Court on Trial*, 182; Mark Tushnet makes a similar observation but argues that "judicial overhang" is an argument *against* judicial interpretive supremacy. See *Taking the Constitution away from the Courts* and "Legislative and Judicial Interpretation," in Bauman and Kahana, eds., *The Least Examined Branch*, 357.
76 Roach, *Supreme Court on Trial*, 182.
77 Whittington, *Political Foundations of Judicial Supremacy*.
78 Bessette, *The Mild Voice of Reason*; Devins and Fisher, *The Democratic Constitution*; Fisher, *Constitutional Dialogues*.
79 Forsey, "The Courts and the Conventions of the Constitution," 22. Emphasis added.
80 Greene et al., *Final Appeal*, 6.
81 Allan, *Law, Liberty and Justice*, 8.

CHAPTER THREE

1 Hogg, *Constitutional Law*, 7–24; as noted in the Introduction, this comment has been repeatedly cited in Supreme Court judgments.
2 Hogg, *Constitutional Law*, 14–15. Hogg argues that the permission to delegate legislative authority in the Canadian constitution (contrary to the U.S. doctrine of non-delegation) is definitive proof that there is no separation of powers in Canada. As in chapter 4, the delegation (which can be withdrawn) can be better understood as another example of a "partial agency" which does not constitute the "whole" of the legislative power and thus does not violate Canada's separation-of-power principle.
3 Hogg, *Constitutional Law*, 7–24.
4 Ibid. Emphasis added.

5 Laurence Claus describes this as the "essentialist" approach and argues that Montesquieu chose to "pretend" that "Britain's constitution separated three essentially different governmental activities and then subjected their performance to supervisory checks designed to protect the primary separation" ("Montesquieu's Mistakes," 425). Claus suggests that a more accurate description of Britain's separation would simply note that it provided "for multiple actors to participate in every governmental action" (425). As I argue below, it is not necessary to abandon the essentialist tripartite division of power in order to accommodate significant inter-branch exercises of power.

6 Lorne Sossin notes that "the executive represents the institution invested with the most power in Canada's political system and yet takes up the least space in Canada's constitutional texts" ("The Ambivalence of Executive Power," 53). For Sossin, this is a "puzzle" that might reflect "Canada's institutionalized ambivalence" (53).

7 Adding to an already confused terminology, this means that in Canada the term "Parliament" in its most formal sense is the equivalent of the British King-in-Parliament or Queen-in-Parliament formulation.

8 The key elements of responsible government; Janet Ajzenstat, *The Political Thought of Lord Durham*, 7. As Montesquieu notes, the monarch "is frequently obliged to give his confidence to those who have the most offended him, and to disgrace the men who have best served him: he does that by necessity which other princes do by choice" (*The Spirit of the Laws*, bk XIX, ch. XXVII, 308) (Claus, "Montesquieu's Mistakes," 424). This acknowledgment is significant because Montesquieu might otherwise be charged with failing to note the nascent elements of responsible government in the English constitution at the time of his writing.

9 For a period following confederation, the separation between legislators and executives was highlighted by the requirement that any member joining cabinet must resign his seat and win a subsequent by-election.

10 *Westergard-Thorpe*, para 28 (Strayer J.A.).

11 Ibid.

12 Vile, *Constitutionalism*, 14. In such a "pure" separation, "checks and balances" are impossible because they would constitute interference. For this reason, Vile prefers to keep the separation of powers analytically distinct from "checks and balances" but, as we shall see, they are so intimately connected that separating them is actually more confusing than considering them in tandem.

13 The employment of justices of the Supreme Court of Canada as deputies of the governor general (as permitted by s.14 of the BNA Act) may also violate the strict application of a "separation of persons" doctrine since the justices may grant royal assent to legislation that they may then be called upon to scrutinize in their judicial capacity. Presented with the separation-of-power implications of such a dual role, the Federal Court of Appeal found the practice "legal" but "undesirable" in *Tunda v. Canada* 2001 FCA 151. See Forcese and Freeman, *The Laws of Government*, 37.
14 Vile, *Constitutionalism*, 14.
15 Ibid. After recognizing that the separation of powers is often amalgamated with the principle of checks and balances and mixed government, Vile notes that "these modifications of the doctrine have of course been much more influential than the doctrine in its pure form" (20). Vile's acceptance that the pure doctrine "has rarely been put into practice" leads one to question whether the pure form's theoretical usefulness is worth all the confusion it has caused (14). Eric Barendt makes a similar point using Vile's categories when he argues that "defenders of the separation principle [in the United Kingdom] should not rely on ... the 'pure separation of powers' [since] another version of the theory, 'the partial separation of powers,' in my view better captures its underlying values." Barendt, "Separation of Powers," 601.
16 Vile claims that the Cromwellian constitution (the 1653 Instrument of Government) embodies "on paper at least" a close attempt at a pure separation. Vile, *Constitutionalism*, 52.
17 Vile suggests that the pre-confederation constitution of Pennsylvania approximates the "pure" form of the separation doctrine. Ibid., 149.
18 Claus, "Montesquieu's Mistakes," 419.
19 Vile, *Constitutionalism*, 107–92.
20 Gordon, *Controlling the State*, 224.
21 Vile, *Constitutionalism*, 13.
22 Ibid., 40; Vile notes that the "critical difficulty of the transition from [the ancient to the modern] is that the three agencies of the mixed government, King, aristocratic assembly, and popular assembly, do not correspond to the executive, legislature, and judiciary in the doctrine of the separation of powers."
23 Despite their obvious and significant differences, the Canadian and American constitutions are squarely based on the English constitution. The high regard for the English constitution by the American founders is demonstrated by this exchange between John Adams and Alexander

Hamilton: Adams argues that the English constitution "would be the most perfect constitution ever devised by the wit of man" if one could "purge that constitution of its corruption, and give to its popular branch equality of representation," to which Hamilton responds, "Purge it of its corruption, and give to its popular branch equality of representation, and it would become an impractical government: as it stands at present, with all its supposed defects, it is the most perfect government which ever existed" (Jefferson, "The Anas," in *Life and Selected Writings*, 117). The Canadian constitution is, of course, explicitly based on the English constitution as indicated in the preamble to the BNA Act (which calls for a constitution "similar in principle to the United Kingdom"). Certainly, the Canadian founders (according to Ajzenstat et al, *Canada's Founding Debates*) and the jurists of the late eighteenth and early nineteenth centuries (Risk, *A History of Canadian Legal Thought*) had no doubt that the English constitution had been received in Canada. A number of these early legal scholars took great umbrage at A.V. Dicey's suggestion that the inclusion of a federal principle fundamentally transformed their system from the English model (Risk, *History of Canadian Legal Thought*, 37).

24 Scott Gordon, for one, begins his exploration of the "countervailing" principle even earlier with the ascendance of imperial Rome (*Controlling the State*, 86–107).

25 The difficulty of finding an appropriate "starting point" is complicated by the fact that the nineteenth-century advocates of "responsible government" declared themselves to be advancing an older and well-understood principle instead of articulating something novel. (As Ajzenstat notes, "Durham dates 'responsible government' from 1688, to the utter confusion of his commentators." "Canada's First Constitution," 46n.20.)

26 It is the *model* and not necessarily the *reality* of early-eighteenth-century English political life that Montesquieu admired. Despite the "long controversy over the correctness of Montesquieu's description," it is the constitutional principle – and not the historical practices that failed to meet the principle – which concerns us here. Vile, *Constitutionalism*, 93. See also Franz Neumann's introduction to *The Spirit of Laws* (New York: Hafner 1949), liv–lv.

27 The influence of Montesquieu on the American founders is well known and noted by Vile (*Constitutionalism*, 83) and, more recently, by Paul O. Carrese (*The Cloaking of Power*, 6, 180). Montesquieu's connection to the Canadian founders is slightly more obscure but only because the

Canadians accepted the English model with very little controversy. Philip Resnick finds Montesquieu indirectly influencing English Canadian founders ("Montesquieu Revisited," 99) and Ajzenstat notes that the early French Canadian constitutionalists (Étienne Parent and Pierre Bédard among them) explicitly cited Montesquieu ("Comment: The Separation of Powers in 1867," 117). See also Ajzenstat, *The Once and Future Canadian Democracy*, 74.

28 Resnick argues that section 6 of this book "is a seminal text for an understanding of the Canadian political order, more so than the passages we can glean from Hobbes or Locke or any of the other major theorists." Resnick, "Montesquieu Revisited," 99.
29 Montesquieu, *Spirit of the Laws*, 150.
30 Vile, *Constitutionalism*, 15.
31 Montesquieu, *Spirit of the Laws*, 150.
32 Ibid., 150. It is clear from this quotation that Montesquieu, unlike Vile, believes that the idea of "checks and balances" is inseparable from the separation of powers in theory and in practice.
33 Ibid., 151. Montesquieu's England, Pangle writes, makes "government the product of an institutionalized competition of selfish individuals and private factions whose struggle checks the possibility of oppression without destroying the force necessary to government" (*Montesquieu's Philosophy*, 116).
34 Some of the present-day confusion over whether or not the English constitution includes such a separation is surely due to the pervasive influence of Sir Ivor Jennings's text, *The Law and the Constitution*. Jennings was of the view that "there are no *material* differences between the three functions, so the separation principle fails to explain why certain tasks should be given to one body rather than another" and thus the principle is "incoherent or hopelessly ambivalent" (Barendt, "Separation of Powers and Constitutional Government," 603). Like Barendt, I argue that a general separation-of-powers principle is not as normatively empty as Jennings suggests.
35 This is an expansion of Montesquieu's judicial power. He restricted judicial power to the punishment of criminals and disputes between citizens. In the modern regulatory state, it makes some sense to include a limited power of adjudication between citizen and state.
36 A.H.F. Lefroy's 1897 text, *The Law of Legislative Power in Canada*, emphasizes that "the Founders of Confederation faithfully followed by preference, and with much ingenuity, the principles of the British Constitution" and stressed the way the BNA Act emulated the "matchless

Constitution" (Lefroy, *The Law of Legislative Power in Canada*, xvi). Risk argues that Lefroy demonstrates "little understanding of the ways his ideal had been transformed, especially by the powers of the cabinet and by political parties" (Risk, *History of Canadian Legal Thought*, 74).

37 *Fraser v. P.S.S.R.B.* [1985] 2 S.C.R. 455 at 469–70 (Dickson C.J.).

38 Montesquieu, *Spirit of the Laws*, 151–2.

39 Fears that were further confirmed by the attempts of Charles II to expand monarchical authority in the Restoration period and then amplified by the possibility of a Catholic line of succession from James II. See Harris, *Restoration* and *Revolution*.

40 Vile, *Constitutionalism*, 46; the Long Parliament, which could be dissolved only with the consent of its members, had declared in 1642 that its "Parliamentary Ordinances" held the force of law even though they were not given royal assent.

41 Allan, *Law, Liberty and Justice*, 49 (citing Blackstone, *Commentaries*, i. 154).

42 This notion of the judiciary as a potentially moderating influence over the other branches runs counter to the Supreme Court of Canada's approach to the separation of powers. In *Babcock v. Canada (Attorney General)*, for example, Justice McLachlin (as she then was) argues that "it is well within the power of the legislature to enact laws, even laws which some would consider draconian, as long as it does not fundamentally alter or interfere with the relationship between the courts and the other branches of government" ([2002] 3 S.C.R. 3 at para 57). "Draconian" laws are precisely those that the Court should mitigate through the use of its own powers.

43 One might object on Hobbesian or Bodinian grounds that this means there is no sovereign in the English constitution. Clearly, however, the "King-in-Parliament" fulfils this need for an unqualified, indivisible sovereign but, as indicated by the compound formulation itself, the King-in-Parliament implies a separation of powers.

44 Shackelton notes that Bolingbroke was a significance influence on Montesquieu. Shackleton, "Montesquieu, Bolingbroke and the Separation of Powers," 25; Barendt, "Separation of Powers and Constitutional Government," 601n.16.

45 Vile, *Constitutionalism*, 95.

46 *Youngstown Sheet & Tube Co. v. Sawyer* 345 US 579 at 635 (1952) (Jackson J.); Allan, *Law, Liberty and Justice*, 53.

47 Claus, "Montesquieu's Mistakes," 424–5.

48 Speech by James Madison to the House of Representatives on the Removal Power of the President (17 June 1789), in *Papers of Madison*,

12: 238. See Kramer, *The People Themselves*, 106, and Clinton, *Marbury v. Madison*, 27.
49 *Rex v. Halliday* [1917] A.C. 260 (Lord Dunedin) (emphasis added). This classic statement of "parliamentary sovereignty" demonstrates that such sovereignty is consistent with a functional separation of power because the real sovereign is the compound "King-in-Parliament." Barendt relies upon a similar formulation to argue that, even though "there is in practice a fusion of legislative and executive *powers*, there is in principle a distinction between the two *functions* ... In other words, government may control the legislature (and certainly there is overlapping membership), but it must still legislate through Acts of Parliament" ("Separation of Powers and Constitutional Government," 615). For greater clarity, I prefer the informal/formal terminology, as used below, instead of Barendt's power/function distinction.
50 Kelly, *Governing with the Charter*, 12.
51 For example, Anti-Federalist Robert Yates (Brutus) claimed that separation of powers would be violated because the "the supreme court under this constitution would be exalted above over all other power in the government and subject to no controul" (Burt, *The Constitution in Conflict*, 53). The U.S. constitution, of course, is the constitution that Hogg insists *does* have a general separation of powers. The existence of the Anti-Federalist argument proves that the notion of separated powers pre-dates the American constitution and that the American text is simply one variation of a larger theme.
52 *The Federalist*, No. 47 (attributed to Madison), 309.
53 Ibid.
54 Hogg, *Constitutional Law*, 7–24.
55 Ajzenstat, "Canada's First Constitution," 44.
56 Ibid.
57 Ibid., 46.
58 Ajzenstat notes that this distinction is crucial to political freedom: "Given that the majority in the popular house usually supports the political executive, the minority is nevertheless free to oppose – exactly because the two bodies, political executive and lower house, are not 'fused'" (ibid.).
59 Smith, *The Invisible Crown*, 121. It was, instead, the federal compromise that dominated the debates surrounding the 1867 act. A number of other issues (direct vs. representative democracy, protection for minorities, etc.) were also discussed but the desirability of responsible government was pretty much assumed by all. One notable exception

was the question of whether less populous colonies – like British Columbia – were ready for the burden of responsible government. Ajzenstat et al., *Founding Debates*.

60 Codifying the assembly of Lower Canada's successful overturning of the governor's rejection of Speaker Louis-Joseph Papineau in 1828–29. Nowadays, reflecting the continuing separation of the House from the government, the speaker is elected by secret ballot.

61 Ajzentstat, *Once and Future Canadian Democracy*, 65. The increasing use of special warrants amounts to an executive infringement of this constitutional restraint and is no less offensive than the judicial circumvention of this provision. For the problem of special warrants, see Smith, *Invisible Crown*, 82–5.

62 "Appropriation of any Part of the Public Revenue, or of any Tax or Impost."

63 Specifically, the bill must be "first recommended to [the] House by Message of the Governor General in the Session in which such ... Bill is proposed."

64 Ajzenstat, *Once and Future Canadian Democracy*, 65.

65 In *Kingstreet Investments Ltd. v. New Brunswick (Department of Finance)* 2007 SCC 1, Justice Bastarache notes that "the Crown may not levy a tax except with authority of the Parliament or the legislature ... This principle of 'no taxation without representation' is central to our conception of democracy and the rule of law" (at para 14).

66 Ajzenstat, *Once and Future Canadian Democracy*, 65.

67 This division of taxing power is of continuing importance. In 1998 the Supreme Court of Canada invalidated an Ontario probate fee on the grounds that the fee constituted a tax and could not therefore be levied by the lieutenant governor-in-council without statutory authority. To do otherwise would violate the "constitutional imperative" of section 53 that is necessary to "ensure parliamentary control over, and accountability for taxation" (*Re Eurig Estate* [1998] 1 S.C.R. 565 para 34, 30 [Major J.]). It should be noted, however, that four members of the *Eurig* Court dissented on this point on the grounds that section 53 has no application to the provincial level since there are no provincial upper houses (Gonthier and Bastarache) or that section 53 has no application to taxing measures that do not take statutory form (Binnie and McLachlin).

68 Political scientist Tom Flanagan wrongly attributes this feature to the "fusion" of legislative and executive power under "responsible government" instead of noting the explicit constitutional provision (s.54) of

the British North America Act, 1867. See Tom Flanagan, "Liberal Tactics," A19.
69 Hogg, *Constitutional Law*, 14–16 to 14–16.2.
70 Ajzenstat, "Canada's First Constitution," 47. The mismanagement of funds in United Canada was also a central preoccupation of the Charlottetown delegates.
71 Tellingly, the primary non-pecuniary area of legislation – criminal law – was subject to a "separation of power" on federalism grounds, by virtue of sections 91(27) and 92(14).
72 The inclusion of the crown as part of "Parliament" in section 17 means that the Canadian and English definitions are not necessarily consistent. Thus, "Parliament" in Canada can be equated to the English notion of the King-in-Parliament but is commonly used to mean the Houses of Parliament or even the House of Commons alone. There is much mischief in this imprecision but such definitional slippage is almost unavoidable when discussing Canadian institutions.
73 Some elements of executive prerogative persist in Canada but they are mainly restricted to the granting of honours and the conduct of foreign affairs (including the power to send troops abroad). Sossin, "Ambivalence of Executive Power," 59.
74 Docherty, *Mr. Smith Goes to Ottawa*, 11, 27.
75 Despite the responsible government convention that the governor general must acquiesce to the demands of the executive and legislature, the governor general is not a "rubber stamp" (Forsey, *Freedom and Order*, 34–5). Forsey argues against the "rubber stamp" theory by recognizing Lord Aberdeen's refusal to appoint senators as requested by the newly-defeated-but-still-in-office Prime Minister Charles Tupper in 1896 (*Freedom and Order*, 38). Patricia Hughes argues that a governor general might refuse to proclaim "clearly unconstitutional legislation ... although this constitutionally correct manoeuvre may itself result in constitutional crisis" (Hughes, "Legislatures and Constitutional Agnosticism," 217). A governor general who proceeded in such a fashion would be wise to find a coalition of elected representatives that might take the burden of responsibility for his/her action.

CHAPTER FOUR

1 Robson, *Justice and Administrative Law*, 16. Cited by Allan, *Law, Liberty and Justice*, 54.
2 [1999] 3 S.C.R. 199.

3 Ibid., para 54 (emphasis in the original) (Major J.). On earlier occasions, the Court had suggested that "it is no avail to point to the fusion of powers which characterizes the Westminster system of government. That the executive through its control of a House of Commons majority may in practice dictate the position the House of Commons takes ... is not ... constitutionally congnizable by the judiciary" (*Canada [Minister of Energy, Mines and Resources] v. Canada [Auditor General]* [1989] 2 S.C.R. 49 at 103 (Dickson C.J.). See Sossin, "Ambivalence of Executive Power," 59.
4 Montesquieu, *Spirit of the Laws*, 156; Vile, *Constitutionalism*, 99–102.
5 Carrese discusses Montesquieu's (and Blackstone's) alleged "sloppiness or conservative obfuscation" on this point in *Cloaking of Power*, 136–7.
6 Russell, "Overcoming Legal Formalism," 6.
7 Cairns, "Judicial Committee."
8 A group that includes A.H.F. Lefroy, Edward Blake, and a number of early Canadian legal scholars. Lefroy's 1897 text exhibits an attachment to such formalities as the "literary theory." Risk argues that the early Canadian formalist legal scholars shared an "integrated set of assumptions (or constraints on vision)" that viewed individual rights as "threatened primarily by the Crown and protected by responsible government ... in sum, the ideal constitution was the Whig constitution as described by eighteenth- and early-nineteenth British writers" (Risk, *History of Canadian Legal Thought*, 120).
9 Clement, *Law of the Canadian Constitution*.
10 Russell, "Overcoming Legal Formalism," 6.
11 Cairns, "Judicial Committee," 319; Knopff and Morton, *Charter Politics*, 67.
12 Clement, *Law of the Canadian Constitution*, 19.
13 Ibid.
14 Bagehot, *The English Constitution*, 48 (emphasis added); Bagehot refers to the fusion of the legislative powers five times: once with the qualifier "nearly" (48) and four times without (50, twice on 51, 60).
15 Ibid., 50.
16 Vile argues that Bagehot's target was the straw man of the "extreme doctrine of the separation of powers ... these claims of Bagehot have been too easily accepted, and therefore the false alternatives that he presented, of the complete separation or the complete fusion of powers in British government, have been over-influential" (*Constitutionalism*, 235).

17 Miriam Smith posits that the early adoption of the behaviouralist approach occurred "because the gap between the formal operation of political institutions and the living realities of constitutional conventions meant that scholars of Canadian political institutions could never ignore the actual behaviour of the political actors such as political parties." Smith, "Institutionalism," 105.
18 Russell, "Overcoming Legal Formalism," 9.
19 Pritchett, "The Development of Judicial Research," 31. Discussed in Devins and Fisher, *The Democratic Constitution*, 218.
20 Russell, "Overcoming Legal Formalism," 9.
21 Brooks and Gagnon (*Social Scientists and Politics in Canada*, 82) cite Smiley, "Contributions to Canadian Political Science." Dawson continues to be criticized for his emphasis on the "dry legalities of political institutions" and for his strong normative approach (he is guilty of situating "Canadian government within the context of the British inheritance, which he largely viewed in a positive light"). Smith, "Institutionalism," 105.
22 Tocqueville, *Democracy in America*, 264. See also Knopff and Morton, *Charter Politics*, 235–9. Montesquieu also emphasizes the "forms of justice" and notes that, while we may find them "doubtless too numerous" while we are litigating them, "if we consider them in the relation they bear to the liberty and security of every individual, we shall often find them too few" (*Spirit of the Laws*, 73–4). He concludes by noting that "the trouble, expense, delays, and even the very dangers of our judiciary proceedings are the price that each subject pays for his liberty" (74). See also Carrese, *Cloaking of Power*, 36.
23 Tocqueville, *Democracy in America*, 256; Carrese, *Cloaking of Power*, 214.
24 Kronman, *The Lost Lawyer*, 4.
25 Stoner, *Common Law Liberty*, 121.
26 A notable Canadian exception is Ernest Weinrib's *The Idea of Private Law* but its argument extends, as the title suggests, only to private law and the author has been reluctant to discuss the implications of his argument for public law.
27 Green, "Legal Realism as Theory of Law"; Llewellyn, "The Constitution as an Institution"; Llewellyn, *Bramble Bush*; Jerome Frank, *Law and the Modern Mind*.
28 *Southern Pacific Co. v. Jensen* (1917) 244 U.S. 205 at 222 (Holmes J., dissenting); See also Holmes, "The Path of Law."
29 Posner, *Economic Analysis of Law*.

30 Dworkin, *Law's Empire* and *Freedom's Law*.
31 Kennedy, *A Critique of Adjudication*.
32 Posner, *Problematics of Moral and Legal Theory* and *Law, Pragmatism and Democracy*.
33 Evans, Rueschemeyer, and Skocpol, *Bringing the State Back In*.
34 Knopff and Morton, *Charter Politics*, 67.
35 Cairns, "Judicial Committee," 319.
36 Knopff and Morton, *Charter Politics*, 70–1.
37 Mansfield, *Taming of the Prince*, xxiii.
38 Ibid., xxiii.
39 In making the argument for "responsible government," proponents like Pierre Bédard were careful to separate the "executive proper" from the executive, which retained a role in legislating as part of Parliament. In this regard, Bédard was following the model laid out by Blackstone and De Lolme – the king is "irresistible" in the enforcement of the law but "the legislative power belongs to Parliament and no individual, least of all the monarch, can demand obedience to laws to which parliament has not assented" (Ajzenstat, "Canada's First Constitution," 52).
40 Mansfield, *Taming of the Prince*, xxiii.
41 Ibid.
42 Ibid., 30.
43 Ibid.
44 Mansfield, *Statesmanship and Party Government*, 3.
45 *Friesen v. Hammell* (2000) 2000 BCSC 1185 (CanLII); see also *McKinney v. Liberal Party of Canada, et al.* (1987) 43 D.L.R. (4th) 706 (O.S.C.) and *Canadian Taxpayers Federation v. Ontario (Minister of Finance)* 2004 CanLII 48177 (Ontario S.C.) at para 58 (Rouleau J.).
46 Mansfield, *America's Constitutional Soul*, 149.
47 Ibid., 150.
48 Prime ministers with only *minority* partisan support are *regularly* reminded of the limits of their power. See Baker, "The Real Protection of the People" (forthcoming).
49 http://www.parl.gc.ca/information/about/process/info/ParlBills.asp?Language=E; Forcese and Freeman note that "government bills receive royal assent on a relatively regular basis" (*The Laws of Government*, 638).
50 Dawson and Dawson, *Democratic Government*, 47.
51 Ibid.
52 Gordon, *Controlling the State*, 336.

53 Donald Savoie, *Governing from the Centre*. Cited in this fashion by Elliot, "Charter Revolution and the Court Party," 324n.185, and Kelly, *Governing with the Charter*, 225–6.
54 Savoie, "The Managerial Prime Minister," 10.
55 Chase, "Endangered Species Bill Trouble," A1.
56 Tibbits and Bronskill, "Terror Bill Gets Facelift," A13.
57 Jaimet, "Liberals Demanded Favours to Pass Bill," A1.
58 Hebert, "Chrétien Regime Limps along," A15.
59 Tibbetts, "PM Rejects 'Sunset Clause' in Terror Law," A5.
60 Held 9 and 10 November 2001. The essays presented at this conference can be found in Daniels, Macklem, and Roach, *The Security of Freedom*. Cotler's contribution is entitled "Thinking outside the Box: Foundational Principles for a Counter-Terrorism Law and Policy."
61 McCarthy, "No Sunset Clause for Antiterror Bill, PM Tells His Caucus," A7.
62 Leblanc, "Ottawa Softens Terror Bill," A1. Emphasis added.
63 Philip Authier, "The Man in the Middle," A1.
64 Jaimet, "Species at Risk Bill," A5.
65 Chase, "Endangered Species Bill Trouble," A1.
66 Jaimet, "Species at Risk Bill," A5.
67 Ibid.
68 Ibid.
69 Chase, "Endangered Species Bill Trouble," A1.
70 Jaimet, "Liberals Demanded Favours to Pass Bill," A1.
71 http://www.parl.gc.ca/information/about/process/info/Parl-Bills.asp?Language=E; see also Forcese and Freeman, *The Laws of Government*, 638.
72 Hogg, *Constitutional Law*, 14-4-5.
73 Ibid., 14-4.
74 War Measures Act, 1914, s.6.
75 *Re Gray* (1918) 42 D.L.R. 1, 12 (Duff J.).
76 Ibid., 11. Emphasis added.
77 Ibid., 12.
78 As Tetley points out in his memoir of the 1970 October Crisis, the invocation of the War Measures Act was followed by a series of regulations that construed the emergency powers in a much narrower fashion than critics have suggested (*The October Crisis*, 89–92).
79 Hogg, *Constitutional Law*, 14-4.
80 Ibid., 14-5.
81 Ibid.

82 Ibid.
83 Franks, "The Canadian Senate," 151.
84 At the time of the 1984 general election, seventy-three senators identified themselves as Liberal, twenty-five as Conservative, and four as independent.
85 In this skirmish, Prime Minister Mulroney responded to the Senate's formal power with one of his own, section 26 of the BNA Act, which allowed for the appointment of eight new Conservative senators to assist the passage of the legislation through the Upper House.
86 Franks, "The Canadian Senate," 156–8.
87 Ibid., 158.
88 White, *Voice of Region*, 220, cited in Franks, "The Canadian Senate," 158.
89 Mansfield, *America's Constitutional Soul*, 150.
90 Dicey, *Introduction*, xxxviii.

CHAPTER FIVE

1 *Mackin v. New Brunswick (Minister of Finance); Rice v. New Brunswick* [2002] 1 S.C.R. 405 at para 39 (Gonthier J.). See also *Valente v. the Queen* [1985] 2 S.C.R. 673 and *Reference re Remuneration of Judges of the Provincial Court of Prince Edward Island* [1997] 3 S.C.R. 3. The Court has also invoked the separation of powers to protect the independence of crown prosecutors (*R. v. Power* [1994] 1 S.C.R. 601), labour arbitrators (*Douglas/Kwantlen Faculty Assn. v. Douglas College* [1990] 3 S.C.R. 570), and human-rights tribunals (*Cooper v. Canada [Human Rights Commission]* [1996] 3 S.C.R. 854).
2 McCormick, "New Questions," 857.
3 Thus, while "the separation of powers is a defining feature of our constitutional order" (*Newfoundland [Treasury Board] v. N.A.P.E.* [2004] 3 S.C.R. 381 at para 104), it has little practical effect on the Court's interpretation of the constitution since "the separation of powers cannot be invoked to undermine the operation of a specific written provision of the Constitution like s. 1 of the Charter." This comment was made by Justice Binnie in response to Newfoundland Court of Appeal Judge W.W. Marshall's suggestion that the *Oakes* test should be modified to accommodate a more nuanced understanding of the separation of powers.
4 Montesquieu, *Spirit of the Laws*, 151–2.
5 Some of the labels attached to Canadian courts reflect this subordination to executive power – the "Court of Queen's Bench," for example –

and the underdeveloped judicial branch in the BNA Act may also be attributed to this secondary character of the judiciary. The independence of the judicial power from the executive began with the establishment of courts of common pleas by the Magna Carta (1215) and was extended by the security of tenure for judges granted as part of the settlement of the Glorious Revolution of 1688. By the time of Canadian confederation in 1867, judicial independence was a well-understood and accepted principle of governance.

6 Hennigar, "Players and the Process," 92; Mitchell, "The Impact of the *Charter*."
7 Blackstone, *Commentaries*, i, 267. For Blackstone, this is true even though the courts are a subordinate part of the crown (the king "has alone the right of erecting courts of judicature"). The independence of the courts exists, therefore, to help the king deliver justice ("to assist him in executing this power," as Blackstone delicately puts it). The capacity of the king to administer English law was doubted by Coke when he remarked to King James in 1608 that "God had endowed His Majesty with excellent science, and great endowments of nature; but his Majesty was not learned in the laws of his realm of England ... which law is an act which requires long study and experience before that a man can attain to the cognizance of it" (Boyer, ed., *Law, Liberty, and Parliament*, ix).
8 Montesquieu, *Spirit of the Laws*, 152.
9 Legislatures may, however, bestow benefits on individuals or corporations through "private bills." While such bills are still found in British law (where they often deal with matters of incorporation), they are rarely used in Canada (where some consider them unconstitutional) and the United States. From the Canadian perspective, the most notable use of private bills was as the sole means of obtaining a divorce prior to the 1968 Divorce Act (Hogg, *Constitutional Law*, 9–18). It is also permissible to direct certain laws at particular industries or groups (see *British Columbia v. Imperial Tobacco Canada Ltd.* [2005] 2 S.C.R. 473 [*Imperial Tobacco*]) and *Authorson v. Canada [Attorney General]* [2003] 2 S.C.R. 40) [*Authorson*].
10 Allan, *Law, Liberty and Justice*, 73.
11 The last English bill of attainder was enacted in 1789 and the practice was officially abolished in 1870. The convention against usage was adopted upon reception of English law in Canada and reflected in the constitutional prohibitions found in section 11 of the Charter of Rights and Freedoms. Attainder bills are prohibited by Article I, section 9 of

the United States constitution. There are many historical antecedents of the prohibition against attainder bills, the most famous of which is the Roman constitutional rule of *Privilegia ne Inroganto* ('no law may be passed against an individual'). See Clinton, *Marbury v. Madison*, 33.
12 Fuller, *The Morality of Law*, 46–9. In Fuller's account, such fairness belongs to the external morality of law (47).
13 Laws are general but they are applied in particular instances, as explained in the case-and-controversy section below. The relationship between the generality of law and the particularity of the application is aptly summarized by Lord Mansfield: "The law does not consist in particular instances, though it is explained by particular instances and rules, but the law consists of principles which govern specific and individual cases, as they happen to arise" *R.v. Bembridge* (1783) 22 How. St. Tr. 155.
14 For this reason, there is a *presumption* that all laws apply prospectively but it may be rebutted if the legislature explicitly declares the law to be retroactive. The Supreme Court of Canada recently rejected a challenge to a retroactive law permitting actions against tobacco manufacturers in *Imperial Tobacco*.
15 As Clinton argues, the application of general law to particulars is not simply "linguistic" but, rather, "ethical or political." "The idea of interpretation as an enterprise primarily devoted to resolving linguistic uncertainties and ambiguities has resulted from twentieth-century fashions" unknown to the classic jurisprudential tradition. Clinton, "Classical Legal Naturalism," 948.
16 Allan, *Constitutional Justice*, 15.
17 Ibid., 14.
18 Ibid.
19 Ibid., 15.
20 Sir Philip Warwick, *A Discourse of Government ... Written in the Year 1678*, quoted in Harris, *Restoration*, 57.
21 Tardi, *The Law of Democratic Governing*, xxxiv.
22 Allan, *Constitutional Justice*, 15.
23 *Roncarelli v. Duplessis* [1959] S.C.R. 121 is the classic Canadian statement of this principle.
24 *The Federalist*, No. 22 (attributed to Hamilton), 136–7.
25 Carrese, *Cloaking of Power*, 204.
26 "General propositions do not decide concrete cases": *Lochner v. New York* 198 U.S. 45 at 75 (Holmes J., dissenting); Fuller, *Morality of Law*, 82–3.

27 *Beaver v. The Queen* [1957] S.C.R. 531. On the unconstitutionality of absolute-liability offences punishable by imprisonment, see *Re B.C. Motor Vehicle Act* [1985] 2 S.C.R. 486.
28 Weiler, *In the Last Resort*, 95–7.
29 The latter is the opinion of the Supreme Court of Canada in *R. v. Vaillancourt* [1987] 2 S.C.R. 636.
30 A.V. Dicey notes that "a large proportion of English law is in reality made by judges ... The appeal to precedent is in the law courts merely a useful fiction by which judicial decision conceals its transformation into judicial legislation" (see Gordon, *Controlling the State*, 50).
31 Benjamin Hoadley, bishop of Bangor, sermon before the king of England (31 March 1717), in Wills, *Explaining America*, 130. Clinton notes that this comment was "often recalled" by the American founders (Clinton, *Marbury v. Madison*, 7).
32 Justice O.W. Holmes, Jr: "I recognize without hesitation that judges do and must legislate, but they can do so only interstitially; they are confined from molar to molecular motions." *Southern Pacific Co. v. Jensen* (1917) 244 U.S. 205 at 221 (dissenting).
33 Cairns, "Judicial Committee," 319–20.
34 One may, for example, litigate on the basis of "public interest standing": *Thorson v. Attorney General of Canada* [1975] 1 S.C.R. 138, *Nova Scotia Board of Censors v. McNeil* [1975] 2 S.C.R. 265, *Minister of Justice of Canada v. Borowski* [1981] 2 S.C.R. 575, and *Finlay v. Minister of Finance of Canada* [1986] 2 S.C.R. 607. "The result of these four cases," Hoggs says, "is to establish a very liberal rule for public interest standing" (*Constitutional Law*, 56–9). Despite the clear rule against deciding moot cases announced in *Borowski v. Attorney General for Canada* [1989] 1 S.C.R. 342, the Court has often used its discretion to hear moot cases: *Tremblay v. Daigle* [1989] 2 S.C.R. 530, *New Brunswick (Minister of Health and Community Services) v. G. (J.)* [1999] 3 S.C.R. 46, and *Doucet-Bourdreau* are just some examples.
35 Roach, *Supreme Court on Trial*, 143.
36 *A.G. (Ontario, et al.) v. A.G. (Dominion of Canada)* 3 D.L.R. 509 at 515 (J.C.P.C.) (Loreburn L.C.): "No one who has experience of judicial duties can doubt that, if an Act of this kind were abused, manifold evils might follow, including undeserved suspicion of the course of justice and much embarrassment and anxiety to the Judges themselves" (at 512).
37 "The answers are only advisory, and will have no more effect than the opinions of the Law Officers" (ibid., 517) and "no direct effect is to

result from the answers so given, and no right or property is thereby to be adjudged" (ibid., 512).
38 This terminology is a bit unwieldy in that it might be taken to imply broader judicial scope than justicable cases because of its inclusion of "controversies." The "controversies" aspect refers, however, to legal issues within the cases themselves (essentially establishing judicial power over the *whole* case, in all of its essence) and nothing further. The Article III restriction has also been understood as prohibiting the federal judiciary from delivering "advisory" opinions in reference cases. See *Muskrat v. United States* (1911) 219 U.S. 346 and Clinton, et al., *Federal Courts*, 993–1001.
39 *The Federalist*, No. 81 (attributed to Hamilton), 517–18.
40 The Canadian constitution does permit ex post facto laws so long as they are explicitly retroactive and are not criminal law (which would then engage s.11[g] of the Charter), but that permissiveness does nothing to remedy overly specific ex post facto laws. See *Imperial Tobacco*, para 69–72 (Major J.) and Edinger, "Retrospectivity in Law."
41 Dicey, *Introduction*, 92.
42 Montesquieu, *Spirit of the Laws*, 153. The Supreme Court of Canada recently reaffirmed that a jury acquittal may not be overturned by judges: "When ... would a verdict of guilty be directed? Would it be permitted whenever the evidence is overwhelming *in the eyes of the judges*? Under our Constitution, the plain answer to this last question is 'no'" (emphasis in the original): *R. v. Krieger* (2006) SCC 30950 at para 9 (Fish J.). Larry Kramer argues that the American framers relied upon the moderating effect of juries to temper judicial activism even in constitutional cases (*The People Themselves*, 135).
43 Gutmann, "Legislatures in the Constitutional State," x.
44 Clinton, *Federal Courts*, 992.
45 Ibid.
46 Ibid.
47 *Cohens v. Virginia* (1821) 6 Wheat. 264 at 405. See also Clinton, *Marbury v. Madison*, for a compelling explanation of Marshall's views on the limitations of judicial review (according to Clinton, *Marbury* "entitles the Court to disregard legislation in resolving particular controversies *only where such legislation bears directly upon the performance of judicial functions*" [18]).
48 Clinton, *Marbury v. Madison*, 29.
49 Ibid.
50 Ibid.

51 Murphy, "Who Shall Interpret?" 406–7.
52 The doctrine of *stare decisis* is, however, intimately connected with the case-and-controversy restriction: "The doctrine of precedent in fact *implies* that the main function of any court is the narrow one of ruling upon the particular case before it. If a court's decision automatically extended beyond the case at hand, then it would make no sense to invoke the principle of 'deciding similar cases similarly' in *justification* of a future judgment." Clinton, *Marbury v. Madison*, 22.
53 Manfredi, *Judicial Power*, 147.
54 This certainly was the case with the *O'Connor-Mills* sequence, where the deficiencies with the Court's *O'Connor* regime formed part of the attorney general's case in *Mills*. Catherine Kane of the Justice Department argues that the legislation in *Mills* was based on "present knowledge" gained through "public hearings on the impact of [O'Connor]" and with "a better idea of the practical impacts of the changes." Baer, "Striking the Balance in Sexual Assault Trials."
55 Bickel, *The Least Dangerous Branch*, 115.
56 Ibid., 133–56.
57 As noted below, one might accept inter-institutional participation only prior to a Supreme Court ruling and reject it thereafter. In other words, all judicial insularists are judicial supremacists but not all judicial supremacists are judicial insularists.
58 Knopff and Morton, *Charter Politics*, 177.
59 Ibid., 177–8.
60 Walter Murphy argues that "even if one believes judges are the ultimate constitutional interpreters, government cannot halt and await a judicial decision whenever a constitutional problem arises." Since "deciding what policies government may legitimately pursue, whether to enact, sign, veto, or enforce a law, all create problems of interpretation," the call for judicial insularity is impractical at best. ("Who Shall Decide?" 401).
61 Makin, "Harper Blasted on Gay Marriage," A1.
62 *Reference Re Same-Sex Marriage* [2004] 3 S.C.R. 698.
63 The text of the letter can be found at http://www.law.utoronto.ca/samesexletter.html.
64 Ibid.
65 Makin, "Harper Blasted on Gay Marriage," A1. For an empirical examination of legislative responses to lower-court rulings (including examples of "creative" or "positive" responses), see Hennigar, "Expanding the 'Dialogue' Debate."

66 Brudner, "Notwithstanding Not Needed on Marriage," *Globe and Mail*, 1 February 2005, http://www.theglobeandmail.com/servlet/story/RTGAM.20050201.wbrudner01/BNStory/Front/.
67 Ibid. In December 2005 Patrick Monahan introduced an important qualifier to Choudhry's argument by noting that Harper's strategy was "technically" legal before noting that it is "highly unlikely you're going to be able to reinstitute the opposite-sex definition of marriage without using the notwithstanding clause." Canadian Press, "Notwithstanding Clause Required to Overturn Same-Sex Marriage Law, says Dean Patrick Monahan," D11.

CHAPTER SIX

1 Some dialogue theorists suggest that inter-institutional exchanges are still possible at this point but they explicitly disavow any further debate over the meaning of the constitution (this is, the dialogue must continue within the constitutional boundaries established by the Court's ruling) unless section 33 is invoked. Roach, *Supreme Court on Trial*, 287.
2 Kent Roach, for one, bemoans "unnecessary and duplicative litigation" and "province-by-province litigation and re-litigation of issues already decided by the Supreme Court" ("Remedial Consensus," 231). One might respond to Roach through Montesquieu, arguing that "the trouble, expense, delays, and even the very dangers of our judiciary proceedings are the price that each subject pays for his liberty" (*Spirit of the Laws*, 74).
3 Hogg, Thornton, and Wade argue that, under their dialogue theory, the representative branches can legitimately advance an interpretation inconsistent with a judicial decision as long as there has been "a material change in circumstances or new evidence that justifies reconsideration by the courts of the original decision" ("Dialogue Revisited," 34). Doing so purely on the basis of changeover in the Court's membership or changes in popular opinion would reduce dialogue to a rule of "if at first you don't succeed, try, try again." The institutional argument for testing the Court's resolve, as presented in this study, is not considered by Hogg et al.
4 Gordon, *Controlling the State*, 52.
5 There is, of course, considerable scope for lower-court disagreement since the question of whether a Supreme Court precedent applies to the case at hand is entirely within the lower court's discretion, at least until *that* case rises through the judicial hierarchy.

6 *R. v. Demers* [2004] 2 S.C.R. 489.
7 Gray, "The Sovereignty of Parliament Today," 60.
8 James Madison accepted this de facto power of the courts: "As the Courts are generally the last in making their decisions, it results to them by refusing or not refusing to execute a law, to stamp it with its final character." Madison's Observations on Jefferson's Draft of a Constitution for Virginia, in *The Papers of Thomas Jefferson*, 6: 308 (cited by Kramer, *The People Themselves*, 105).
9 The term "constitutional hints" is used by Duclos and Roach to argue for more aggressive judicial remedies in "Constitutional Remedies." See note 28, below, for a potential relationship between their use of the term and my own.
10 This is not to suggest that Lincoln's view is widely accepted in the United States today. It is not uncommon for legal commentators to suggest that a Lincolnian approach to institutions would lead to considerable confusion: "Lincoln's view – which would allow the political branches to defy the courts' rulings each time a new party were involved – would make the orderly administration of justice nearly impossible: The Executive Branch could continually attempt to enforce laws already ruled unconstitutional, necessitating fresh litigation each time." Dorf, "Bloomberg's Response," http://writ.news.findlaw.com/dorf/20050214.html.
11 The quotations are from Supreme Court Justice Catron's letter to President Buchanan. From Jaffa, *A New Birth of Freedom*, 305.
12 Ibid., 305.
13 A tact his chief Republican rival, William Seward, took. Goodwin, *Team of Rivals*, 191.
14 Lincoln's first inaugural address, 4 March 1861. Stern, *Lincoln*, 653–4.
15 Manfredi quotes part of this passage in *Judicial Power*, 22.
16 *Luther v. Borden* (1849) 48 U.S. 1 was available as a precedent for Lincoln; *Nixon v. United States* (1993) 506 U.S. 224 is a recent statement of the doctrine. *Operation Dismantle v. The Queen* [1985] 1 S.C.R. 441 is commonly understood as establishing that Canada has no comparable doctrine but Lorne Sossin detects a nascent but vague version in recent jurisprudence on justiciability (*Boundaries of Judicial Review*, 199).
17 This is not all that different from Bickel's argument that the Court should exercise the "passive virtues" until an agreed-upon principle emerges: "Over time, as a problem is lived with, the Court does not work in isolation to divine the answer that is right. It has the means to elicit partial answers and reactions from the other institutions and to

try tentative answers itself. When at last the Court decides that 'judgment cannot be escaped – the judgment of this Court,' the answer is likely to be a proposition 'to which widespread acceptance may fairly be attributed,' because in the course of a continuing colloquy with the political institutions and with society at large, the Court has shaped and reduced the question, and perhaps because it has rendered the answer familiar if not obvious": Bickel, *Least Dangerous Branch*, 240 (see also Burt, *Constitution in Conflict*, 23).

18 Goodwin, *Team of Rivals*, 674.
19 Ibid.
20 Ibid.
21 The Lincoln administration also refused to adopt the *Dred Scott* reasoning in the issuance of passports and patents and in laws passed to abolish slavery in the territories and the District of Columbia. See Whittington, "Extrajudicial Constitutional Interpretation," 785.
22 From Lincoln's 1858 speech at Chicago, in Stern, *Lincoln*, 445.
23 Tocqueville, *Democracy in America*, 103; Knopff and Morton, *Charter Politics*, 178.
24 From Lincoln's 1858 speech at Chicago, in Stern, *Lincoln*, 446.
25 Speech by John Breckenridge, in 11 *Annals of Congress* (February 1802): 179–80. Cited by Kramer, *The People Themselves*, 108.
26 Devins and Fisher, *The Democratic Constitution*, 20. Emphasis added.
27 Kramer, *The People Themselves*, 217.
28 Such hints can be understood as the flipside of another instance of partial agency in the judicial-legislative relationship: the ability of courts to suggest a "constitutional road map" for the drafting of future legislation when the instant legislation is held to be invalid. See Duclos and Roach, "Constitutional Remedies," and Luna, "Road Maps." The Supreme Court of Canada's recommendation of a special-counsel provision in *Charkaoui v. Canada (Citizenship and Immigration)* 2007 SCC 9 is among the most recent "road maps" provided. Such advice to the legislature is a form of judicial agency over the legislative power but it is partial because it does not wholly assume the legislative power.
When Duclos and Roach state that they "believe that legislative action informed by careful analysis not only of what judges think the *Constitution requires*, but also what judges think it *prefers*, can foster a better institutional relationship ... reducing the need to test legislation in the courts" (24–5, emphasis in the original), they appear to suggest remedial powers for the Court that exceed partial agency.
29 Makin, "Harper Blasted on Hay Marriage," A1.

30 Ibid.
31 Ibid.
32 Canadian Press, "Notwithstanding Clause Required to Overturn Same-Sex Marriage Law, says Dean Patrick Monahan," D11.
33 Simpson, "The Same-Sex Debate Is a Meaningless Charade," A31.
34 Ibid.
35 Makin, "Harper Blasted on Gay Marriage," A1.
36 Ibid.
37 Gibson, "Founding Fathers-in-Law," 261.
38 The exception is the revision to section 91 that transferred power over unemployment insurance from the provinces to the federal government.
39 *Hogan v. Newfoundland* (2000) 183 D.L.R. (4th) 225 (Nfld. C.A.).
40 Waldron, "Some Models of Dialogue," 36–7; Manfredi, *Judicial Power*, 192–4.
41 Roach, *Supreme Court on Trial*, 189–93. Prime Minister Mulroney contributed to the override's poor reputation by calling it the "major fatal flaw of 1981" that made the entire constitution "not worth the paper it is printed on" (House of Commons, *Debates*, 6 April 1989, 153).
42 Cameron, "The Charter's Legislative Override," 140, 158. Similarly, Andrew Heard suggests that a convention against using section 33 has begun to crystallize (*Canadian Constitutional Conventions*, 147).
43 Manfredi, "Strategic Behaviour"; c.f. Roach, *Supreme Court on Trial*, 191–2: "[Section 33's] use is certainly not politically fatal ... all three provincial governments that have used it have been reelected shortly thereafter." On the usage of section 33 generally, see Kahana, "The Notwithstanding Clause and Public Discussion."
44 Manfredi, "Strategic Behaviour," 148.
45 Ibid., 158–65.
46 Todd, "O'Connor Appeal Dropped after Healing Circle," A1.
47 Weber, "Man Who Fought Rape Shield Law Cleared of Assault," A7.
48 *United States v. Butler*, 297 U.S. 1 (1936) at 62 (Roberts J.); Nagel, *Constitutional Cultures*, 132.
49 Morton and Knopff, *The Charter Revolution*, 149.
50 The acceptance of judicial supremacy may also erode democratic habits since that principle allows government to avoid controversial issues by arguing that it must be deferential to the Court. The Chrétien government's reaction to *M. v. H.* is a ready example; see Knopff, "A Delicate Dance."
51 Baer, "Striking the Balance in Sexual Assault Trials."
52 Ibid.

53 *Canada (Attorney General) v. Hislop* 2007 SCC 10 at para 94 (LeBel and Rothstein JJ.). Emphasis added.
54 Devins and Fisher, *The Democratic Constitution*, 7.
55 Ibid.
56 Ibid.

CHAPTER SEVEN

1 *The Federalist*, No. 78 (attributed to Hamilton), 496.
2 Ibid., No. 49 (attributed to Madison), 322; Madison reiterates this point in a 1789 speech: "If the constitutional boundary of either [department] can be brought in to question, I do not see that any of these independent departments has more right than another to declare their sentiments on that point." Speech by James Madison to the House of Representatives on the Removal Power of the President (17 June 1789), in *Papers of Madison*, vol. 12 (Robert A. Rutland et al., eds., 1975), 238. Cited in Kramer, *The People Themselves*, 106.
3 *Mills v. The Queen* [1986] 1 S.C.R. 863 at 965 (McIntyre J) [*Mills v. The Queen*]. Quoted in *Doucet-Boudreau*, para 52 (Iacobucci and Arbour JJ.).
4 *Doucet-Boudreau*, para 42 (Iacobucci and Arbour JJ.): "As a basic rule, no part of the Constitution can abrogate or diminish another part of the Constitution." See *New Brunswick Broadcasting Co. v. Nova Scotia (Speaker of the House of Assembly)* [1993] 1 S.C.R. 319 at 373 (McLachlin J.) and *Reference re Bill 30, An Act to Amend the Education Act (Ont.)* [1987] 1 S.C.R. 1148.
5 *Doucet-Boudreau*, para 56 (Iacobucci and Arbour JJ.).
6 Ibid., para 53 (Iacobucci and Arbour JJ.).
7 An earlier version of section 24(1) made the connection to traditional judicial remedies even stronger: the court could "define or enforce any of the individual rights or freedoms ... *by means of an injunction or similar relief*" (emphasis added) (Bayefsky, *Canada's Constitution Act*, 545).
8 *Mills v. The Queen*, para 262 (McIntyre J.)
9 Hogg, *Constitutional Law*, 37-2.
10 *R. v. 974649 Ontario Inc. ("Dunedin")* [2001] 3 S.C.R. 575, para 22 (McLachlin C.J.).
11 Roach, "Do We Want Judges with More Muscle?" A27.
12 Ibid.
13 Morton and Knopff, *The Charter Revolution*, 15. Even repealing legislation does not guarantee that judicial creativity will be curbed; see *Dunmore v. Ontario (Attorney General)* [2001] 1 S.C.R. 1016.

14 *Re Philips and Lynch* (1986) 27 D.L.R. (4th) 156 (NSSC).
15 Manfredi, *Judicial Power*, 164.
16 *Schachter*, 701 (Lamer C.J.): "The irony of this result is obvious" and "the nullification of benefits to single mothers does not sit well with the overall purpose of s. 15 of the Charter and for s. 15 to have such a result clearly amounts to 'equality with a vengeance.'"
17 Ibid., 696 (Lamer C.J.).
18 Ibid., 697 (Lamer C.J.).
19 Ibid., 715 (Lamer, C.J.).
20 *Vriend*, para 4 (Cory and Iacobucci JJ.); Macklem, "*Vriend v. Alberta*: Making the Private Public."
21 Kelly suggests that the recommendations of the Alberta Human Rights Commission provide a clear democratic foundation for the Court's activism in *Vriend* (*Governing with the Charter*, 101–2). His argument attempts to justify judicial power with elite bureaucratic opinion and therefore does nothing to address the counter-majoritarian difficulty since such an approach continues to bypass the legislature, denying it a legitimate role in rights-disputes.
22 Roach, *Supreme Court on Trial*, 201.
23 Ibid., 202.
24 Ibid.
25 Manfredi, *Judicial Power*, 165.
26 *Eldridge*, para 80 (La Forest J.).
27 Ibid., para 95 (La Forest J.).
28 Ibid., para 82 (La Forest J.). Byron Sheldrick argues that the *Eldridge* Court's "focus is clearly and exclusively on the individuals before the court, for it is their rights entitlements about which the court is being asked to rule. The issue of how to deal with future claimants, and the budgetary implications of the decision, are considered to be the state's concern, not the courts" ("Judicial Review and the Allocation of Health Care Resources," 160). Sheldrick is half-right – the Court is not concerned with the budgetary implications – but, as the statement by La Forest makes clear, the remedy in *Eldridge* is clearly meant to apply to future claimants.
29 Ibid., para 85 (La Forest J.). See also *Singh v. Minister of Employment and Immigration*.
30 *Eldridge*, para 77 (La Forest J.).
31 Ibid., para 96 (La Forest J.).
32 Breckenridge, *United States Government and Politics*, 169–74.
33 A result that has driven defenders of judicial power to advocate more intrusive judicial remedies. See Roach, "Remedial Consensus," 224.

34 *Eldridge*, para 87 (La Forest J.).
35 *Martin*, para 5 (Gonthier J.).
36 Assuming, of course, that the complainant can overcome the doctrine of crown immunity. See Hogg and Monahan, *Liability of the Crown*.
37 The *Schachter* decision left open the "rare" possibility of conjunctive remedies (720) but subsequent cases (*Guimond v. Quebec [Attorney General]* para 18–19; *Mackin v. New Brunswick [Minister of Finance]*; and *Rice v. New Brunswick* [2002] 1 S.C.R. 405, 2002 SCC 13, para 80–1) have interpreted *Schachter* as denying conjunctive remedies in all but the rarest of circumstances.
38 Manfredi notes that the Court arrived at its assessment of the costs in *Eldridge* "by simply extrapolating to the entire province the costs incurred by a private institution to provide interpretation services on the lower BC mainland. The Court did not engage in any obvious analysis of whether those services would be adequate or could be provided at the same cost in more remote regions of the province than the densely populated mainland." Manfredi, *Judicial Power*, 156.
39 *Auton v. British Columbia (Attorney General)* (BCSC), para 64–5.
40 Roach, "Remedial Consensus," 230.
41 Ibid., 229.
42 Ibid., 230.
43 Ibid., 238–9.
44 The trial court judge's power to issue new orders was expressly rejected by the Nova Scotia Court of Appeal but the Supreme Court of Canada hinted that this power was never seized as part of the remedy.
45 *Doucet-Boudreau*, para 56 (Iacobucci and Arbour JJ.).
46 *Doucet-Boudreau* (NSCA), para 16 (Flinn J.A.).
47 Ibid., para 16 (Flinn J.A.).
48 *Doucet-Boudreau*, para 56 (Iacobucci and Arbour JJ.).
49 Maltzman, et al., *The Collegial Game*. Such collective activity is not incompatible with a preferential model, as argued in Segal and Spaeth, *The Supreme Court and the Attitudinal Model Revisited*, 100n.50, 404.
50 *Mahe v. Alberta*.
51 *Doucet-Boudreau* (NSCA), para 73 (Freeman J.A., dissenting).
52 Ibid., para 83 (Freeman J.A., dissenting).
53 Pilkington notes that "it still seems unlikely that Canadian governments will refuse or fail to comply with court orders declaring constitutional rights" and this is "far beyond the facts of *Doucet-Boudreau*." Pilkington, "Enforcing," 90.

54 Berryman, *The Law of Equitable Remedies*, 156.
55 *Doucet-Boudreau*, para 36 (Iacobucci and Arbour JJ.).
56 *The Federalist*, No. 49 (attributed to Madison), 322.
57 *Doucet-Boudreau*, para 91 (LeBel and Deschamps JJ.).
58 Ibid., para 110 (LeBel and Deschamps JJ.).
59 Ibid., para 112 (LeBel and Deschamps JJ.).
60 Ibid., para 124 (LeBel and Deschamps JJ.).
61 Pilkington, "Enforcing," 85.
62 Ibid.

CONCLUSION

1 The notion of rights-as-trumps is well known. Classic accounts include Ronald Dworkin, *Taking Rights Seriously*, and Mary Ann Glendon, *Rights Talk*. Waldron, *Law and Disagreement* identifies Hobbes as an early observer of this tendency: "And when men that think themselves wiser than all others, clamor and demand right Reason for judge; yet seek no more, but that things should be determined, by no other mens reason but their own, it is as intolerable in the society in of men, as it is in play after trump is turned, to use the trump on every occasion, that suite whereof they have most in their hand" (*Leviathan*, chapter V).
2 Nanos, "Charter Values Don't Equal Canadian Values," 53.
3 Kramer, *The People Themselves*, 32.
4 Subject, of course, to the powers of reservation and disallowance. Sections 55, 56, and 57 of the BNA Act once permitted the United Kingdom government to "disallow" (56) and "reserve" (57) Canadian legislation but the imperial use of these provisions was expressly disavowed at the Imperial Conference of 1930 (even prior to 1930, the imperial powers were used sparingly – the power of reservation had not been used since 1878 and the power to disallow had been used only once, in 1878) (Hogg, *Constitutional Law*, 3-2n.4). Section 90 allows for the federal government, acting through the governor general, to disallow or reserve provincial legislation but those powers have also "fallen into disuse" (*The Queen v. Beauregard* [1986] 2 S.C.R. 56 at 72), although there have been "wholly frivolous" reservations in "modern times" (Hogg, *Constitutional Law*, 5-20). For the history of federal disallowance of provincial legislation, see Forsey, *Freedom and Order*, 177–91, and Mallory, *Social Credit and the Federal Power*. In addition, provincial acts are vulnerable to the "declaratory" power in

section 92(10)(c), which can bring a local work into federal jurisdiction by declaring it to be "for the general advantage of Canada."

5 Goldsworthy, *The Sovereignty of Parliament*, 3.
6 "*Dr. Bonham's Case*" (1610) 8 Co. Rep. 107a-121a, 77 Eng. Rep. See Cook, "Against Common Right and Reason," 301, and Plucknett, "*Bonham's Case* and Judicial Review."
7 Allan, *Law, Liberty and Justice* and *Constitutional Justice*; Barendt, "Separation of Powers and Constitutional Government."
8 *Roncarelli v. Duplessis* [1959] S.C.R. 121; *Reference re Alberta Statutes* [1938] S.C.R. 100.
9 Gray, "Sovereignty of Parliament Today," 60.
10 Cameron, "Dialogue and Hierarchy," 1051, 1062.
11 *N.A.P.E.*, para 111 (Binnie J.).
12 DeCoste, "The Separation of State Powers," 6.
13 Forcese and Freeman, *The Laws of Government*, 37–8.
14 Ibid., 37–8.
15 [1990] 3 F.C. 465 (F.C.A.).
16 Ibid., 485–6.
17 Ibid., 486.
18 Huscroft, "Constitutionalism from the Top Down," 100.
19 Ibid.
20 Ibid., 100.
21 Hogg et al., "Dialogue Revisited," 38n.133.
22 Huscroft, "Thank God We're Here," 255.
23 *Canada (Attorney General) v. Hislop* [2007] 1 S.C.R. 429 at para 111 (Le Bel and Rothstein JJ.).

Bibliography

BOOKS AND ARTICLES

Agresto, John. *The Supreme Court and Constitutional Democracy.* Ithaca, N.Y.: Cornell University Press 1984.
Ajzenstat, Janet. *The Once and Future Canadian Democracy.* Montreal and Kingston: McGill-Queen's University Press 2003.
– "Reconciling Parliament and Rights: A.V. Dicey Reads the Canadian Charter of Rights and Freedoms." 30(4) *Canadian Journal of Political Science* (1997): 645.
– "Canada's First Constitution: Pierre Bédard on Toleration and Dissent." 23(1) *Canadian Journal of Political Science* (1990): 39.
– *The Political Thought of Lord Durham.* Montreal and Kingston: McGill-Queen's University Press 1988.
– "Comment: The Separation of Powers in 1867." 20(1) *Canadian Journal of Political Science* (1987): 117.
Ajzenstat, Janet, Paul Romney, Ian Gentles, and William D. Gairdner. *Canada's Founding Debates.* Toronto: Stoddart 1999.
Alexander, Larry, and Frederick Schauer. "On Extrajudicial Constitutional Interpretation." 110(7) *Harvard Law Review* (1997): 1359.
Allan, T.R.S. *Constitutional Justice: A Liberal Theory of the Rule of Law.* Oxford: Oxford University Press 2001.
– *Law, Liberty, and Justice: The Legal Foundations of British Constitutionalism.* Oxford: Clarendon Press 1993.
Authier, Philip. "The Man in the Middle: Civil-Rights Lawyer Trod a Fine Line in Debate." Montreal *Gazette*, 8 December 2001, A1.
Baer, Nicole. "Striking the Balance in Sexual Assault Trials." 1(1) *Justice Canada*.

Bagehot, Walter. *The English Constitution.* Cambridge: Cambridge University Press 2001.

Barendt, Eric. "Separation of Powers and Constitutional Government." 98 *Public Law* (1995): 599.

Bayefsky, Anne F. *Canada's Constitution Act 1982 & Amendments: A Documentary History.* Toronto: McGraw-Hill Ryerson 1989.

Berg, Thomas C. "What Hath Congress Wrought? An Interpretive Guide to the Religious Freedom Restoration Act." 39 *Villanova Law Review* (1994): 1.

Berman, Mitchell N. "Constitutional Decision Rules." 90(1) *Virginia Law Review* (2004): 1.

Berryman, Jerry. *The Law of Equitable Remedies.* Toronto: Irwin Law 2000.

Bessette, Joseph M. *The Mild Voice of Reason: Deliberative Democracy and American National Government.* Chicago: University of Chicago Press 1994.

Bickel, Alexander. *The Least Dangerous Branch: The Supreme Court at the Bar of Politics.* Indianapolis, Ind., and New York: Bobbs-Merrill 1962.

Blackstone, William. *Commentaries on the Laws of England, in Four Books.* London: A. Strahan and W. Woodfall; Gale-Thomson, Eighteenth Century Collections Online, http://galenet.galegroup.com/servlet/ECCO.

Boyer, Allan D., ed. *Law, Liberty, and Parliament: Selected Essays on the Writings of Sir Edward Coke.* Indianapolis, Ind.: Liberty Fund 2004.

Bradley, Craig M. "Behind the *Dickerson* Decision." *Trial* (October 2000): 81.

Breckenridge, George. *United States Government and Politics.* Toronto: McGraw-Hill Ryerson 1998.

Brodie, Ian. *Friends of the Court: The Privileging of Interest Group Litigants in Canada.* Albany: SUNY Press 2002.

Brooks, Stephen, and Alain G. Gagnon. *Social Scientists and Politics in Canada: Between Clerisy and Vanguard.* Montreal and Kingston: McGill-Queen's University Press 1988.

Brudner, Alan. "Notwithstanding Not Needed on Marriage." *Globe and Mail*, 1 February 2005 (online edition).

Burt, Robert A. *The Constitution in Conflict.* Cambridge, Mass.: Harvard University Press 1992.

Cairns, Alan. "The Judicial Committee and Its Critics." 4(3) *Canadian Journal of Political Science* (1971): 301.

Cameron, Jamie. "The Charter's Legislative Override: Feat or Figment of the Constitutional Imagination?" In Grant Huscroft and Ian Brodie,

eds., *Constitutionalism in the Charter Era*. Markham, Ont.: LexisNexis-Butterworths 2004.
- "Dialogue and Hierarchy in Charter Interpretation: A Comment on *R. v. Mills*." 38 *Alta. L. Rev.* (2000): 1051.
Canada, House of Commons, *Debates*, 6 April 1989, 153.
Canadian Press. "Notwithstanding Clause Required to Overturn Same-Sex Marriage Law, Says Dean Patrick Monahan." Regina *Leader-Post*, 17 December 2005, D11.
Carrese, Paul O. *The Cloaking of Power: Montesquieu, Blackstone, and the Rise of Judicial Activism*. Chicago: University of Chicago Press 2003.
Chase, Stephen. "Endangered Species Bill Trouble: Chrétien Said to Be Unhappy That Caucus Could Not Reach Consensus on Environment." *Globe and Mail*, 1 May 2002, A1.
Chemerinsky, Erwin. "The Court Should Have Remained Silent: Why the Court Erred in Deciding Dickerson v. United States." 149(1) *University of Pennsylvania Law Review* (2000): 287.
- *Interpreting the Constitution*. New York: Praeger 1987.
Choudhry, Sujit, and Claire E. Hunter. "Measuring Judicial Activism on the Supreme Court of Canada: A Comment on *Newfoundland (Treasury Board) v. N.A.P.E.*" 48 *McGill Law Journal* (2003): 525.
Claus, Laurence. "Montesquieu's Mistakes and the True Meaning of Separation." 25(3) *Oxford Journal of Legal Studies* (2005): 419.
Clement, W.H.P. *The Law of the Canadian Constitution* (2nd ed.). Toronto: Carswell 1904.
Clinton, Robert Lowry. "Classical Legal Naturalism and the Politics of John Marshall's Constitutional Jurisprudence." 33 *John Marshall Law Review* (1999–2000): 935.
- *Marbury v. Madsion and Judicial Review*. Lawrence: University of Kansas Press 1989.
Clinton, Robert N., Richard A. Matasar, and Michael G. Collins. *Federal Courts: Theory and Practice*. Boston: Little, Brown 1996.
Conant, Michael. *Constitutional Structure and Purposes: Critical Commentary*. Westport, Conn.: Greenwood Press 2001.
Cook, Harold J. "Against Common Right and Reason: *The College of Physicians v. Dr. Thomas Bonham*." 29 *American Journal of Legal History* (1985): 301.
Cooper, Barry. "Limitations and Ambiguities." In Gordon Gibson, ed., *Fixing Canadian Democracy*. Vancouver: Fraser Institute 2003.
Cotler, Irwin. "Thinking outside the Box: Foundational Principles for a Counter-Terrorism Law and Policy." In Ronald J. Daniels, Patrick Macklem, and

Kent Roach, eds., *The Security of Freedom: Essays on Canada's Anti-Terrorism Bill*. Toronto: University of Toronto Press 2001.

Coughlan, Stephen G. "Half-Full Glasses, Pendulums and Individual Rights: The First Twenty Years of the *Charter*." 52 *University of New Brunswick Law Journal* (2003): 299.

Dawson, R. MacGregor, and W.F. Dawson, revised by Norman Ward. *Democratic Government in Canada* (5th ed.). Toronto: University of Toronto Press 1989.

DeCoste, Frederick C. "The Separation of State Powers in Liberal Polity: *Vriend v. Alberta*." 44 *McGill Law Journal* (1991): 231.

Devins, Neal, and Louis Fisher. *The Democratic Constitution*. New York: Oxford University Press 2004.

Dicey, A.V. *Introduction to the Study of the Law of the Constitution*. Indianapolis, Ind.: Liberty Fund 1982.

Docherty, David. *Mr. Smith Goes to Ottawa: Life in the House of Commons*. Vancouver: UBC Press 1997.

Dorf, Michael C. "New York Mayor Michael Bloomberg's Response to a Same-Sex Marriage Ruling: Should Executive Officials Defend Laws They Consider Unconstitutional?" *Writ*, 14 February 2005.

Dorf, Michael C., and Barry Friedman. "Shared Constitutional Interpretation." 61 *Supreme Court Review* [2000].

Duclos, Nitya, and Kent Roach. "Constitutional Remedies as 'Constitutional Hints': A Comment on *R. v. Schachter*." 36(1) *McGill Law Journal* (1991): 1.

Dworkin, Ronald. *Freedom's Law: The Moral Reading of the American Constitution*. Cambridge, Mass.: Harvard University Press 1996.

– *Law's Empire*. Cambridge, Mass.: Harvard University Press 1986.

– *Taking Rights Seriously*. London: Duckworth 1977.

Edinger, Elizabeth. "Retrospectivity in Law." 29 *University of British Columbia Law Review* (1995): 5.

Eisgruber, Christopher L. "The Most Competent Branches: A Response to Professor Paulsen." 83 *Georgetown Law Journal* (1994): 348.

Elliot, Robin. "Charter Revolution and the Court Party": Sound Critical Analysis or Blinkered Political Polemic?" 35 *University of British Columbia Law Review* (2001–02): 271.

Ely, John Hart. *Democracy and Distrust: A Theory of Judicial Review*. Cambridge. Mass.: Harvard University Press 1980.

Evans, Peter B., Dietrich Rueschemeyer, and Theda Skocpol. *Bringing the State Back In*. Cambridge: Cambridge University Press 1985.

Feldthusen, Bruce. "Access to the Private Therapeutic Records of Sexual Assault Complainants." 75 *Canadian Bar Review* (1996): 537.

Fisher, Louis. *Constitutional Dialogues: Interpretation as Political Process.* Princeton, N.J.: Princeton University Press 1988.
Flanagan, Tom. "Liberal Tactics Amount to Constitutional Back-Seat Driving." *Globe and Mail,* 20 February 2007, A19.
Forcese, Craig, and Aaron Freeman. *The Laws of Government: The Legal Foundations of Canadian Democracy.* Toronto: Irwin Law 2005.
Forsey, Eugene. "The Courts and the Conventions of the Constitution." 33 *University of New Brunswick Law Journal* (1984): 11.
– *Freedom and Order: Collected Essays.* Toronto: McClelland and Stewart 1975.
Frank, Jerome. *Law and the Modern Mind.* New York: Tudor Publishing 1935.
Frankfurter, Felix. "The United States Supreme Court Molding the Constitution." 32 *Current History* (1930): 235.
Franks, C.E.S. "The Canadian Senate in Modern Times." In Serge Joyal, ed., *Protecting Canadian Democracy: The Senate You Never Knew.* Montreal and Kingston: McGill-Queen's University Press 2003.
Friedman, Barry. "The History of the Countermajoritarian Difficulty, Part One: The Road to Judicial Supremacy." 73 *New York University Law Review* (1998): 333.
Fuller, Lon L. *The Morality of Law* (rev. ed.). New Haven, Conn.: Yale University Press 1969.
Gant, Scott. "Judicial Supremacy and Nonjudicial Interpretation of the Constitution." 24 *Hastings Constitutional Law Quarterly* (1997): 359.
Gibson, Dale. "Founding Fathers-in-Law: Judicial Amendment of the Canadian Constitution." 55(1) *Law and Contemporary Problems* (1992): 261.
Glendon, Mary Ann. *Rights Talk: The Impoverishment of Political Discourse.* New York: Free Press 1991.
Goldsworthy, Jeffrey. *The Sovereignty of Parliament: History and Philosophy.* Oxford: Oxford University Press 1999.
Goodwin, Doris Kearns. *Team of Rivals: The Political Genius of Abraham Lincoln.* New York: Simon and Schuster 2005.
Gordon, Scott. *Controlling the State: Constitutionalism from Ancient Athens to Today.* Cambridge, Mass.: Harvard University Press 1999.
Gray, Hamish R. "The Sovereignty of Parliament Today." 10(1) *University of Toronto Law Journal* (1953): 54.
Green, Michael Steven. "Legal Realism as Theory of Law." 46 *William and Mary Law Review* (2004–05): 1917.

Greene, Ian, Carl Baar, Peter McCormick, George Szablowski, and Martin Thomas. *Final Appeal: Decision-Making in Canadian Courts of Appeal.* Toronto: Lorimer 1998.
Gutmann, Amy. "Legislatures in the Constitutional State." In Richard W. Bauman and Tsvi Kahana, eds., *The Least Examined Branch: The Role of Legislatures in the Constitutional State.* Cambridge: Cambridge University Press 2006.
Hamilton, Alexander, John Jay, and James Madison. *The Federalist.* New York: Modern Library 2001.
Harris, Tim. *Revolution: The Great Crisis of the British Monarchy 1685–1720.* London: Penguin Books 2006.
– *Restoration: Charles II and His Kingdoms 1660–1685.* London: Penguin Books 2005.
Heard, Andrew. *Canadian Constitutional Conventions: The Marriage of Law and Politics.* Oxford: Oxford University Press 1991.
Hébert, Chantal. "Chrétien Regime Limps Along." Kitchener *Record*, 3 May 2002, A15.
Hennigar, Matthew A. "Expanding the 'Dialogue' Debate: Canadian Federal Government Responses to Lower Court Charter Decisions." 37(1) *Canadian Journal of Political Science* (2004): 3.
– "Players and the Process: *Charter* Litigation and the Federal Government." 21 *Windsor Yearbook of Access to Justice* (2002): 91.
Hiebert, Janet. *Charter Conflicts: What Is Parliament's Role?* Montreal and Kingston: McGill-Queen's University Press 2002.
Hogg, Peter W. *Constitutional Law of Canada*, 4th ed. (looseleaf). Scarborough, Ont.: Carswell 1997.
Hogg, Peter W., and Allison A. Bushell (Thornton). "The Charter Dialogue between Courts and Legislatures (or Perhaps the Charter of Rights Isn't a Bad Thing after All." 35 *Osgoode Hall Law Journal* (1997): 75.
Hogg, Peter W., Allison A. Bushell Thornton, and Wade K. Wright. "*Charter* Dialogue Revisited – Or, 'Much Ado about Metaphors.'" 45(1) *Osgoode Hall Law Journal* (2007): 1.
Hogg, Peter W., and Patrick J. Monahan. *Liability of the Crown* (3rd ed.). Scarborough, Ont.: Carswell 2000.
Holmes, Oliver W., Jr. "The Path of Law." 10 *Harvard Law Review* (1897): 457.
Hughes, Charles Evans. *The Supreme Court of the United States.* New York: Columbia University Press 1928.
Hughes, Patricia. "Legislatures and Constitutional Agnosticism." In Richard W. Bauman and Tsvi Kahana, eds., *The Least Examined Branch: The*

Role of Legislatures in the Constitutional State. Cambridge: Cambridge University Press 2006.
Huscroft, Grant. "Constitutionalism from the Top Down." 45(1) *Osgoode Hall Law Journal* (2007): 91.
– "'Thank God We're Here': Judicial Exclusivity in Charter Interpretation and Its Consequences." 25 *Supreme Court Law Review* (2d) (2004): 241.
Jaffa, Harry V. *A New Birth of Freedom: Abraham Lincoln and the Coming of the Civil War*. Lanham, Md.: Rowman and Littlefield 2000.
Jaimet, Kate. "Liberals Demanded Favours to Pass Bill." Ottawa *Citizen*, 27 December 2002, A1.
– "Species at Risk Bill Gets House's OK: Compromises Calm Grit Turmoil." Calgary *Herald*, 12 June 2002, A5.
Jefferson, Thomas. "The Anas." In *Life and Selected Writings*. New York: Modern Library 2004.
Jennings, Ivor, Sir. *The Law and the Constitution* (5th ed.). London: University of London Press 1959.
Kahana, Tsvi. "The Notwithstanding Clause and Public Discussion: Lessons from the Ignored Practice of S.33 of the *Charter*." 44 *Canadian Public Administration* (2001): 255.
Kahn, Ronald. "Institutional Norms and Supreme Court Decision-Making: The Rehnquist Court on Privacy and Religion." In Cornell W. Clayton and Howard Gillman, eds., *Supreme Court Decision-Making: New Institutionalist Approaches*. Chicago: University of Chicago Press 1999.
Kelly, James B. *Governing with the Charter: Legislative and Judicial Activism and Framers' Intent*. Vancouver: UBC Press 2005.
Kennedy, Duncan. *A Critique of Adjudication [fin de siècle]*. Cambridge, Mass.: Harvard University Press 1998.
Knopff, Rainer. "A Delicate Dance: The Courts and the Chrétien Government." In Les Pal, ed., *How Ottawa Spends*. Toronto: Oxford University Press 2001.
Knopff, Rainer, and F.L. Morton. *Charter Politics*. Scarborough, Ont.: Nelson Canada 1992.
Komesar, Neil K. *Imperfect Alternatives: Choosing Institutions in Law, Economics, and Public Policy*. Chicago: University of Chicago Press 1994.
– "Slow Learning in Constitutional Analysis." 88 *Northwestern Law Review* (1993): 212.
Kramer, Larry D. *The People Themselves: Popular Constitutionalism and Judicial Review*. Oxford: Oxford University Press 2004.

Kronman, Anthony T. *The Lost Lawyer: Failing Ideals of the Legal Profession*. Cambridge. Mass.: Harvard University Press 1995.
Laycock, Douglas. "Federalism as a Structural Threat to Liberty." 22(1) *Harvard Journal of Law & Public Policy* (1998): 67.
Leblanc, Daniel. "Ottawa Softens Terror Bill." *Globe and Mail*, 21 November 2001, A1.
Lefroy, A.H.F. *The Law of Legislative Power in Canada*. Toronto: Toronto Law Book and Publishing 1897.
Levinson, Sanford. *Constitutional Faith*. Princeton, N.J.: Princeton University Press 1988.
Llewellyn, Karl. *Bramble Bush: On Our Law and Its Study*. Cambridge: Oxford University Press 1953.
– "The Constitution as an Institution." 34 *Columbia Law Review* (1934): 4.
Luna, Erik. "Constitutional Road Maps." 90(4) *Journal of Criminal Law & Criminology* (2000): 1125.
Macklem, Timothy. "*Vriend v. Alberta*: Making the Private Public." 44 *McGill L.J.* (1999): 197.
Makin, Kirk. "Senior U.S., Canadian Judges Spar over Judicial Activism." *Globe and Mail*, 17 February 2007, A2.
– "Harper Blasted on Gay Marriage." *Globe and Mail*, 25 January 2005, A1.
Malleson, Kate, and Peter Russell. *Appointing Judges in an Age of Judicial Power: Critical Perspectives from Around the World*. Toronto: University of Toronto Press 2006.
Mallory, J.R. *Social Credit and the Federal Power in Canada*. Toronto: University of Toronto Press 1976.
Maltzman, Forrest, James F. Spriggs II, and Paul Wahlbeck. *The Collegial Game*. New York: Cambridge University Press 2000.
Manfredi, Christopher P. "The Day Dialogue Died: A Comment on *Sauvé v. Canada*." 45(1) *Osgoode Hall Law Journal* (2007): 105.
– "The Life of a Metaphor: Dialogue in the Supreme Court, 1998–2003." In Grant Huscroft and Ian Brodie, eds., *Constitutionalism in the Charter Era*. Markham, Ont.: LexisNexis-Butterworths 2004.
– "Strategic Behaviour and the Canadian *Charter of Rights and Freedoms*." In Patrick James, Donald E. Abelson, and Michael Lusztig, eds., *The Myth of the Sacred: The Charter, the Courts, and the Politics of the Constitution in Canada*. Montreal and Kingston: McGill-Queen's University Press 2002.
– *Judicial Power and the Charter: Canada and the Paradox of Liberal Constitutionalism*. Don Mills, Ont.: Oxford University Press 2001.

Manfredi, Christopher P., and James B. Kelly. "Misrepresenting the Supreme Court's Record? A Comment on Sujit Choudhry and Claire E. Hunter, 'Measuring Judicial Activism on the Supreme Court of Canada.'" 49 *McGill Law Journal* (2004): 741.
– "Dialogue, Deference and Restraint: Judicial Independence and Trial Procedures." 64 *Saskatchewan Law Review* (2001): 323.
– "Six Degrees of Dialogue: A Response to Hogg and Bushell." 37 *Osgoode Hall Law Journal* (1999): 513.
Mansfield, Harvey C., Jr. *America's Constitutional Soul*. Baltimore: Johns Hopkins University Press 1991.
– *The Taming of the Prince: The Ambivalence of Modern Executive Power*. New York: Free Press 1989.
– *Statesmanship and Party Government: A Study of Burke and Bolingbroke*. Chicago: University of Chicago Press 1965.
Mathen, Carissima. "Dissent and Judicial Authority in *Charter* Cases." 52 *University of New Brunswick Law Journal* (2003): 321.
Mayhew, David. *Congress: The Electoral Connection*. New Haven, Conn.: Yale University Press 1974.
McCarthy, Shawn. "No Sunset Clause for Antiterror Bill, PM Tells His Caucus." *Globe and Mail*, 1 November 2001, A7.
McConnell, Michael. "Institutions and Interpretation: A Critique of *City of Boerne v. Flores*." 111 *Harvard Law Review* (1997): 153.
McCormick, Peter. "New Questions about an Old Concept: The Supreme Court of Canada's Judicial Independence Decisions." 37(4) *Canadian Journal of Political Science* (2004): 839.
McLachlin, Beverley, Rt. Hon., "Respecting Democratic Roles." Speech to the Conference on "The Law and Parliament." Ottawa, Ont., 22 November 2004.
Mitchell, Graeme G. "Developments in Constitutional Law: The 2002–2003 Term: A Tale of Two Courts." 22 *Supreme Court Law Review* (2d) (2003): 83.
– "The Impact of the *Charter* on the Public Policy Process: The Attorney General." In P. Monahan and M. Finkelstein, eds., *The Impact of the Charter on the Public Policy Process*. Toronto: York University Centre for Public Law and Public Policy 1993.
Monahan, Patrick. *Constitutional Law* (2nd ed.). Toronto: Irwin Law 2002.
Montesquieu, Charles de Secondat Baron de. *The Spirit of the Laws*. New York: Prometheus Books 2002.
Morton, F.L., and Rainer Knopff. *The Charter Revolution and the Court Party*. Peterborough, Ont.: Broadview Press 2000.

Murphy, Walter F. "Who Shall Interpret?: The Quest for the Ultimate Constitutional Interpreter." 48(3) *Review of Politics* (1986): 401.
Nagel, Robert F. "Judicial Supremacy and the Settlement Function." 39(3) *William and Mary Law Review* (1997–98): 849.
– *Constitutional Cultures: The Mentality and Consequences of Judicial Review*. Berkeley: University of California Press 1993.
– "Disagreement and Interpretation." 56 *Law & Contemporary Problems* (1993): 11.
Nanos, Nik. "Charter Values Don't Equal Canadian Values: Strong Support for Same-Sex and Property Rights." *Policy Options* (February 2007): 50.
Pangle, Thomas L. *Montesquieu's Philosophy of Liberalism*. Chicago: University of Chicago Press 1973.
Paulsen, Michael Stokes. "The Most Dangerous Branch: Executive Power to Say What the Law Is." 83 *Georgetown Law Journal* (1994): 217.
Pilkington, Marilyn L. "Enforcing the Charter: The Supervisory Role of Superior Courts and the Responsibility of Legislatures for Remedial Systems." 25 *Supreme Court Law Review* (2d) (2004): 77.
Plucknett, Theodore F.T. "*Bonham's Case* and Judicial Review." 40 *Harvard Law Review* (1926): 30.
Posner, Richard. *Law, Pragmatism and Democracy*. Cambridge, Mass.: Harvard University Press 2003.
– *The Problematics of Moral and Legal Theory*. Cambridge, Mass.: Harvard University Press 2001.
– *Economic Analysis of Law* (3rd ed.). Boston: Little, Brown 1986.
Pritchett, C. Herman. "The Development of Judicial Research." In Joel B. Grossman and Joseph Tanenhaus, eds., *Frontiers of Judicial Research*. New York: J. Wiley 1968.
Reid, Mitch. "*United States v. Dickerson*: Uncovering *Miranda*'s Once Hidden and Esoteric Constitutionality." 38 *Houston Law Review* (2001): 1343.
Resnick, Phillip. "Montesquieu Revisited, or the Mixed Constitution and the Separation of Powers in Canada." 20(1) *Canadian Journal of Political Science* (1987): 97.
Risk, R.C.B. *A History of Canadian Legal Thought: Collected Essays*. Toronto: University of Toronto Press 2006.
Roach, Kent, "Sharpening the Dialogue Debate: The Next Decade of Scholarship." 45(1) *Osgoode Hall Law Journal* (2007): 169.
– "Dialogue or Defiance: Legislative Reversals of Supreme Court Decisions in Canada and the United States." 4(2) *International Journal of Constitutional Law* (2006): 347.

- "Dialogic Judicial Review and Its Critics." In Grant Huscroft and Ian Brodie, eds., *Constitutionalism in the Charter Era*. Markham, Ont.: LexisNexis-Butterworths 2004.
- "Do We Want Judges with More Muscle?" *Globe and Mail*, 13 November 2003, A27.
- "Remedial Consensus and Dialogue under the *Charter*: General Declarations and Delayed Declarations of Invalidity." 35(2) *University of British Columbia Law Review* (2001–02): 211.
- "Constitutional and Common Law Dialogues between the Supreme Court and Canadian Legislatures." 80(1–2) *Canadian Bar Review* (2001): 481.
- *The Supreme Court on Trial: Judicial Activism or Democratic Dialogue*. Toronto: Irwin Law 2001.
- "The Uses and Audiences of Preambles to Legislation." 47 *McGill Law Journal* (2001): 129.

Romney, Paul. *Getting It Wrong: How Canadians Forgot Their Past and Imperilled Confederation*. Toronto: University of Toronto Press 1999.

Russell, Peter H. "Overcoming Legal Formalism: The Treatment of the Constitution, the Courts and Judicial Behaviour in Canadian Political Science." 1 *Canadian Journal of Law and Society* (1986): 5.

Savoie, Donald. "The Managerial Prime Minister." *Policy Options* (November 2000): 10.
- *Governing from the Centre: The Concentration of Power in Canadian Politics*. Toronto: University of Toronto Press 1999.

Schmitz, Cristin. "Tertiary Ground for Denying Bail Upheld by Supreme Court, 5–4.' 22(23) *Lawyers Weekly* (18 October 2002): 1.

Segal, Jeffrey, and Howard Spaeth. *The Supreme Court and the Attitudinal Model Revisited*. Cambridge: Cambridge University Press 2002.

Shackleton, Robert. "Montesquieu, Bolingbroke and the Separation of Powers." 3(1) *French Studies* [1949]: 25.

Sheldrick, Byron M. "Judicial Review and the Allocation of Health Care Resources in Canada and the United Kingdom." 5(2–3) *Journal of Comparative Policy Analysis* (2003): 149.

Simpson, Jeffrey. "The Same-Sex Debate Is a Meaningless Charade." *Globe and Mail*, 6 December 2006, A31.
- *The Friendly Dictator*. Toronto: McClelland and Stewart 2001.

Smith, David E. *The Invisible Crown: The First Principle of Canadian Government*. Toronto: University of Toronto Press 1995.

Smith, Miriam. "Institutionalism in the Study of Canadian Politics: The English-Canadian Tradition." In André Lecours, ed., *New Institutionalism: Theory and Analysis*. Toronto: University of Toronto Press 2005.

Snowiss, Sylvia. *Judicial Review and the Law of the Constitution.* New Haven, Conn.: Yale University Press 1990.
Sonenshein, David. "*Miranda* and the Burger Court: Trends and Countertrends." 13 *Loyola University Law Journal* (1982): 405.
Sossin, Lorne. "The Ambivalence of Executive Power in Canada." In Paul Craig and Adam Tomkins, eds., *The Executive and Public Law.* Oxford: Oxford University Press 2006.
– *Boundaries of Judicial Review: The Law of Justiciability in Canada.* Scarborough, Ont.: Carswell 2000.
Stern, Philip Van Doren. *The Life and Writings of Abraham Lincoln.* New York: Modern Library 2000.
Stoner, James R., Jr. *Common Law Liberty: Rethinking American Constitutionalism.* Lawrence: University of Kansas Press 2003.
Strauss, David A. "Miranda, the Constitution and the Congress." 99(5) *Michigan Law Review* (2001): 958.
– "The Ubiquity of Prophylactic Rules." 55 *University of Chicago Law Review* (1988): 190.
Sunstein, Cass. *One Case at a Time: Judicial Minimalism on the Supreme Court.* Cambridge, Mass.: Harvard University Press 1999.
Surowiecki, James. *The Wisdom of Crowds: Why the Many Are Smarter Than the Few.* New York: Random House 2004.
Tardi, Gregory. *The Law of Democratic Governing (Volume 1: Principles).* Scarborough, Ont.: Thomson-Carswell 2004.
Tetley, William. *The October Crisis, 1970: An Insider's View.* Montreal and Kingston: McGill-Queen's University Press 2007.
Tibbetts, Janice. "Public Fear Overrides Right to Bail: Court." *National Post*, 11 October 2002, A1.
– "PM Rejects 'Sunset Clause' in Terror Law." Ottawa *Citizen*, 22 October 2001, A5.
Tibbetts, Janice, and Jim Bronskill. "Terror Bill Gets Facelift: Minister Offers 5-Year Sunset Clause on Some Provisions, Refines Wording." Montreal *Gazette*, 21 November 2001, A13
Tocqueville, Alexis de. *Democracy in America*, ed. J.P. Mayer, trans. George Lawrence. Garden City, N.Y.: Anchor 1969.
Todd, Douglas. "O'Connor Appeal Dropped after Healing Circle." Vancouver *Sun*, 18 June 1998, A1.
Tribe, Lawrence. *Constitutional Choices.* Cambridge, Mass.: Harvard University Press 1985.
Trotter, Garry T. *The Law of Bail in Canada* (2nd ed.). Scarborough. Ont.: Carswell 1999.

Tushnet, Mark. "Legislative and Judicial Interpretation." In Richard W. Bauman and Tvsi Kahana, eds., *The Least Examined Branch: The Role of Legislatures in the Constitutional State*. Cambridge: Cambridge University Press 2006.
- *Taking the Constitution away from the Courts*. Princeton, N.J.: Princeton University Press 1999.
- "Two Versions of Judicial Supremacy." 39(3) *William and Mary Law Review* (1997–98): 945.
Vicini, James. "Meese Scoured for Saying High Court Rulings Not Law of Land." New York *Times*, 24 October 1986, A17.
Vile, M.J.C. *Constitutionalism and the Separation of Powers* (2nd ed.). Indianapolis, Ind.: Liberty Fund 1998.
Waldron, Jeremy. "Some Models of Dialogue between Judges and Legislators." In Grant Huscroft and Ian Brodie, eds., *Constitutionalism in the Charter Era*. Markham, Ont.: LexisNexis-Butterworths 2004.
- *The Dignity of Legislation*. Cambridge: Cambridge University Press 1999.
- *Law and Disagreement*. Oxford: Oxford University Press 1999.
Weber, Bob. "Man Who Fought Rape Shield Law Cleared of Assault." *National Post*, 10 February 2001, A7.
Weiler, Paul. *In the Last Resort: A Critical Study of the Supreme Court of Canada*. Toronto: Carswell 1974.
Weinrib, Ernest. *The Idea of Private Law*. Cambridge, Mass.: Harvard University Press 1995.
Weinrib, Lorraine. "The Loophole That Holds the Charter Together." *Globe and Mail*, 2 April 1998, A23.
White, Graham. *Cabinets and First Ministers* (The Canadian Democratic Audit). Vancouver: UBC Press 2005.
White, Randall. *Voice of Region: The Long Journey to Senate Reform in Canada*. Toronto: Dundurn Press 1999.
Whittington, Keith E. *Political Foundations of Judicial Supremacy: The Presidency, the Supreme Court, and Constitutional Leadership in U.S. History*. Princeton, N.J.: Princeton University Press 2008.
"Extrajudicial Constitutional Interpretation: Three Objections and Responses." 80 *North Carolina Law Review* (2001–02): 773.
Whyte, John. "Not Standing for Notwithstanding." In Mark Charlton and Paul Barker, eds., *Crosscurrents 1: Contemporary Political Issues*. Scarborough, Ont.: Nelson Canada 1991.
Wills, Garry. *Explaining America: The Federalist*. Garden City, N.Y.: Doubleday 1981.

Wilson, Bertha, Hon. "We Didn't Volunteer." In Paul Howe and Peter H. Russell, eds., *Judicial Power and Canadian Democracy.* Montreal and Kingston: McGill-Queen's University Press 2001.

Wolfe, Christopher. *The Rise of Modern Judicial Review: From Constitutional Interpretation to Judge-Made Law.* Lanham, Md.: Rowman and Littlefield 1994.

CASES CITED

A.G. (Ontario, et al.) v. A.G. (Dominion of Canada) (1912) 3 D.L.R. 509 (J.C.P.C.).

Authorson v. Canada (Attorney General) [2003] 2 S.C.R. 40.

Auton (Guardian ad litem of) v. British Columbia (Attorney General) (2001), 197 D.L.R. (4th) 165 (BCSC); [2004] 3 S.C.R. 657.

Babcock v. Canada (Attorney General) [2002] 3 S.C.R. 3.

Beaver v. The Queen [1957] S.C.R. 531.

Borowski v. Attorney General for Canada [1989] 1 S.C.R. 342.

British Columbia v. Imperial Tobacco Canada Ltd. [2005] 2 S.C.R. 473.

Canada (Attorney General) v. Hislop [2007] 1 S.C.R. 429.

Canada (Minister of Energy, Mines and Resources) v. Canada (Auditor General) [1989] 2 S.C.R. 49.

Charkaoui v. Canada (Citizenship and Immigration) 2007 SCC 9.

City of Boerne v. Flores (1997) 521 U.S. 507.

Cohens v. Virginia (1821) 6 Wheat. 264.

Cooper v. Aaron (1958) 358 U.S. 1.

Cooper v. Canada (Human Rights Commission) [1996] 3 S.C.R. 854.

Dickerson v. United States (2000) 120 S. Ct. 2326.

Doucet-Boudreau v. Nova Scotia (Minister of Education) 2001 NSCA 104 (N.S.C.A.); [2003] 3 S.C.R. 3.

Douglas/Kwantlen Faculty Assn. v. Douglas College [1990] 3 S.C.R. 570.

"Dr. Bonham's Case" (1610) 8 Co. Rep. 107a-121a, 77 Eng. Rep.

Dred Scott v. Sandford (1856) 60 U.S. 393.

Dunmore v. Ontario (Attorney General) [2001] 1 S.C.R. 1016.

Eldridge v. British Columbia (Attorney General) [1997] 3 S.C.R. 624.

Employment Division v. Smith (1990), 494 U.S. 872.

Re Eurig Estate [1998] 1 S.C.R. 565.

Evans v. Gore (1920) 253 U.S. 245.

Finlay v. Minister of Finance of Canada [1986] 2 S.C.R. 607.

Fitzgerald v. Alberta 2004 ABCA 184.

Fraser v. P.S.S.R.B. [1985] 2 S.C.R. 455.
Friesen v. Hammell (2000) 2000 BCSC 1185 (CanLII).
Gonzales v. O Centro Espitita Beneficente Uniao Do Vegetal (21 February 2006), no. 04–1084 (U.S.S.C).
Graves v. New York (1939) 306 U.S. 466.
Hogan v. Newfoundland (2000) 183 D.L.R. (4th) 225 (Nfld. C.A.).
Irwin Toy v. Quebec [1989] 1 S.C.R. 927 at 983.
Kingstreet Investments Ltd. v. New Brunswick (Department of Finance) 2007 SCC 1.
Law Society of Upper Canada v. Skapinker [1984] 1 S.C.R. 357.
Lochner v. New York 198 U.S. 45.
Mackin v. New Brunswick (Minister of Finance) [2002] 1 S.C.R. 405.
MacMillan Bloedel Ltd. v. Simpson [1995] 4 S.C.R. 725.
Marbury v. Madison 5 U.S. (1 Cranch) 137.
McKinney v. Liberal Party of Canada, et al. (1987) 43 D.L.R. (4th) 706 (O.S.C.).
Michigan v. Tucker (1974) 417 U.S. 433.
Mills v. The Queen [1986] 1 S.C.R. 863.
Minister of Justice of Canada v. Borowski [1981] 2 S.C.R. 575.
Miranda v. Arizona (1966) 384 U.S. 436.
Multani v. Commission scolaire Marguerite-Bourgeoys 2006 SCC 6.
Muskrat v. United States (1911) 219 U.S. 346.
New Brunswick Broadcasting Co. v. Nova Scotia (Speaker of the House of Assembly), [1993] 1 S.C.R. 319.
New Brunswick (Minister of Health and Community Services) v. G. (J.) [1999] 3 S.C.R. 46.
Newfoundland (Treasury Board) v. N.A.P.E. [2004] 3 S.C.R. 381.
Nixon v. United States (1993) 506 U.S. 224.
Nova Scotia Board of Censors v. McNeil [1975] 2 S.C.R. 265.
Nova Scotia (Workers' Compensation Board) v. Martin 2003 SCC 54.
O'Malley v. Woodrough (1939) 307 U.S. 277.
Operation Dismantle v. The Queen [1985] 1 S.C.R. 441.
Pollock v. Farmers' Loan and Trust Co. (1895) 158 U.S. 601.
R. v. 974649 Ontario Inc. ("Dunedin") [2001] 3 S.C.R. 575.
R. v. Bembridge (1783) 22 How. St. Tr. 155 (Lords).
R. v. Bray [1983] 2 C.C.C. (3d) 325 (Ont. C.A.).
R. v. Demers [2004] 2 S.C.R. 489.
R. v. Hall [2002] 3 S.C.R. 309.
R. v. Krieger (2006) SCC 30950.
R. v. Mills 56 Alta. L.R. (3d) 277 (Q.B.) (Belzil J.); [1999] 3 S.C.R. 668.

R. v. Morales [1992] 3 S.C.R. 711.
R. v. Nova Scotia Pharmaceutical Society [1992] 2 S.C.R. 606.
R. v. O'Connor [1995] 4 S.C.R. 411.
R. v. Pearson [1992] 3 S.C.R. 665.
R. v. Power [1994] 1 S.C.R. 601.
R. v. Vaillancourt [1987] 2 S.C.R. 636.
Re B.C. Motor Vehicle Act [1985] 2 S.C.R. 486.
Re Gray (1918) 42 D.L.R. 1 at 12.
Re Philips and Lynch (1986) 27 D.L.R. (4th) 156 (NSSC).
Re Residential Tenancies Act 1979 [1981] 1 S.C.R. 714.
Re: Remuneration of Judges [1997] 3 S.C.R. 3.
Reference re Alberta Statutes [1938] S.C.R. 100.
Reference re Bill 30, An Act to Amend the Education Act (Ont.) [1987] 1 S.C.R. 1148.
Reference Re Same-Sex Marriage [2004] 3 S.C.R. 698.
Rex v. Halliday [1917] A.C. 260.
RJR-MacDonald Inc. v. Canada (Attorney General) [1995] 3 S.C.R. 199.
Rodriguez v. British Columbia (Attorney General) [1993] 3 S.C.R. 519.
Roncarelli v. Duplessis [1959] S.C.R. 121.
Sauvé v. Canada (Attorney General) [1993] 2 S.C.R. 438.
Savué v. Canada (Chief Electoral Officer) [2002] SCC 68.
Schachter v. Canada [1992] 2 S.C.R. 679.
Sherbert v. Verner (1963) 374 U.S. 398.
Singh v. Minister of Employment and Immigration [1985] 1 S.C.R. 177.
Sobeys Stores Ltd. v. Yeomans and Labour Standards Tribunal (N.S.) [1989] 1 S.C.R. 238.
Southam Inc. v. Canada (Attorney General) [1990] 3 F.C. 465 (F.C.A.).
Southern Pacific Co. v. Jensen (1917) 244 U.S. 205.
Thorson v. Attorney General of Canada [1975] 1 S.C.R. 138.
Tremblay v. Daigle [1989] 2 S.C.R. 530.
Tunda v. Canada 2001 FCA 151 (F.C.A.).
United States v. Burns [2001] 1 S.C.R. 283, 2001 SCC 7.
United States v. Butler (1936) 297 U.S. 1.
Valente v. the Queen [1985] 2 S.C.R. 673.
Vriend v. Alberta [1998] 1 S.C.R. 493.
Wells v. Newfoundland [1999] 3 S.C.R. 199.
Westergard-Thorpe et al. v. Attorney General of Canada et al.; Jones et al. v. The Queen et al. 183 D.L.R. (4th) 458 (F.C.A.).
Youngstown Sheet & Tube Co. v. Sawyer 345 US 579.

Index

Agresto, John, 5
Ajzenstat, Janet, 50, 61–2, 172n5, 175n58, 180n39
Alexander, Larry, 41–2, 50
Allan, T.R.S., 9, 86–8, 146
ambivalent model. *See* neo-institutionalism
Anderson, David, 76–7
Anti-Terrorism Act, 74–7
attainder, bills of, 85–6, 183n11
Auton v. British Columbia, 133, 137

Bagehot, Walter, 66–7, 178n14, 178n16
bail (judicial interim release), 30–6, 118. *See also R. v. Morales* and *R. v. Hall*
Barendt, Eric, 146, 171n15
Bédard, Pierre, 61, 180n39
behaviouralism, 66–7
Bickel, Alexander 3, 97, 109, 189n17
Binnie, Ian, 142, 147, 164n2
Blackstone, William, 58, 85, 88
Bolingbroke, Henry St John, 59
Bradley, Craig, 28

Breckenridge, John, 112–13
British North America Act, 1867: protecting judicial independence, 9; section 9 ("executive power"), 54, 139; section 17 ("legislative power"), 54, 63; sections 53 and 54 ("public finance" provisions), 61–2, 132–6; and the separation of powers, 8, 53–4
Brudner, Alan, 100
Burt, Robert, 5, 175n51

Cairns, Alan, 65–6, 69–70, 92
Cameron, Jamie, 19, 36, 41, 47, 147
Canada Evidence Act, 50–1
Carrese, Paul, 88, 179n22
case-and-controversy constraint, 14, 86–7, 92–6, 104–11; and confining mistakes, 109–10; and judicial remedies, 125–6
Cassell, Paul, 27
Catron, John, 107
Charlottetown Accord, 116
Charter of Rights and Freedoms, 9–10; section 1 ("reasonable

limits"), 6, 9, 17, 23–4; section 3 ("right to vote"), 25, 36–7; section 7 ("fundamental justice"), 22, 90, 92; section 11(e) ("reasonable bail"), 30–6, 45; section 15 ("equality"), 128–38; section 23 ("minority language education rights"), 139; section 31 ("legislative powers"), 126. *See also* notwithstanding clause
checks and balances. *See* separation of powers
Choudry, Sujit, 19, 99–101, 114–15, 158n7
Chrétien, Jean, 74–6
City of Boerne v. Flores, 17, 19–23, 26, 46, 105
Claus, Laurence, 55, 59, 170n5, 170n8
Clement, W.H.P., 65–7
Clinton, Robert Lowry, 95, 186n 47, 154n7, 184n15
Constitution Act, 1791, 61
Constitution Act, 1867. *See* British North America Act, 1867
Constitution Act, 1982, section 24 ("remedies clause"), 15, 124–8, 136–7, 147; section 52 ("supremacy clause"), 15, 39–40, 125–8, 136–7, 147
constitutional interpretation. *See* coordinate interpretation, dialogue theory, judicial interpretive supremacy, legal pluralism
constitutional supremacy, 40, 151–2
Cooper v. Aaron, 4
coordinate interpretation, 3–7, 10, 17–19, 23–4, 34, 37–8; advocates in United States and Canada, 5; and constitutional supremacy, 40–1; criteria for responses, 117–22; defined, 4; and dialogue theory, 3–4, 6; hostility to, 39–52; and legal pluralism, 102–22; Lincoln's approach, 106–11; and rule of law, 41–4; after Supreme Court rules, 103–15
Cotler, Irwin, 75, 114
Cover, Robert, 42

Dawson, R. MacGregor, 67, 73
Dawson, W.F., 73
DeCoste, Frederick, 147, 157n50
Department of Justice (Canada), 33, 47, 121
Deschamps, Marie, 142–3
Devins, Neal, 5, 48, 112, 122
dialogue theory: and coordinate interpretation, 3–4, 6, 10, 17; defined, 6; and judicial supremacy, 23–4, 36–7, 150, 188n3; in *R. v. Mills*, 23–4, 35 ; in *R. v. Hall*, 30, 35–6; in *Sauvé*, 36–7; as second-order rule, 125; in *Vriend*, 130
Dicey, A.V., 14, 81, 94
Dickerson v. United States, 18, 26–9, 105; approval of by Canadian scholars, 36
Dickson, Brian, 57
direct democracy, 13
Doucet-Boudreau v. Nova Scotia (Minister of Education), 15, 139–44
Douglas, Stephen, 110
Dr. Bonham's Case, 146
Dred Scott v. Sandford, 103; Lincoln's response, 106–12

Index

Duff, L.P., 78
Durham, Lord (John George Lambton), 61, 172n25
Dworkin, Ronald, 68, 167n41, 195n1

Eisgruber, Christopher, 5
Eldridge v. British Columbia (Attorney General), 15–16, 133–9
Employment Division v. Smith, 17, 20–2
executive, 8–15, 40, 54; ambivalent power, 70–1; as distinct from judicial power, 84–9; domination of legislature, 9–13, 64, 72–7; and judicial remedies, 139–44; and responsible government, 54, 61–3. *See also* separation of powers

Federalist Papers, 60, 88–9, 93, 124
Fisher, Louis, 5, 48, 112, 122
Flanagan, Tom, 12, 176n68
Forcese, Craig, 148–9
Forsey, Eugene, 9, 52, 177n75
Frankfurter, Felix, 18
Franks, C.E.S., 79–80
Freeman, Aaron, 148–9
Freeman, Gerald, 141–2
Free Trade Agreement, 80–1
fusion of executive and legislature. *See* separation of powers

Garton, Graham, 121
Ginsburg, Ruth Bader, 21
Goldsworthy, Jeffey, 146
Gonthier, Charles, 30–2, 34
Gordon, Scott, 73, 172n24, 185n30

Gray, Hamish, 105, 147
Greene, Ian, 9

Hall, David, 32, 34
Hamilton, Alexander, 88–9, 93, 103; on remedies, 124
Harper, Stephen, 99–101, 114–15
Hiebert, Janet, 160n34
Hogg, Peter: on civil liberties, 51; dialogue theory, 4, 23, 150, 154n10, 154n11, 155n26; on interdelegation, 77–9, 169n2; on separation of powers, 8–9, 53–4, 61–2, 156n36; on supremacy clause, 40, 126
Holmes, Oliver Wendell, Jr, 68
Hughes, Charles Evans, 3, 153n5, 166n26
Huscroft, Grant, 5, 150, 153n5, 155n23; on judicial exclusivity, 39, 152

Iacobucci, Frank, 23, 35–6, 149

Jackson, Andrew, 40
Johnson, William Samuel, 95
Judicial Committee of the Privy Council, 65–6, 93
judicial independence, 9, 83, 182n1
judicial invalidations, 43, 96. *See also* remedies
judicial supremacy 4–5, 17–19, 23–6, 34, 147–8; application beyond particular case, 95–6; and constitutional supremacy, 40, 148–52; and judicial insularity, 98–101; and legal pluralism, 15, 98–101; as required by constitutional text, 39–41; as required

for principled outcomes, 46; as required by rule of law, 41–4; in U.S. jurisprudence, 21–2, 27–9, 51–2

Kahn, Ronald, 21
Kane, Catherine, 47, 121
Kelly, James, 8, 12, 60, 155n24, 164n108
Kennedy, Anthony, 21, 23
Knopff, Rainer, 49, 70, 98, 120, 191n50
Komesar, Neil, 48–9
Kramer, Larry, 5, 41–3, 146
Kronman, Anthony, 68

La Forest, Gérard, 25, 133
Lamer, Antonio, 30–1, 35, 118, 129
Law Society of Upper Canada v. Skapinker 153n6, 154n7
LeBel, Louis, 142–3, 152
LeBlanc, Arthur, 140, 142
legal formalism, 65–8
legal pluralism, 14, 106–15, 120–1; after Supreme Court rules, 102–22
legal realism, 68–9
L'Heureux-Dubé, Claire, 22, 30
Lincoln, Abraham, 14, 107–11, 122, 189n10
Lochner v. New York, 103
Locke, John, 56, 122

MacEachen, Allan, 80
Madison, James, 14, 59, 78, 122, 124; on case-and-controversy constraint, 95; and partial agency, 11–12, 60, 62, 108, 140–2

Mahe v. Alberta, 139
Major, John, 23, 131, 142
Manfredi, Christopher, 5, 36, 155n24, 155n28; on dialogue, 36, 159n29; on notwithstanding clause, 116; on remedies, 132, 194n38
Mansfield, Harvey, on institutional ambivalence, 12–13, 65, 70–2, 77, 151; on social science, 72–4, 80, 105–6, 151
Marbury v. Madison, 4, 95
Marshall, John, 4, 95
Martin, Paul, 74
Mayhew, David, 46
McConnell, Michael, 21
McCormick, Peter, 83, 156n44
McIntyre, W.R., 125–6
McLachlin, Beverley, 23, 32–7, 40, 127, 174n42
McLellan, Anne, 75
Meech Lake Accord, 116
Mills, Brian, 23, 118
minority retort, 6, 15, 17–24, 37–9, 43, 45–7, 51; criteria for coordinate response, 117–22; defined 19; and legal pluralism, 101; and notwithstanding clause, 24. See also *R. v. Mills*
Miranda v. Arizona, 18, 26–9
Mitchell, Graeme, 33, 36
Monahan, Patrick, 8, 188n67
Montesquieu, Charles de Secondat Baron de, 73, 122, 144; influence on U.S. and Canadian framers, 56, 172n27; Madison explains, 60; on moderate government, 57, 88–9, 109, 149; on the separation of powers, 57–60, 64–5, 84–5, 170n8

Index

Morales, Maximo, 30, 118
Morton, F.L. (Ted), 49, 70, 98, 120
Mulroney, Brian, 80, 182n85
Murphy, Walter, 5, 96

Nagel, Robert, 5, 37, 41, 165n19
neo-institutionalism, 12–13, 69–70; ambivalent model, 12–13, 70–2
Newfoundland [Treasury Board] v. N.A.P.E., 133
notwithstanding clause (s.33), 44–5, 99–100, 102–3; and dialogue theory, 6–7, 9, 17, 23–4, 36; inadequacy for coordinate responses, 114–17, 166n30
Nova Scotia (Workers' Compensation Board) v. Martin, 135

O'Connor, Hubert, 22, 118
O'Connor, Sandra Day, 21

Parliament of Canada, 25, 31, 33, 36, 44; bicameralism, 79–81; composition, 177n72; dependence on judicial enforcement, 105; and dialogue theory, 6–7, 114–15; and interdelegation, 77–9; and lower court judgments, 98–101; and majoritarianism, 45–8, 49; and prime minister, 73–7; response to *Morales*, 7, 31, 35, 47; response to *O'Connor*, 6–7, 22–4, 47; role in protecting civil liberties, 50–1; and separation of powers, 8–16, 40, 54
partial agency. *See* separation of powers
Paulsen, Michael Stokes, 5

Pilikington, Marilyn, 8, 143–4, 194n53
political parties, 13, 66, 71
Porter, John, 67
prime minister. *See* executive
Pritchett, C. Herman, 67

R. v. Hall, 7–8, 18–19, 26, 29, 32–7, 47, 52; as coordinate response, 118–22; as example of judicial reconsideration, 102–4, 113–14. *See also* textual retort
R. v. Mills, 6–8, 17–20, 22–4, 34–7, 46–7, 52; as coordinate response, 118–22; as example of judicial reconsideration, 26, 32, 102–4, 113–14. *See also* minority retort
R. v. Morales, 7, 18, 26, 30–6, 47
R. v. Morgentaler, 116
R. v. O'Connor, 7, 17, 22–4; as perceived by Justice Department, 47, 121
R. v. Pearson, 30
R. v. Sharpe, 98–9
R. v. Vaillancourt, 49, 90
reading-in. *See* remedies
reasonable limits clause (s.1). *See* Charter of Rights and Freedoms
reference decisions. *See* Supreme Court of Canada
Re Gray, 77–8
Rehnquist, William, 21, 27
religious freedom, 20–1, 158n8
Religious Freedom Restoration Act (RFRA), 20–1
remedies, constitutional, 15, 123–44; delayed declarations of invalidity, 16, 105, 131; reading-in, 15, 117, 128–32

Re Philips and Lynch, 128,
  193n14
Resnick, Philip, 172n27, 173n28
responsible government, 8, 11–13,
  54, 177n75; and separation of
  powers, 61–3
*R.J.R.-MacDonald Inc. v. Canada
  [Attorney General]*, 49
Roach, Kent, on dialogue theory,
  23–4, 36–7; on fusion, 12; on
  legislatures, 46–7, 49, 51; on
  remedies, 127–8, 131–2, 137–9;
  on standing, 93
Roberts, Owen, 119
Roosevelt, Franklin, 113
Rothstein, Marshall, 152
rule of law, 14, 16, 41–4, 86–7;
  in British system, 43, 146–7
Russell, Peter, 65–7

same-sex marriage, 99–101,
  114–15
*Sauvé v. Canada (Chief Electoral
  Officer)*, 36–7
Savoie, Donald, 74
Scalia, Antonin, 20, 28–9
Schachter v. Canada, 15, 128, 131,
  135
Schauer, Frederick, 41–2, 50
Senate of Canada, 13, 79–81
separation of powers, 8–16,
  53–63; and behaviouralism,
  66–8; and bicameralism, 79–81;
  in British constitutionalism,
  59–60, 64; in British North
  America Act, 1867, 8, 53–4,
  57, 61–3; Canadian doctrine
  defined, 13, 40, 57; checks
  and balances, 9–14, 57, 48–52,
  83; executive domination of
  legislature, 9–13, 64, 72–7; fusion theory, 12–13, 64–7, 72–7,
  144, 148; and interdelegation,
  77–9; and judicial remedies,
  15–16, 123–4, 142–3; and the
  mixed constitution, 56, 171n22;
  and partial agency, 11–13, 15,
  59–60, 64–5, 141–2; in the
  United States, 11, 51–2, 59, 78–
  9. *See also* judicial independence
sexual-assault records, 22, 118
Shaw, Duncan, 98
Sherbert v. Verner, 20
Simpson, Jeffrey, 73, 114
slavery. See *Dred Scott v. Sandford*
Smiley, Donald, 67
Sossin, Lorne, 9, 156n42, 170n6,
  189n16
Species-at-Risk legislation, 74,
  76–7
standing, 93, 185m34
Stevens, John Paul, 21
Stoner, James, 68
Strayer, Barry, 8, 54, 149
Stuart, Donald, 36
supremacy clause (s.52). *See*
  Constitution Act, 1982
Supreme Court of Canada, 5,
  17–19, 22–4, 29–37, 77; as apex
  of judiciary, 97, 101; and dialogue theory, 6–7, 23–4, 29–38,
  125; and majoritarianism, 45–8;
  reference decisions, 13, 93; remedies jurisprudence, 124–44; on
  separation of powers, 83–4,
  156n36, 174n42, 182n1, 182n3

Tardi, Gregory, 88
textual retort, 7, 15, 18–19, 24–39,
  43, 51; criteria for coordinate

response, 117–22; defined 24;
and legal pluralism, 101; and
notwithstanding clause, 44–5;
and principled outcomes, 47
Thomas, Clarence, 21
Thornton, Allison, 4, 23, 154n10,
  154n11, 155n26
Tocqueville, Alexis de, 68–9, 111
Tribe, Lawrence 41, 153n3
Trotter, Gary, 31
Tushnet, Mark, 5, 42, 50

United States Congress, 27–9, 62,
  113, 134
United States constitution, 59; Article I, section 9, 86; Article III, section 2, 92–6; First Amendment, 20–1; Fifth Amendment, 26–9; Sixteenth Amendment, 29; interdelegation, 78–9
United States Supreme Court,
  17–18, 20–2, 26–9, 36, 105; on
constitutional supremacy, 119;
  reversals, 102–3

vagueness, 30–4
Vile, M.J.C., 11, 55–7, 59,
  170n12
Vriend, Delwin, 129–30
Vriend v. Alberta, 15, 117,
  129–32, 166, 157n50

Waldron, Jeremy, 45–6, 50, 195n1
War Measures Act, 77–8
Warren, Earl, 26–7
Warwick, Sir Philip, 88
Wells v. Newfoundland, 64
White, Graham, 12
White, Randall, 80
Whittington, Keith, 51, 167n41,
  167n42, 190n21
Wilson, Bertha, 40, 44, 153n6

Young Offenders Act, 50